Alone with Nature

Also available from Bloomsbury:

Aesthetics and Nature by Glenn Parsons
Aesthetics of Care by Yuriko Saito
How to Think about the Climate Crisis by Graham Parkes

Alone with Nature

The Psychology of Environmental Attunement

Eugene Hughes

BLOOMSBURY ACADEMIC
LONDON · NEW YORK · OXFORD · NEW DELHI · SYDNEY

BLOOMSBURY ACADEMIC
Bloomsbury Publishing Plc, 50 Bedford Square, London, WC1B 3DP, UK
Bloomsbury Publishing Inc, 1359 Broadway, New York, NY 10018, USA
Bloomsbury Publishing Ireland, 29 Earlsfort Terrace, Dublin 2, D02 AY28, Ireland

BLOOMSBURY, BLOOMSBURY ACADEMIC and the Diana logo are trademarks
of Bloomsbury Publishing Plc

First published in Great Britain 2026

Cover design by Louise Dugdale
Cover image: Distant walking on Black Sand Diamond Beach Iceland
Eystri-Fellsfjara at Jökulsárlón, Southern Iceland/Getty Images

ISBN: HB: 978-1-3504-9994-2
PB: 978-1-3504-9995-9
ePDF: 978-1-3504-9997-3
eBook: 978-1-3504-9996-6

Typeset by Newgen KnowledgeWorks Pvt. Ltd., Chennai, India
Printed and bound in Great Britain

For product safety related questions contact productsafety@bloomsbury.com.

To find out more about our authors and books visit www.bloomsbury.com
and sign up for our newsletters.

Contents

Are you bowed down in heart?
Do you but hear the clashing discords and the din of life?
Then come away, come to the peaceful wood.
Here bath your soul in silence. Listen! Now,
From out the palpitating solitude
Do you not catch, yet faint, elusive strains?
They are above, around, within you, everywhere.
Silently listen! Clear, and still more clear, they come.
They bubble up in rippling notes, and swell in singing tones.

James Weldon Johnson
Extract from Deep in the Quiet Wood

Foreword

Arnold Berleant

Alone with Nature offers an environmental approach to well-being through a direct, full, solitary involvement with a natural environment through environmental attunement. This is not a passive absorption but an active, sensory, participatory engagement, typically solitary, with a natural environment. While deeply personal, it is not subjective but active as well as receptive, and thoroughly sensory.

This extraordinary book makes the case for a fresh, comprehensive path to environmental experience through achieving environmental attunement. Hughes describes the rationale of environmental attunement theory, which is an ecological approach that seeks to encounter nature as a whole through perceptual engagement, always acknowledging its complexities and interdependencies within ecological systems. Not only does this encourage full perceptual involvement, but it also enables one to achieve an experience of being fully alive. Of value as a psychotherapeutic process, it is of still more general significance in exhibiting the possibilities for enhancing lived experience.

The scope of *Alone with Nature* is both full and illuminating. Its message is worked out carefully and systematically, starting with an account of the experience of environmental attunement. This recognizes its strong emphasis on sensory perception and the active and open engagement of the participant in environmental experience. Hughes extends his account of environmental experience to embrace the full range of sensory awareness and the active, participatory nature of such experience. The theoretical account presented in the central chapter provides coherent and full support for this distinctive environmental experience.

Environmental attunement theory proposes an ecological approach to environmental experience that acknowledges the totality of nature and the complexities and interdependencies within ecological systems. This approach encourages an appreciation that goes beyond the visual or aesthetic values, implanting human experience within the full environmental complex.

Achieving such attunement carries psychotherapeutic benefits and so becomes a therapeutic resource. But more, environment attunement carries intrinsic benefits to human beings-in-the-world. 'This heightened awareness ... allows for a more embodied sense of engagement with our physical surroundings.' As Hughes summarizes, attunement states provide a heightened awareness of the physicality of a body directly engaged with its surroundings and a more vivid sense of things happening between the space and self interdependently (115). Environmental attunement promotes a perceptual participation that is human experience at its most fulfilling: the condition of being most fully alive.

Of special significance are the applications of this approach to environmental experience. Not only are these applications psychotherapeutic, which one might anticipate, but also social. Opportunities for environmental attunement can be embedded in urban settings, and Hughes' account of the Barbican Centre in Central London reveals the surprising possibilities of environmental attunement in a dense urban context.

Here is a theoretical account grounded in concrete experience and wide research. Informed by a large literature in psychology, psychotherapy and aesthetics, Hughes offers an original contribution to understanding and experiencing the natural environment that is rich with insights and applications. At the same time, reading this book is as pleasurable as it is illuminating. Expressed with flair and passion, as well as broad and profound understanding, *Alone with Nature* is a unique and valuable addition to the literature on environment.

Acknowledgements

In hindsight, this book began, unbeknown to me, as a young child running wild in the west of Ireland. These early experiences formed a lifelong love for nature. So, when I found myself at my computer struggling to translate my thoughts into words, the forests where I live called me. I have walked this book far more than I have typed it. In those woods, I do not need to speak or explain; it is a place where I can just be and be nurtured, arriving back to my desk with fresh spirits. The process of writing *Alone with Nature* has brought me even closer to my old and loyal friend – nature.

Over the years, the lion's share of my career has been dedicated to helping people heal and grow. In that work, I have been fortunate to find ways to incorporate my love for nature. Along the way, my colleague and cherished friend, author and environmentalist Trebbe Johnson, has been my mentor on this path. The deepening of my nature-based practice would not be as wholesome without Trebbe's wisdom. Equally, all my collaborations and conversations with Jungian scholar Dr Louise Austin have helped me maintain a deep connection to the soul of my work. Their wisdom has greatly enriched the ideas in this book, while their friendship has turned much of the work into an exciting adventure.

The PhD in Creativity, which started at the University of the Arts in Philadelphia and subsequently moved to Rowan University in Pennsylvania, provided the container for much of my academic research. The brainchild of Professor Jonathan Fineberg, this unique programme gave me the interdisciplinary and creative space to break free from conventional ways of looking at the human-nature relationship. Although the focus of my research was psychological, Professor Fineberg encouraged me to engage with diverse fields to challenge my thinking and find something universal and essential in the exchange – a rare gem in the conventionally siloed world of academia.

Thanks to this process, Professor Paul Stoller introduced me to the ideas of sensory anthropology, which made me question the abject lack of the sensual in much contemporary psychological research, in its focus on the purely cognitive. In a similar vein, philosopher Professor Arnold Berleant opened my eyes to experiencing experience as a continuum, rather than devolving into what he describes as the black hole of psychology and philosophy – subjectivism. It's one thing to appreciate the senses; it's quite something else for a psychologist to give them primacy. Yet, shifting my attention from purely mental processes to sensory perception has been instrumental in letting go of my anthropocentric worldview in favour of one of kinship with a more-than-human world.

This book, however, would float above real life without the grounding of the experiences of those I interviewed over the years – from the people who dedicate much of their lives to being alone with nature, to those whose life circumstances make nature contact challenging, yet still manage to find precious moments of attunement to this more-than-human world. These are the wonderful people who give my work deep roots.

I also want to acknowledge my partner, Mirko, who has been my rock throughout the research and writing of this book. His uncanny intuition knew when I needed to be a recluse, when to tease me from my cave and when to lift me up with kind words of encouragement. I feel very lucky indeed to have received these gifts.

There are many unexplored avenues, unanswered questions and shortcomings in this book, all of which are down to me. For all the insight and good this book brings, I am eternally grateful to all the beings – human and otherwise – mentioned here. The deep sense of gratitude I have for these beings is hard to put into words. But here it goes. Thank you from the bottom of my heart.

Introduction

A strange phenomenon

When the Land Artist Nancy Holt first ventured alone into the Great Basin Desert in Utah, United States, she recalled an extraordinary feeling of her inner world merging with the outer landscape, an experience that lasted for several days (Williams et al., 2015). Holt's experience, although extraordinary, is not unique. In his autobiographical account of a year spent in solitude in the Patagonian wilderness, Robert Kull eloquently describes similar encounters (Kull, 2009). In my role as a psychologist working with individuals in nature, for close to two decades, I have heard many people describe similar experiences. However, despite extensive research on the benefits of exposure to green spaces over the past forty years, these types of experiences have largely been overlooked in psychological literature. What is this strange phenomenon that blurs the line between self and nature? Why does it occur when we are alone in nature? And what value does it hold for modern human society?

Over the course of three years, I conducted interviews with people who sought solitude in some of the world's most secluded locations. These included shamans who ventured deep into the Amazon rainforest for extended periods to communicate with ancestral spirits, land artists residing in caves perched on high cliffs and wilderness rites of passage guides who considered the desert their home. The findings from these interviews identified how intentionally spending time alone in nature can produce a unique state of consciousness. This state is marked by heightened sensations, memories and imagination, along with an embodied sense of attunement to the immediate surroundings. Furthermore, the findings highlight how these states significantly influence our sense of self, extending far beyond the cognitive effects documented in existing research.

However, over 55 per cent of the world's population lives in urban areas (exceeding 75 per cent in wealthier nations), and quality access to nature is increasingly shaped by social and environmental inequities. The question looms large as to what value these extraordinary states hold for wider populations than elite groups (Colley et al., 2022). On that basis, following my initial research, I interviewed a wider range of people and carried out several experiments in less remote, more accessible, everyday nature settings and situations. The outcomes led to several fresh discoveries, including the identification of micro-attunements, shorter and less intense states accessible in more accessible settings, that nonetheless have a remarkably positive effect on the self.

These research findings form the foundation of Environmental Attunement Theory, a theoretical framework that contains the core characteristics of the state itself, the conditions that bring it about and the ways in which it impacts our sense of self. This book provides a comprehensive overview of the theory. Unfolding in three parts, the book covers the phenomenology of environmental attunement, its philosophical and psychological implications, and its practical applications in contemporary therapy, urban environmental design and environmental justice.

Some notes on solitude and nature

This is a psychology book about two outliers in the canon of psychological literature and research: solitude and the other-than-human world. Both the experience of being alone and that of being in nature are seldom credited as having much psychological depth. When it comes to solitude, more has been written on its possible psychopathologies than on any potential benefits (Coplan & Bowker, 2014). Nature, on the other hand, has been well covered by cognitive studies over the past forty years (Capaldi et al., 2014; Bowler et al., 2010), is treated as the mindless other, and therefore offers a relationship incapable of psychological depth. This may seem a harsh critique, but over the chapters of the book, I share the philosophical, psychological and cultural reasoning behind it in greater detail. In advance, the following paragraphs provide some highlights.

Psychology's problem with solitude

The twentieth century saw a major shift in psychology away from studying the intrapsychic reality of individuals to understanding them as inherently relational beings shaped by social interactions. Three major factors shaped this shift. The first was the introduction of Edmund Husserl's intersubjective philosophy, which had a profound influence on theories of mind and human development that followed (Stolorow & Atwood, 2002). The second was the infant research of child development psychologists such as Donald Winnicott (Winnicott et al., 1990) and John Bowlby (Bowlby, 2005) responding to the devastating effects of institutionalized care systems on orphans in the aftermath of the Second World War. The third was the cognitive turn in the late twentieth century, in which cognitive scientists, aided by advances in neuroimaging technology, looked to the workings of the brain to understand these relational bonds (Cozolino, 2014).

Today, human relations are seen as the basic building blocks of human development – critical to our cognitive and social development and psychological health throughout our life cycle. The more fragile or disturbed these relationships, the greater the risk of psychopathologies taking root. This idea of the self as cognitively constructed within the dynamics of social interactions has fundamentally shaped our understanding of human psychology. In the context of this understanding of the self, it is little wonder that the costs of solitude are perceived as far outweighing any benefits in the psychological discourse. Most studies argue that, at any age, it is one of the strongest risk factors for psychological ill-being (Long et al., 2003; O'Day & Heimberg, 2021; Averill & Sundararajan 2014; Coplan & Bowker, 2014). Although solitude comes in many different forms – from occurrences of other-imposed and self-sought solitude – the literature rarely focuses on the latter and any of its potential benefits.

There is little doubt that imposed isolation – being cut off from others against one's will – can be deeply distressing and damaging. Throughout my years in clinical practice, for example, I have personally observed the heartbreaking impact of families isolating victims of sexual abuse because of a fear of social disgrace that outweighs their familial bonds. This form of isolation is both cruel and damaging. Solitude can also manifest as a more familiar type of loneliness stemming from a perceived mismatch between the social connections we desire and those we actually have. The real difficulty arises when these feelings become acute and chronic. While we cannot entirely stop the shadows of loneliness from passing by, most people can prevent them from settling permanently.

Then, there is a self-sought solitude – a form of aloneness we actively choose for rest, reflection or creative pursuits, which can be deeply nourishing. Most of us can recall playing on our own as a kid, happily lost in our imagination, as adolescents increasingly need and enjoy our privacy, and as adults cherishing moments of aloneness lost in a book or film. This type of aloneness takes us away from the distractions of everyday life and affords us the freedom to engage with something other, a state of *being alone with*. With a handful of exceptions which I draw upon later in the book, this type of self-enhancing solitude is largely ignored in psychology literature. This is where *Alone with Nature* sits, exploring a form of self-sought aloneness motivated by the desire to engage with nature.

Psychology's approach to nature

The psychology of humans' relationship to nature started to gain traction in the 1980s, with seminal studies on stress relief and attention restoration (Kaplan, 1995; Ulrich et al., 1991). As outlined in the following chapters, the research literature has grown steadily over the decades. Where we stand today, there is substantial evidence of the benefits of short-term exposure to green space. Through this lens of exposure, nature is treated broadly as a passive provider of cognitive effects – a soothing backdrop to alleviate the stresses and strains of our busy human lives, a sort of 'green-pill' to address life's milder symptoms. This benign representation ignores the complex dynamics of environments as living systems and human multisensory involvement within it. The treatment of nature as a living ecology, of which we are part, has to date proven too dangerous a proposition for a field dedicated to the workings of the human mind.

The challenges of the twenty-first century call for the field of psychology to re-evaluate its stance on nature. The top of the list is the most pressing existential issue of our time – the environmental polycrisis driven by global warming, deforestation, pollution and biodiversity loss. Paul Crutzen, the Nobel Prize-winning atmospheric chemist who brought the term 'Anthropocene' into common use, describes this geological epoch as one where human activity is the primary force shaping Earth's environment and ecosystems (Benner et al., 2022). He asserted that humanity's control over biological, chemical and geological processes on the planet is already an undeniable and devastating fact.

With such pressing needs, scientists are answering the call for action, and new discoveries are being made. Sentient creatures from the octopus to insects are accepted into the consciousness club (O'Shaughnessy, 2003). The vast fungal networks that use mycorrhizal fungi to facilitate nutrient sharing, chemical warnings and electrical signalling between trees suggest that plants communicate (Kohn, 2013). However, as the boundaries traditionally placed between humans and non-human life are under scrutiny by most sciences, the field of psychology lags.

However, the biggest disruptor to anthropocentric psychology theories and models comes from the cognitive sciences and the emerging interdisciplinary field of embodied cognition (Froese, 2018; Fuchs, 2018; Fuchs & De Jaegher, 2009; Varela et al., 2016). Their chief claim is that the mind is not located in the brain but embodied and enacted through our interactions with the environment, blurs the hard lines between mind and matter, cognition and sensation, perceiver and environment, and presents something of a game changer to the psychological study of humans' relationship with nature. As a result, the idea of reciprocity between humans and non-humans, rather than woolly rhetoric, can now be empirically grounded.

Overall, Environmental Attunement Theory contributes to this shifting focus in the field of psychology in several substantive ways. First, Environmental Attunement Theory frees the psychology of the human-nature relationship from anthropocentric dualistic frameworks that have governed the field to date. In doing so, this theory helps advance a new understanding of human consciousness by identifying a distinct embodied state that emerges when individuals are intentionally alone in nature. The theory, therefore, contributes to growing voices in the interdisciplinary field of embodied cognition and our understanding of the role of multisensory perception in self-experience.

Second, attunement states are not merely restorative or cognitive in effect; they fundamentally enhance and expand one's sense of self. This finding has important implications for both individual psychological development and public mental health more broadly. Third, the principles of Environmental Attunement Theory offer a bridge between psychology and urban design, digital technology, public health and education, in humanity's search for new ways of existing in cohabitation with this more-than-human world.

A brief note on the linguistic challenge of nature

The question 'what is nature?' recurs throughout this book, and is specifically addressed in Chapter 4. Traditionally, psychology has viewed humans as distinct from nature – a viewpoint that I contend stems from Cartesian dualism, which prioritizes the mind over the physical world. I advocate for psychology to align with most sciences that classify everything, including humans and their actions, as a part of nature. I recognize that this leads to an apparent contradiction in the phrase 'alone with nature'. Linguistically, 'nature' commonly denotes everything excluding humans and is frequently used in this manner throughout the existing psychological literature. For clarity and simplicity, I adopt the same approach, using 'nature' as a shorthand for environments where non-human life prevails.

At points where it is necessary to move beyond binary definitions, I explicitly distinguish between different types of environments and describe their multifactorial composition. Chapter 4 introduces a framework for identifying the specific environmental factors and affordances necessary for attunement states to occur. With that said, I suspect that any reader of this book in years to come will use fresh nomenclature around the human-nature relationship. Language has limitations in exploring new grounds. At present, we are stuck between the past and future.

With that said, the terms 'environmental attunement' and 'attunement states' are introduced and used throughout this book. They are used to describe a specific state of consciousness that is identifiable and distinguishable from other states and, therefore, are integral to the chief claim of this book. The choice of words was not taken lightly and is the result of much scholarly discourse and peer review. I return to this choice of terminology at several points.

A personal reflection

When close to finishing the final draft of this book, I was unexpectedly diagnosed with a serious spinal condition. Without surgery, I ran the risk of paralysis of the spine which would disrupt communication between the brain and the body, leading to a loss of voluntary movement and sensation from the neck down. Within three weeks of diagnosis, I underwent surgery. The last thing I remember was the anaesthetist counting me back from ten before going under. How far removed from being alone in nature could I be, and the embodied states of environmental attunement I have researched for years. There, I lay an anaesthetized body contained within one of the most sanitized and sterile places on the planet. Next, I remember coming around in the intensive care unit of the hospital, linked up to various machines, and attended to by a team of medical professionals.

The operation was successful, and within a few days, I was released from the hospital, albeit completely dependent on the support of my loved ones for the weeks that followed. Throughout my experience, I felt lucky to be alive and profoundly grateful to everyone involved in my care, from the consultants, doctors and nurses to my partner, loved ones, friends and neighbours who showed such kindness and support. It took a community to help me heal, and the experience served as a real-life reminder that nothing and no one can exist in isolation. Within two months, I could walk alone again in the woods near where I live. The woods' familiar sensuous murmur greeted me back. And in that moment, there was no place or time else I needed to be; I was home.

The reason for sharing my personal experience here is to underline the point that interdependence is fundamental to life. Humans need humans not just for the provision of food, shelter and care, but also for kindness, compassion and love. We are relational creatures who need human society to survive and thrive from cradle to grave. By proposing that there is more to the psychological life of humans than other people, Environmental Attunement Theory does not aim to present as an 'either or' proposition. Instead, it is a 'yes and' proposition that aims to expand psychology's focus beyond human relations to embrace this more-than-human world.

Being alone with nature is not the panacea to all ailments in life; it cannot cure the world's big illnesses, resolve conflicts or fix the environmental poly-crises that we face. That said, through my research, I am confident in my convictions that attunement states can profoundly affect our sense of self. Whereas most scientific studies quantify the human-nature relationship as improvements to cognitive processing, Environmental Attunement Theory paves the way for a fresh understanding of its psychological value. By reframing the human-nature relationship as reciprocal, embodied and central to selfhood, Environmental Attunement Theory offers a new paradigm for psychology – one that recognizes the existential and ethical stakes of modern society's connection to the rest of life around us.

References

Averill, J. R., & Sundararajan, L. (2014). Experiences of solitude: Issues of assessment, theory, and culture. In *The handbook of solitude: Psychological perspectives on social isolation, social withdrawal, and being alone* (pp. 90–108). Wiley Blackwell.

Benner, S., Lax, G., Crutzen, P. J., Pöschl, U., Lelieveld, J., Brauch, H. G., Töpfer, K., & Renn, J. (Eds.). (2022). *Paul J. Crutzen and the anthropocene: A new epoch in Earth's history. The Anthropocene* (Volume 1). Springer.

Bowlby, J. (2005). *The making and breaking of affectional bonds*. Routledge Classics. Routledge.

Bowler, D. E., Buyung-Ali, L. M., Knight, T. M., & Pullin, A. S. (2010). A systematic review of evidence for the added benefits to health of exposure to natural environments. *BMC Public Health, 10*(1), 456. https://doi.org/10.1186/1471-2458-10-456.

Capaldi, C. A., Dopko, R. L., & Zelenski, J. M. (2014). The relationship between nature connectedness and happiness: A meta-analysis. *Frontiers in Psychology, 5* (September). https://doi.org/10.3389/fpsyg.2014.00976.

Colley, K., Irvine, K. N., & Currie, M. (2022). Who benefits from nature? A quantitative intersectional perspective on inequalities in contact with nature and the gender gap outdoors. *Landscape and Urban Planning, 223* (July), 104420. https://doi.org/10.1016/j.landurbplan.2022.104420.

Coplan, R. J., & Bowker, J. C. (2014). *The handbook of solitude: Psychological perspectives on social isolation, social withdrawal, and being alone*. Wiley Blackwell.

Cozolino, L. J. (2014). *The neuroscience of human relationships: Attachment and the developing social brain* (2nd ed.). The Norton Series on Interpersonal Neurobiology. W.W. Norton & Company.

Froese, T. (2018). Book review: Ecology of the brain: The phenomenology and biology of the embodied mind. *Frontiers in Psychology* 9. https://doi.org/10.3389/fpsyg.2018.02174.

Fuchs, T. (2018). *Ecology of the brain: The phenomenology and biology of the embodied mind* (1st ed.). Oxford University Press.

Fuchs, T., & De Jaegher, H. (2009). Enactive intersubjectivity: Participatory sense-making and mutual incorporation. *Phenomenology and the Cognitive Sciences, 8*(4), 465–486. https://doi.org/10.1007/s11097-009-9136-4.

Kaplan, S. (1995). The restorative benefits of nature: Toward an integrative framework. *Journal of Environmental Psychology, 15*(3), 169–182. https://doi.org/10.1016/0272-4944(95)90001-2.

Kohn, E. (2013). *How forests think: Toward an anthropology beyond the human.* University of California Press.

Kull, R. (2009). *Solitude: Seeking wisdom in extremes: A year alone in the Patagonia Wilderness.* New World Library.

Long, C. R., Seburn, M., Averill, J. R., & More, T. A. (2003). Solitude experiences: Varieties, settings, and individual differences. *Personality and Social Psychology Bulletin, 29*(5) 578–583. https://doi.org/10.1177/0146167203029005003.

O'Day, E. B., & Heimberg, R. G. (2021). Social media use, social anxiety, and loneliness: A systematic review. *Computers in Human Behavior Reports, 3*(January), 100070. https://doi.org/10.1016/j.chbr.2021.100070.

O'Shaughnessy, B. (2003). *Consciousness and the world.* Clarendon Press.

Stolorow, R. D., & Atwood, G. E. (2002). *Contexts of being: The intersubjective foundations of psychological life.* The Analytic Press.

Ulrich, R. S., Simons, R. F., Losito, B. D., Fiorito, E., Miles, M. A., & Zelson, M. (1991). Stress recovery during exposure to natural and urban environments. *Journal of Environmental Psychology, 11*(3), 201–230. https://doi.org/10.1016/S0272-4944(05)80184-7.

Varela, F. J., Thompson, E., & Rosch, E. (2016). *The embodied mind: Cognitive science and human experience* (Revised edition). MIT Press.

Williams, A. J. (Ed.). (2011). *Nancy Holt: Sightlines.* University of California Press.

Winnicott, D. W., Winnicott, C., Shepherd, R., & Davis, M. (1990). *Home is where we start from: Essays by a psychoanalyst.* Penguin.

Part 1

In the Field

1

What happens alone with nature?

It is widely accepted that the quality of interpersonal relationships is directly linked to the development and maintenance of a healthy sense of self. When it comes to psychological well-being, the quality of relationships matters. Yet there has been limited research and attention given to the quality of our relationship with the physical world around us. Through my research, I discovered that cultivating our capacity to be alone with nature offers a unique opportunity to experience an exceptional state of consciousness, and with that, a profound sense of our own existence. How does this embodied state of attunement come about? Why does it shine a light on where we make the cut between the self and the rest of life on this planet? And what difference does it make to modern human societies?

There is a short and a long answer to these questions. The short answer I offered in the introduction highlights the gap in the psychology literature on self-sought experiences of solitude in nature and the discovery through my research of a distinct state of consciousness arising from prolonged, multisensory engagement with nature. The long answer is spread across the following nine chapters, providing the background to my research, the findings, their theoretical implications and their applicability to everyday life – and therefore offering the reader the first comprehensive introduction to Environmental Attunement Theory. This chapter begins by providing the context to how my research began, and an overview of the key findings and concepts that are examined in greater detail in the subsequent chapters.

From clinical practice to nature-based inquiry

I have spent most of my career in the field of human development trying to understand the workings of the human mind. I have always held a particular fascination in the relationship between psyche and place. Some of this I attribute to growing up in rural Ireland, running wild through the forests and fields near where I lived. It was during the final years of my clinical training; however, my childhood fascination took a professional turn that changed the trajectory of my career.

I started seeing a patient whom I call Annabel for confidentiality purposes. Aged thirty-nine, Annabel spent most of her adult years in and out of various mental health facilities. On the first day of therapy, Annabel refused to enter the room we were assigned to and asked if we could go outside. For the first couple of sessions, I sat in a nondescript fluorescent-lit room facing an empty chair, as Annabel stood in the doorway. When I asked her why, she sighed and said, 'I just can't stay in that room.' For a trainee trying to do the right thing, Annabel's refusal posed a dilemma. Everything in my training to this point emphasized the importance of the containment provided by the therapy room. Would the containment and safety of the therapy be sacrificed if we abandoned the room for the garden instead? If I pushed us to work indoors, would all chances of a good working relationship be destroyed? After a few weeks of tussling at the threshold, I conceded and set up two chairs in a quiet corner at the back of the garden.

Annabel and I worked together for close to two years and, once a week, we found some open-air position, moving around to avoid rain or gain warmth from the sun. In contrast to the neutral background provided by the consulting room, the garden provided an array of sensory stimuli that were difficult to ignore. Its atmosphere, temperature, smells, lights, colours, shapes and textures constantly shifted with the ever-changing weather of the seasons. While the indoor setting seemed to induce anxiety for Annabel, the whole ambiance of the garden seemed to cultivate ease and emotional reciprocity between us. We accepted and absorbed the elements as they wove their way into how we worked, inspiring the metaphorical language we used between us and encouraging the real and the imagined to coexist comfortably. There was something about working in that space that helped us realize our sentient nature. We were more than two talking heads.

On the surface, it may seem that going outside was the right and easy step to take, but from the early days of psychoanalysis and psychotherapy, the consulting room has been synonymous with the containment of a client's inner world. As the depth psychologist James Hillman points out:

> The traditional argument of psychology says: maintain the closed vessel of the consulting room, of the behavioral lab, of the field itself, for this tradition is born from the nineteenth century science, which continues to define psychology as the 'scientific' study of subjectivity. And science works best in controllable situations, in vito, under the bell jar, where it can carefully observe, predict, and therefore perhaps alter the minutiae of the subject. (Roszak et al., 1995, p. xxii)

On a practical level, the space provides a private, protected place. Scholars note that the physical space has increasingly become associated with professional and ethical practice (Casement, 1990). It also represents the physical manifestation of psychology's focus on humans' internalized worlds. Dissolving the boundaries of the space potentially threatens the containment of the client's inner world and interpersonal world of the patient and therapist. I had two clinical supervisors at the time, both psychoanalytically trained, who guided me through my work with Annabel. In general, they supported the move outdoors, but inevitably, our discussions led to questioning if resistance to the room was a resistance to treatment and the client's conscious and unconscious willingness to doing the inner work of therapy. In this case, however, Annabel engaged in the psychotherapeutic process and seemed to gain some therapeutic benefit, albeit outside the consulting room.

I do not want to imply that the efficacy of the work was solely due to the change in setting or that the surrounding nature had some therapeutic effect. My willingness to work outside may have also played a part in establishing the trust required for a good working relationship. However, the experience made me question the traditional emphasis placed on the consulting room as the physical containment of the 'inner' work, held as sacred in therapy. It also raised my curiosity about why my profession felt threatened by the idea of intimate relations with nature as a source of psychological growth. The net result was that this final case, before qualifying for clinical practice, set me on an unexpected trajectory for the rest of my career.

Initial nature observations

After I qualified, I set up a private clinical practice in Central London, working with people who presented a wide range of mental health issues. From my work with Annabel, in addition to exploring interpersonal dynamics, I maintained my interest in exploring people's relationships with nature, from their early childhood memories to their present lives. Simply discussing people's memories of being in nature seemed to raise their awareness of its value to the quality and texture of their everyday lives. Sometimes, depending on the patient's circumstances and the setting, we worked outside, finding a suitable spot in the gardens of the mental health centres I worked, or walking off the beaten track in Hampstead Heath, a sprawling well-established park filled with ancient trees in North London, UK.

My desire to incorporate nature into my practice increased over time. However, in the early 2000s, very little clinical training on what was then loosely termed outdoor therapy existed in the UK. Instead, my learning route was experiential. I researched and participated in various nature-based programmes, often outside the UK. This is how I met Trebbe Johnson, the acclaimed wilderness rites of passage guide and environmental author. Trebbe led a programme in the Sahara Desert I attended. Our mutual interest in the relationship between place and psyche developed into a working collaboration. We worked together across the globe for over a decade, leading nature-based programmes in a range of different types of natural settings, including the Blue Ridge Mountains in Virginia, the High Atlas Mountains in North Africa and Alpine trails in Switzerland.

Our intent for these nature-based programmes was to provide people with the support and space required to nurture their connection to nature as a source of self-reflection, awareness and growth. Typically, each programme incorporated solo time, anything between six and twenty-four hours alone with nature. Over the years, people repeatedly reported how during these solo experiences, they gained some fresh sense of their own existence in ways unavailable in their everyday lives. Often, I heard people recount the extraordinary phenomena that Nancy Holt and Robert Kull wrote about, that I reference in the opening to the introduction to this book, a form of blurring of worlds, and a deep sense of resonance with their surroundings. While I could speculate, based on my observations of the hundreds of people I worked with over the years, how or why these solo experiences impacted people in the ways they did, my knowledge was anecdotal, and the existing research provided little.

The gap in psychological research on nature and self

It may seem rather ignorant to state that we still know relatively little on how nature affects the self, given the fact environmental psychological studies since the 1980s have overwhelmingly pointed to the benefits of being in nature. On analysis, however, the majority of the research falls within the parameters of time-based exposure to green space. There are three components to this. First, the exposure periods typically range from fifteen to sixty minutes, with an average of twenty minutes (Bowler et al., 2010; Lee & Maheswaran, 2011; Meidenbauer et al., 2020; White et al., 2019). Second, exposure is treated primarily as visual, and therefore, studies can involve watching digital images or videos of nature. Third, green spaces refer to stereotypical images of nature as green, and other types of natural environments that fall outside this stereotype, such as deserts, boglands and rocky shorelines, are seldom studied.

The outcomes of most of these studies since the 1980s can be grouped into two main categories. The first is the psychophysiological reduction of stress and anxiety (Ewert & Chang, 2018; Farrow & Washburn, 2019; Li, 2010; Ulrich, 1981; Ulrich et al., 1991; Ward Thompson et al., 2012). The second is the restoration of cognitive functioning such as attention, memory and creativity (Balcetis & Dunning, 2016; Berman et al., 2008; Berto, 2005; de Keijzer et al., 2016; Hartig et al., 2003; Kaplan & Kaplan, 1989; Ohly et al., 2016). I will go into further depth in subsequent chapters.

The point to underline here is that through the parameters of time-based exposure to green spaces, looking at a video of a mountain scene can yield the same cognitive effects as physically being there. Cross-referencing several studies, for example, demonstrates how watching nature scenes on a computer screen can lower blood pressure and improve levels of attention in similar amounts to walking in real natural environments (Berman et al., 2008; Berto, 2005; Farrow & Washburn, 2019; Hartig et al., 2003; Mostajeran et al., 2021; Park et al., 2010).

From a practical perspective, short-term exposure to nature is relatively easy to study. Neural imaging technology allows us to study participants' responses to computer images of nature in the laboratory (Menser et al., 2021). Cognition tests can be effectively administered before, during and after short exposures to green spaces. The upshot is that there is a wealth of data on the positive physiological and cognitive effects of short-term exposure to natural environments. Long-term experiences in which participants interact with the environment are more challenging to research. Relatively few studies have examined prolonged immersive experiences.

The handful of studies that do exist are based on the personal accounts of people who spent long periods in remote locations. The results of these studies refer to the well-recorded reduction and restoration benefits of most natural studies, but interestingly, they also point to more qualitative outcomes (Averill & Sundararajan, 2014; Fredrickson & Anderson, 1999; Hammitt, 1982; Kull, 2009; Long et al., 2003; Naor & Mayseless, 2020). There were two types of qualitative outcomes. The first type is existential, referencing self-awareness, self-realization and self-transcendence. The second is relational, referring to feelings of intimacy, belonging and harmony (Long et al., 2003; Maes et al., 2016). While these more qualitative effects are mentioned and generally reported as having positive effects, the loadings are modest. This means that concrete definitions, causal factors or any underlying mechanics from a research perspective are non-existent. The upshot is that while floodlights have turned on the cognitive effects of short-term exposure, how prolonged experiences affect the self at deeper relational and existential levels remains a mystery.

Mainstream psychology may be guilty of reducing nature experiences to their cognitive roots, yet there are shelves of books that elevate them to transcendent levels. Such works play an important role in the canon of nature literature. However, romanticizing nature experiences, elevating them to something near spiritual or holding them as universally good, from a psychological point of view, leaves us none of the wiser. Where cognitive approaches are reductive, the glorification of nature similarly inhibits us from understanding what happens alone in nature. Between the reduction of the human-nature relationship to the purely cognitive and their elevation towards the mystical, I believe that there is a need for a middle-ground approach to understand the deeper existential and relational dimensions of the relationship. This gap became the impetus for my initial research to explore what happens during extended periods of solitude in nature, turning to qualitative research with individuals who regularly seek these experiences.

Exploring solitude in nature: Twenty interviews

I decided to start my investigations at the furthest reaches of human experience. Over the course of three years, I interviewed twenty people who had exceptional experiences of solitude in nature: environmental artists, nature therapists, wilderness rites of passage guides and shamanic healers who lived and worked in remote locations on the planet. Although diverse in geographical locations and disciplines, what this population had in common was the regular practice of spending extended periods alone immersed in nature. Collectively, although the sample size was relatively small, it provides a deep reservoir of experience. The protocol was simple: I spent several hours with each participant exploring their experience of being alone with nature, encouraging them to describe in as vivid detail as possible.

The main discovery from this phase of research was that, when alone with nature, people can experience a distinct shift in state. The following account from one participant, Jessica, encapsulates this phenomenon. Jessica travels from her home in Oslo every year to the Helgeland coast in northern Norway to camp on her own for three months. In this secluded landscape, where coastal mountains, deep fjords, and a labyrinth of islands and islets come together, Jessica finds inspiration for her work as an environmental artist. Jessica described her experience as follows:

> When I go to there, I bring with me who I am, and what I have done before. However, gradually, the environment has its own influence. It can take a bit of time to let go, but when I am open enough to experience the land, I can start to really listen. Listening is a better word than looking. Listening describes in a more holistic way how I am physically engaged.

> When I am listening in this way, I feel this resonance between the land
> and my body, my imagination, and my emotions. The experience, when
> it comes, is strong. It's like a door that opens.
>
> Interview extract (Hughes, 2022)

This state appeared in some form in all interviewees' accounts. Sometimes, the feeling was stronger for some than others, and the duration varied, but the feeling was strong enough for people to recognize it as distinct. Based on the musical metaphors that people most commonly use to describe this state, I started to name it attunement, or more precisely, environmental attunement. Based on the musical metaphors that people repeatedly used to describe this state shift, I landed on the name attunement. The word 'attunement' has a long legacy from its French origin. Martin Heidegger's concept of Stimmung, often translated as attunement, draws upon the musical metaphor to describe how our moods interact and shape our experience of the world around us.

In the world of psychotherapy, Daniel Steer describes affect attunement occurring between an infant and its primary caregiver. The term has also been used in contemporary aesthetics. However, I kept returning to attunement as it was most closely aligned with people's descriptions. I return to the naming of attunement at several points throughout the book, but from here on, I refer to environmental attunement as this specific state in which people experience a pattern of perceptual effects and, most noticeably, an embodied sense of resonance with their immediate surroundings.

Defining environmental attunement:
Characteristics, conditions and impact

From this original set of interviews, I extracted three key findings about these exceptional states: the core characteristics of the state itself, the conditions in which it occurs and the ways in which it affects people.

Characteristics of attunement states

The way people experience the world around them, and themselves as part of it, changes. Some participants described this shift in state as sudden, as if a door opens, whereas others described a more gradual process of awareness. Nevertheless, whether sudden or gradual, people were aware that a shift in state has occurred. The study identified four core characteristics of this state: heightened multisensory awareness, vivid mental imagery, altered time perception and an embodied sense of connection to immediate physical surroundings.

The study concluded that these four components operate interdependently, generating a qualitative shift in the individual's overall state such that the individual is conscious that the experience is distinct from their everyday normative state. In essence, what people experience is not simply a heightened affect but an embodied state of consciousness, identifiable by a pattern of effects.

Core conditions

The second significant finding was that simply being alone in nature does not automatically lead to a state of attunement; the quality of contact matters. There are four aspects to this. First, attunement requires time. The deep states of attunement people described take anywhere on average between six and twelve hours, and sometimes longer. Second, multisensory stimulation is required. Visual exposure such as looking out of a window at a natural view is not sufficient. Third, it takes a certain quality of attention, directed towards engaging with the whole of your surroundings, as opposed to focusing on a singular object or activity. Fourth, attunement states occur in environments in which non-human factors dominate a person's perceptual field.

Impact on self

The impact of attunement states on people is threefold. First, people experience a heightened sense of ownership and agency over their bodies and how they move within the environment. Second, people experience a sense of being an active part of their immediate surroundings. Third, participants reported a profound sense of being alive. These embodied, engaged and enlivened factors represent more than a feel-good effect – they represent a shift in the person's overall self and self-and-world perception.

While past research has mentioned people's feelings of harmony and connection when alone in nature, this framework enables us to identify and distinguish attunement states from other types of nature experiences. Notably, the initial study also concluded that spending more time in nature does not automatically produce this state. Attunement states require specific conditions. Together, these findings create a framework for understanding the conditions, characteristics and outcomes of environmental attunement as a distinct state of consciousness.

Chapters 2 and 3 dive into the specifics of this initial study, including the methodology, findings and conclusions. Overall, these initial findings provide a framework for identifying attunement as a distinct state of consciousness, but they also raise deeper theoretical questions about how psychology conceptualizes the self in relation to a more-than-human world.

Part 2: In theory

Adam Grant, a prominent researcher of innovation at Harvard, claims that phenomena outside of our everyday experiences have the unique ability to shed light on our default thinking (2016). Grant used the term 'default thinking' for the concepts and ideas that underpin much of our everyday thinking, ideas that often go unnoticed and unchallenged. In this vein, through my research on attunement, I have come to realize that there are three basic assumptions underpinning contemporary psychology that can hinder our understanding of the phenomenon and the psychology of the human-nature relationship more broadly. It has been by challenging these basic assumptions that I have come closer to a theoretical interpretation of environmental attunement.

The first assumption is that the brain is the seat of the self, which has dominated psychology since the cognitive turn of the 1950s. One consequence of this is that nature experiences are valued primarily for their 'green pill' effect on cognitive functioning. The second is the pervasive belief that humans are relational beings, which advocates for human relationships as the sole source of psychological development and well-being. Consequently, it is difficult to appreciate the rest of life around us as anything other than a restorative backdrop for human endeavours. The third assumption is the Cartesian divide between mind and matter, which negates the possibility of any meaningful reciprocity between the human mind and mindless nature.

These three assumptions are expanded in Part 2 of this book. The task is not easy, as these assumptions underpin much of modern psychology and its theories and models. However, in addressing these assumptions, we move closer to a more theoretical grounding for the phenomenon of attunement, or at least closer to the possibility of positioning the experience of attunement within a less anthropocentric and more ecological frame of reference. As the depth psychologist James Hillman points out, the central question for psychology is not 'who am I?' but rather 'where am I?' – and where we draw the line between the 'me' and the 'not-me' (as cited in Roszak, 1995). The phenomenology of environmental attunement sheds light on where we draw this line.

When I first met philosopher Arnold Berleant, a leading figure in the field of environmental aesthetics and one of my PhD supervisors, he drew my attention to my use of the definite article when talking about 'the' environment. The point he wanted to emphasize is that environments should not be objectified, as we are, in fact, part of our surroundings, fully immersed and actively engaged within them. Consider, for example, the simple act of breathing. With every inhalation, molecules from our surroundings penetrate deep into our bodies, and as we exhale, parts of us are released to merge with particles beyond the boundaries of our skin. The point is that physiological reciprocity occurs, rendering any attempt at finite delineations meaningless. For Berleant, 'what we experience are contracts not opposites, combining in the rich texture of environment experience', and in doing so, he challenges, 'the most illustrious division of them all, that between inside and outside, person and environment, nature and human (p. 45)'.

Berleant's work is not isolated. It is situated within the phenomenological tradition of Maurice Merleau-Ponty, who notably advocated for the primacy of perception in human experience. Merleau-Ponty critiqued the sciences for their detached perspective, which he argued manipulates and relinquishes the immediacy of sensory experience. In the word of Merleau-Ponty 'scientific thinking which looks on from above, and thinks of the object-in-general, must return to the "there is" which underlies it, to the sire, the soul of the sensible and opened world such as it is in our life and for our body – not that possible body which we may legitimately think of as an information machine but that actual body I call mine, this sentinel standing quietly at the commends of my words and my act' (p. 160).

Berleant takes our understanding of environmental engagement beyond the construct of subject and object by orientating our attention towards our multisensory perceptual participation within environments. He proposes a continuum of experience where the in-between is as real as either end. Where sensation ends and cognition begins, it becomes impossible to delineate and irrelevant to the varying and sometimes contrasting textures and qualities of the various aspects of experience. Physical sensations are treated with the same curiosity and interest as emotions and ideas (Hughes & Berleant, 2023). Berleant's work is of particular relevance to environmental attunement as it challenges the dualistic constructs that governed Western philosophy for millennia, and in doing so, paves the way for a fresh understanding of humans' engagement with nature.

Phenomenology's reconfiguration of sensory perception as central to human experience is not only a challenge to philosophers but also to the cognitive sciences, and one which has significantly influenced a branch of cognitive science broadly termed 'embodied cognition' to search for consciousness beyond the confines of the brain. As a result, a new generation of scientists has discovered that the line between sensation and cognition is far less delineated than previously thought (Gallagher, 2023; Varela et al., 2016). With an appreciation that the mind is inextricably linked to the body and its interaction within the environment, research is extended beyond the brain, and as a consequence, new evidence points to a more complex perceptual participation between perceiver and environment (Berger, 2016; Shimojo & Shams, 2001). The senses are not autonomous inputs to be interpreted; rather, perception is a dynamic system of cross-modal activity influenced by memory and imagination, and shaped by its interaction with the environment.

Throughout Part 2, this intersection of phenomenology and embodied cognition is used to inform our understanding of environmental attunement. Chapter 4 challenges the human-nature divide that governs most modern psychology by proposing environments as complex, multifactorial systems that are further animated by the individual's perceptual participation. The chapter identifies how environments with low human impact afford opportunities for attunement that other types of environments do not. Chapter 5 distinguishes between the concept of the self as a purely internalized mental construct and the embodied sense of self, and how this distinction helps us better understand the psychological potential of attunement states. Chapter 6 explores perception as a dynamic multi-modal system and its pivotal role in shaping not only our experience of the world but also our sense of self. Together, the core concepts put forward in these three chapters provide the theoretical foundation for Environmental Attunement Theory.

From theory to practice: Environmental attunement in everyday life

Throughout my career as a psychotherapist, I maintained my clinical practice in Central London, UK. Although I travelled to some of the remotest places on the planet to lead nature-based programmes and carry out my research, I have always returned to this inner-city practice. Consequently, I am acutely aware of how challenging access to nature can occur in many parts of the population. With population growth and urbanization figures mushrooming, nature contact is far from equal. Since I first identified attunement states and their potential psychological benefits, I have felt deep concern about their universal applicability. Part 1 of this book examines the initial discovery of attunement states. Part 2 draws upon philosophical, psychological and cultural sources to provide a theoretical underpinning. Part 3 explores environmental attunement in the context of everyday modern life.

The initial research I carried out focused on individuals who sought solitude in places far removed from human life. Acknowledging the limitations of my original research, I went on to carry out interviews with people in more everyday settings and devised a series of experiments to test the relevance and applicability of environmental attunement to general populations. Chapter 7 explores how Environmental Attunement Theory can inform contemporary psychotherapeutic practice. Chapter 8 discusses the potential for environmental attunement to influence contemporary urban green space design – and the more-than-human city. Chapter 9 discusses the role of environmental attunement in addressing the disparity in access to nature that disproportionately affects certain groups and

Environmental attunement in therapy

Towards the end of his life, Heinz Kohut, the originator of self-psychology, famously predicted the greatest psychological challenge facing modern humans to be the fragmenting self (Kohut, 2009). Kohut's prediction could materialize as the World Health Organization reports the growing burden of a global mental health pandemic (2022). Access to conventional talking therapies and medical treatments is a severe cause of concern. The mental health profession is increasingly challenged to widen its options. In 2020, to address the ever-growing waiting lists, the UK's National Health Service launched a series of outdoor initiatives under the banner of social prescribing, advising people to spend more time in green spaces (Howarth et al., 2020).

This well-intentioned initiative, which is supported by an impressive body of research recommending exposure to nature as an early intervention for general health and well-being, has some limitations. However, initiatives of this kind are often underpinned by deep-rooted philosophical beliefs that reduce humans' relationships with nature to interactions that overlook the complexity of environmental dynamics and human multisensory engagement within them. Such initiatives can lack the variance and distinctions between different types of nature encounters.

In Chapter 7, I argue that, although it is reasonable to assume that outdoor therapies yield positive outcomes, given the evidence to date, the majority of outdoor therapies maintain an anthropocentric stance. Nature remains the backdrop, albeit invigorating and rejuvenating, to our human dynamics. Attunement states teach us, as with human relationships, that the quality of the relationship matters. There is reciprocity involved that requires certain conditions, time and intentionality. Using nature as a backdrop to conventional therapeutic methods may avail of the effects of exposure to nature; however, this approach falls short in availing ways in which our relationship with nature can affect our sense of self. Instead of simply taking therapy outdoors, Chapter 7 explores how Environmental Attunement Theory can be used to bring nature into the therapeutic process.

Chapter 7 discusses a hypothetical case as a vehicle to understand how Environmental Attunement Theory can inform conventional psychotherapies. Challenging the assumption that nature-based therapy must be outdoor, the case study uses Environmental Attunement Theory to inform the dialogic process within the consulting room in three ways. First, how is the field of exploration expanded from the person's intrapersonal and interpersonal dynamics to encompass a more-than-human world? Second, how is attention given to an individual's felt experience and their intentional interaction with other-than-human life? Third, how is the capacity to be alone with nature encouraged as a pathway to experiencing attunement and its effects on our sense of self?

This hypothetical case maps a shift in therapeutic focus from the intersubjective world of the individual towards an ecological appreciation of the self within a more-than-human world. When the case was reviewed by a panel of psychotherapy peers from different subspecialties, several points were raised that never reached a logical conclusion. We practise within our specialist rivers, where currents sweep us along, sometimes knowingly, sometimes not. Exploring environmental attunement in the context of the psychotherapeutic relationship stirs the riverbed by challenging the anthropocentric nature of contemporary psychotherapy and the underlying philosophical dichotomies that prevent the field from truly incorporating nature.

Environmental attunement and urban green space design

At the start of the nineteenth century, most people on the planet could walk out their front door and find untouched land within an hour. Today, the global population has risen from roughly 1 billion to 8 billion, with over half living in urban areas. Very few places remain untouched by human presence. Marine life in some of the deepest oceans is affected by microplastics. As attunement states require freedom from human distraction, we have to question how feasible this is for most people on the planet.

Increasing evidence for the mental and physical benefits of access to nature for urban dwellers, alongside growing environmental concerns, is fuelling major innovations in contemporary urban green space design. Greater biodiversity is being introduced into urban green spaces, for example, to decrease noise and air pollution and improve people's quality of life. With such innovations, can the contemporary urban green space offer the same or similar affordances as remote environments with low human impact? Is it possible to access a state of attunement in a city?

Despite its post-Second World War brutalist architecture, the Barbican Centre in Central London has been transformed into a biodiverse habitat in an initiative called 'The Woodland Edge'. Urban designers have created large areas with woodland-edge planting, intimate places where other-than-human life dominates the perceptual field, and spaces in which residents can find moments of solitude. The critical question in this chapter is whether Barbican's renovated green spaces can facilitate micro-attunement – less intense and momentary states of attunement.

Contemporary urban greenspace design is situated within the context of nature-based solutions, addressing social, environmental, aesthetic and restorative needs. However, this chapter argues that contemporary urban green spaces often lack the essential aloneness and quality of nature contact required for attunement. Through a synthesis of interviews with residents of the Barbican Centre in London and related studies, this chapter identifies specific characteristics of urban green spaces that offer pathways to attunement.

The Barbican Centre's gardens serve as a case study, illustrating how intentional design can provide opportunities for residents to be alone with nature in the heart of a city. The gardens' naturalistic planting, unmanicured aesthetics and skilfully incorporated privacy pockets allow for freedom from human distractions and multisensory engagement with other-than-human life. This chapter proposes how micro-attunements can enhance general urban populations' relationships with nature and the overall quality of life. While acknowledging the limitations of the current research, this chapter concludes with ways in which Environmental Attunement Theory can stimulate interdisciplinary discourse across the fields of psychology, architecture and urban green space design.

Bridging the social divide

Towards the end of his career in 1957, following many volumes he wrote on the importance of early emotional bonds to human development, child psychiatrist Donald Winnicott published a short article entitled 'On the Capacity to Be Alone' (Winnicott, 1990). He proposes that the capacity of a young child to spend time alone is an important marker in the maturation of the self. This early independence and self-drive to explore can determine the desire and capacity to be alone throughout our lives. Winnicott's idea distinguishes between a state of loneliness shaped by the absence and yearning for connection and a type of aloneness that feeds our creativity and sense of fulfilment. Others followed, such as the psychoanalyst Allan Storr (Storr,

1989), psychologist Mihaly Csikszentmihalyi (Csikszentmihalyi, 2000) and a relatively small group of researchers compared to those who researched the pitfalls of loneliness (Averill & Sundararajan, 2014; Long et al., 2003; Naor & Mayseless, 2020).

Winnicott's article is impressive, not least because he wrote it after a career advocating for human connection, in an era when the vast majority of psychological literature champions the idea that we are social creatures, and that we need to belong to be part of society in order to survive and thrive. Throughout Part 3 of the book, I challenge this assumption that we are solely social creatures, not with an opposing proposition, but with 'yes and'. Yes, we are human, and we are part of this more-than-human world. We are ecological beings as well as human beings, with kinship broader than our own, if we choose to appreciate it. To be alone with nature is to be engaged, to be curious, to be energized by and to energize the other-than-human world. This quality of being alone with nature is fundamentally different from the character of loneliness that we fear. Cultivating the capacity to be alone with nature in this manner is essential for attunement.

When surveyed, attitudes towards solitude in nature environments tended to be more favourable than being alone in other settings. People tend to associate being alone in nature with more positive experiences. Natural environments provide stimulation, unlike other types of environments. Biophilia theory posits that humans have an innate sense of connection to the rest of life around us. This trait may be present in a repressed state in modern life, but can be invigorated when in contact with nature. The evidence for biophilia is problematic, although its basic premise is intuitive. Similarly, the emotional and symbolic bonds we hold towards certain types of natural environments based on our past experiences and associations – something referred to as place attachment and place identity in the literature – also play a part in our desire to be alone.

The capacity to be alone with nature is layered and is therefore a topic I weave throughout the chapter in the book. Chapter 9, though, specifically addresses access to and willingness to engage with nature across the general population. Any theory of environmental attunement is destined to remain on the bookshelf if it cannot appreciate the nature gap in modern society. Significant disparities exist in the opportunities to access and engage with nature based on socioeconomic status, gender, sexuality and race. The nature gap disproportionately affects the most disadvantaged and marginalized groups, who are also often the most directly and adversely affected by environmental degradation (Colley et al., 2022; Rigolon, 2016; Wu et al., 2022). For a theory that champions the capacity to be alone with nature, environmental attunement must consider these disparities to make a meaningful contribution. Chapter 9 situates Environmental Attunement Theory within the broader context of social and environmental injustice as the pressing issue of our age and reflects on future paths.

Reflections: The value of environmental attunement in contemporary life

Experiences of attunement are different from what one gets from looking out of the window at a beautiful nature view, sitting in the park on a summer's day with a friend or skiing down a mountain on a clear day. I have spoken with people from different walks of life across the globe who have experienced attunement, and what is common to all is the embodied feeling of being a part of their surroundings. For some, the experience of attunement is intense and can last days. However, over the years, I have interviewed enough people to know that micro-attunements, although more subtle and fleeting, hold value in that they bring a feeling of innate satisfaction and fulfilment in everyday life. It is not that attunement states offer some grand epiphany or life-changing moments, but that they can evoke what Joseph Campbell famously referred to as the rapture of being alive, and with that, the embodied sense that life is worth living (Campbell, 1990).

In an age when humans' relationship with nature seems to be at an all-time low, where social interaction and virtual reality take our attention, cities are the dominant habitat and solitude sits low on our agenda, which is the rapture of being alive that makes us feel in an embodied sense that life is worth living. The task of integrating attunement into daily life may be immense. However, once we succeed in understanding the mechanics of attunement states, we may be able to use its insights and principles across various disciplines, such as education, environmental design and public health. If nothing else, the study of environmental attunement provides the field of psychology with fresh curiosity about nature's impact on the self, and the possibility that there may well be more to our psychological development and fulfilment than other people.

References

Averill, J. R., & Sundararajan, L. (2014). Experiences of solitude: Issues of assessment, theory, and *culture*. In *The handbook of solitude: Psychological perspectives on social isolation, social withdrawal, and being alone* (pp. 90–108). Wiley Blackwell.

Balcetis, E., & Dunning, D. (2016). Cognitive dissonance and the perception of natural environments. *Psychological Science*. Retrieved from (Campbell, 2008).

Berger, C. C. (2016). Where imagination meets sensation: Mental imagery, perception, and multisensory integration. *Inst för neurovetenskap / Dept of Neuroscience*. Retrieved from http://openarchive.ki.se/xmlui/handle/10616/45157.

Berman, M. G., Jonides, J., & Kaplan, S. (2008). The cognitive benefits of interacting with nature. *Psychological Science, 19*(12), 1207–1212. https://doi.org/10.1111/j.1467-9280.2008.02225.

Berto, R. (2005). Exposure to restorative environments helps restore attentional capacity. *Journal of Environmental Psychology, 25*(3), 249–259.

Bowler, D. E., Buyung-Ali, L. M., Knight, T. M., & Pullin, A. S. (2010). A systematic review of evidence for the added benefits to health of exposure to natural environments. *BMC Public Health, 10*(1), 456. https://doi.org/10.1186/1471-2458-10-456.

Campbell, J. (1990). *The hero has a thousand faces*. Fontana Press.

Colley, K., Irvine, K. N., & Currie, M. (2022). Who benefits from nature? A quantitative intersectional perspective on inequalities in contact with nature and the gender gap outdoors. *Landscape and Urban Planning, 223*, 104420. https://doi.org/10.1016/j.landurbplan.2022.104420

Csikszentmihalyi, M. (2000). *FLOW: The psychology of optimal experience*. Ingram International Publisher.

de Bell, S., Alejandre, J. C., Menzel, C., Sousa-Silva, R., Straka, T. M., Berzborn, S., Bürck-Gemassmer, M., Dallimer, M., Dayson, C., Fisher, J. C., Haywood, A., Herrmann, A., Immich, G., Keßler, C. S., Köhler, K., Lynch, M., Marx, V., Michalsen, A., Mudu, P., ... Bonn, A. (2024). Nature-based social prescribing programmes: opportunities, challenges, and facilitators for implementation. *Environment International, 190*, 108801. https://doi.org/10.1016/j.envint.2024.108801.

de Keijzer, C., Gascon, M., Nieuwenhuijsen, M. J., & Dadvand, P. (2016). Long-term green space exposure and cognition across the life course: A systematic review. *Current Environmental Health Reports, 3*(4), 468–477. https://doi.org/10.1007/s40572-016-0116-x.

Ewert, A., & Chang, Y. (2018). Levels of nature and stress response. *Behavioral Sciences, 8*(5), 49. https://doi.org/10.3390/bs8050049.

Farrow, M. R., & Washburn, K. (2019). A review of field experiments on the effect of forest bathing on anxiety and heart rate variability. *Global Advances in Health and Medicine, 8*, 2164956119848654. https://doi.org/10.1177/2164956119848654.

Fredrickson, L. M., & Anderson, D. H. (1999). A qualitative exploration of the wilderness experience as a source of spiritual inspiration. *Journal of Environmental Psychology, 19*(1), 21–39. https://doi.org/10.1006/jevp.1998.0110.

Gallagher, S. (2023). *Embodied and enactive approaches to cognition.* Elements in philosophy of mind. Cambridge University Press. https://doi. org/10.1017/978100920979.

Grant, A. (2016). *Originals: How non-conformists move the world.* Viking.

Hammitt, W. E. (1982). Cognitive dimensions of wilderness solitude. *Environment and Behavior, 14*(4), 478–493. https://doi.org/10.1177/00139 16582144005.

Hartig, T., Evans, G. W., Jamner, L. D., Davis, D. S., & Gärling, T. (2003). Tracking restoration in natural and urban field settings. *Journal of Environmental Psychology, 23*(2), 109–123. https://doi.org/10.1016/ S0272-4944(02)00109-3.

Howarth, M., Griffiths, A., da Silva, A., & Green, R. (2020). Social prescribing: A 'natural' community-based solution. *British Journal of Community Nursing, 25*(6), 294–298. https://doi.org/10.12968/bjcn.2020.25.6.294.

Hughes, E. (2016). Attunement: The psychology of being alone with nature (PhD thesis). The University of the Arts. Available from ProQuest Dissertations & Theses Global. (Accession No. 5328f2e6572e6ca62965ba98e cfb3606).

Hughes, E., & Berleant, A. (2024). Aesthetic engagement as a pathway to mental health and wellbeing. In Y. Saito, J. Douglass, & H. Watanabe (Eds.), *The Oxford Handbook of Mental Health and Contemporary Western Aesthetics* Oxford University Press.

Kaplan, R., & Kaplan, S. (1989). *The experience of nature: A psychological perspective.* Cambridge University Press.

Kohut, H. (2009). *The restoration of the self.* The University of Chicago Press.

Kull, R. (2009). *Solitude: Seeking wisdom in extremes: A year alone in the Patagonia Wilderness.* New World Library.

Lee, A. C. K., & Maheswaran, R. (2011). The health benefits of urban green spaces: A review of the evidence. *Journal of Public Health, 33*(2), 212–222. https://doi.org/10.1093/pubmed/fdq068.

Li, Q. (2010). Effect of forest bathing trips on human immune function. *Environmental Health and Preventive Medicine, 15*(1), 9–17. https://doi. org/10.1007/s12199-008-0068-3.

Long, C. R., Seburn, M., Averill, J. R., & More, T. A. (2003). Solitude experiences: Varieties, settings, and individual differences. *Personality and Social Psychology Bulletin, 29*(5), 578–583. https://doi.org/10.1177/01461672 03029005003.

Maes, M., Wang, J. M., Van den Noortgate, W., & Goossens, L. (2016). *Loneliness and attitudes toward being alone in belgian and chinese adolescents: Examining measurement invariance. Journal of Child and Family Studies, 25*(5), 1408–1415. https://doi.org/10.1007/s10826-015-0336-y.

Meidenbauer, K. L., Stenfors, C. U. D., Bratman, G. N., Gross, J. J., Schertz, K. E., Choe, K. W., & Berman, M. G. (2020). The affective benefits of nature exposure: What's nature got to do with it? *Journal of Environmental Psychology, 72*, 101498. https://doi.org/10.1016/j.jenvp.2020.101498.

Menser, T., Baek, J., Siahaan, J., Kolman, J. M., Delgado, D., & Kash, B. (2021). Validating visual stimuli of nature images and identifying the representative characteristics. *Frontiers in Psychology, 12*. https://www.frontiersin.org/artic les/10.3389/fpsyg.2021.685815.

Mostajeran, F., Krzikawski, J., Steinicke, F., & Kühn, S. (2021). Effects of exposure to immersive videos and photo slideshows of forest and urban environments. *Scientific Reports, 11*(1), Article 1. https://doi.org/10.1038/s41598-021-83277-y.

Naor, L., & Mayseless, O. (2020). *The wilderness solo experience: A unique practice of silence and solitude for personal growth. Frontiers in Psychology, 11*.

Ohly, H., White, M. P., Wheeler, B. W., Bethel, A., Ukoumunne, O. C., Nikolaou, V., & Garside, R. (2016). *Attention restoration theory: A systematic review of the attention restoration potential of exposure to natural environments. Journal of Toxicology and Environmental Health, Part B, 19*(7), 305–343.

Park, B. J., Tsunetsugu, Y., Kasetani, T., Kagawa, T., & Miyazaki, Y. (2010). The physiological effects of Shinrin-yoku (taking in the forest atmosphere or forest bathing): Evidence from field experiments in 24 forests across Japan. *Environmental Health and Preventive Medicine, 15*(1), 18–26.

Rigolon, A. (2016). A complex landscape of inequity in access to urban parks: A literature review. *Landscape and Urban Planning, 153*, 160–169. https://doi.org/10.1016/j.landurbplan.2016.05.017

Roszak, T., Gomes, M. E., & Kanner, A. D. (Eds.). (1995). *Ecopsychology—Restoring the earth, healing the mind.* Sierra Club Books.

Shimojo, S., & Shams, L. (2001). Sensory modalities are not separate modalities: Plasticity and interactions. *Current Opinion in Neurobiology, 11*(4), 505–509.

Stern, D. N. (1985). *Interpersonal world of the infant—A view from psychoanalysis and development.*

Storr, A. (1989). *Solitude.* Flamingo.

Trott, M., Driscoll, R., Iraldo, E., & Pardhan, S. (2022). Changes and correlates of screen time in adults and children during the COVID-19 pandemic: A systematic review and meta-analysis. *eClinicalMedicine, 48*, 101452.

Ulrich, R. S. (1981). Natural versus urban scenes: Some psychophysiological effects. *Environment and Behavior, 13*(5), 523–556.

Ulrich, R. S., Simons, R. F., Losito, B. D., Fiorito, E., Miles, M. A., & Zelson, M. (1991). Stress recovery during exposure to natural and urban environments. *Journal of Environmental Psychology, 11*(3), 201–230.

Varela, F. J., Thompson, E., & Rosch, E. (2016). *The embodied mind: Cognitive science and human experience (revised edition).* MIT Press.

Ward Thompson, C., Roe, J., Aspinall, P., Mitchell, R., Clow, A., & Miller, D. (2012). More green space is linked to less stress in deprived communities: Evidence from salivary cortisol patterns. *Landscape and Urban Planning, 105*(3), 221–229.

White, M. P., Alcock, I., Grellier, J., Wheeler, B. W., Hartig, T., Warber, S. L., Bone, A., Depledge, M. H., & Fleming, L. E. (2019). Spending at least 120 minutes a week in nature is associated with good health and wellbeing. *Scientific Reports, 9*(1), Article 1.

Williams, A. J., Badischer Kunstverein Karlsruhe, Miriam and Ira D. Wallach Art Gallery New York, & Lee, P. M. (2015). *Nancy Holt: Sightlines.* University of California Press.

Winnicott, D. W. (1990). *The maturational processes and the facilitating environment: Studies in the theory of emotional development.* Karnac.

Wu, J., Xu, Z., Jin, Y., Chai, Y., Newell, J., & Ta, N. (2022). Gender disparities in exposure to green space: An empirical study of suburban Beijing. *Landscape and Urban Planning, 222*, 104381. https://doi.org/10.1016/j.landurbplan. 2022.104381.

2

Discovering environmental attunement

It was as if I was looking at a painting and then suddenly the painting starts to move. And I'm conscious of the land pulsating in response to my steps. It was like my movements were somehow resonating with the land, like a dance, in this rhythm, me and the land.

Research Participant

This chapter focuses on the phenomenon of environmental attunement as it emerged in the personal accounts of the artists, wilderness rites of passage guides, nature therapists and ancestral healers I interviewed over the course of three years who seek solitude in nature. The chapter explores the specific circumstances and qualities that characterize these extraordinary states of attunement – moments in which people report an embodied sense of participation with the land. By systematically analysing these first-hand accounts, this chapter outlines not only the features that distinguish this state from others, and specific conditions required, but also how these findings lay the groundwork for future research initiatives and their relevance to wider population groups.

The chapter begins by introducing the research and the diverse individuals involved in the study. I then outline the methodological approach before moving to the heart of the chapter: a systematic analysis of interview data that identifies four core characteristics of attunement states: heightened sensations, vivid mental imagery, time fluidity and an embodied sense of participation. The chapter also details the four core conditions necessary for attunement to arise: the physical composition of the environment, the multisensory stimulation, the duration of time and the individual's intentionality. I draw on first-hand accounts to illustrate how these characteristics and conditions interact to produce a state that leads to an expanded, enlivened sense of self. The chapter concludes by pointing to the broader theoretical and practical implications of these findings, which are taken up in the following chapters.

Research overview

People seek solitude for various reasons, including respite, time away from others and focus on solo activities. Over the course of three years, I interviewed twenty people who intentionally sought solitude in nature. For this group of individuals, their goal was to be alone 'with' nature for its own sake, a relational, rather than a transactional act. These individuals are extraordinary in that the extremes they go to connect with nature are far outside the type of everyday nature experience that most of us can access. To realize this ambition, they travel to some of the remotest places on the planet and the farthest edges of human experience. Consequently, their collective experiences provide us with unique insights into what happens at the extreme end of solitude in nature.

The line of enquiry for my research was straightforward – to understand what happens when people spend prolonged and intentional periods alone in nature. Each interviewee was asked to describe their lived experiences in as vivid detail as possible. Whether interviewing shamans from Peru, land artists in England, nature therapists based in Europe or wilderness rites of passage guides located in various locations worldwide, what jumped out from people's descriptions was the point at which they became aware of feelings of heightened sensitivity and receptivity towards their immediate surroundings. For some, the process was gradual, while for others, it was sudden. The intensity and duration of the experiences varied. However, these moments of heightened awareness were present in each interview.

People described how sometimes it takes a few days to shake off the structures of their everyday routines. But slowly they dissolve, and they start to feel all the sensations the land has to offer and its effect on them. When they are open with all of these senses in that way, as one participant put it 'listening with my whole body', the place comes alive. People describe becoming part of this pulsating land, part of its beat and feeling this embodied sense of resonance with their immediate surroundings. This kind of connection can feel intense, as every part of their being, physical and emotional, past and present, is folded into the landscape.

It is important to point out that this is not the first time that participants in nature studies describe out-of-ordinary phenomena. Of the handful of studies on prolonged solitude in nature, several record people experiencing strong positive feelings of harmony and connection that they do not feel in their everyday lives (Hammitt, 1982; *Hollenhorst*, n.d.; Korpela & Staats, 2014; Kull, 2009; Long et al., 2003; Mateer, 2022; Naor & Mayseless, 2020). However, these references show up as having very modest loadings across studies, and their descriptions are vague. Moreover, we know very little about the environmental conditions and the quality of interaction that cause these feelings.

The unique aspect of this study lies in its articulation of the phenomenon as a distinct, identifiable and distinguishable state because of its unique set of characteristics. The study also identifies the specific circumstances and actions that bring about this state. In addition to identifying the core characteristics and conditions, the findings point to the ways in which this state can affect our sense of self. Although my research on the phenomenon extended beyond this original study, I used the findings as a framework for subsequent research and as the basis of Environmental Attunement Theory. This chapter provides an overview of the original study's approach and a summary of the main findings and conclusions.

The sample selection

I used two main criteria to identify individuals for this initial study: repeated experiences of spending extended periods alone in remote locations and a conscious desire to engage with nature. In the initial stages, I targeted individuals broadly termed nature-based practitioners such as environmental artists, nature-based psychotherapists, wilderness rites of passage guides and shamanic healers, as they fulfilled the criteria. I also paid attention to the diversity in gender, culture and geographical location. Due to the nature of their work, many of these people were difficult to reach and were often out of contact for long periods of time. However, over the course of one year, an initial sample of twelve came together. After these interviews were completed, common themes started to emerge, therefore I expanded the sample beyond nature-based practitioners to others who met the criteria. This next wave included, for example, a poet who spent a year in nature following a major accident and a psychologist who takes several months out of their work every year to walk 'the Camino', the ancient pilgrim route through rural Spain to Santiago de Compostela.

Here are two snapshots of some of the people I interviewed. The first is Sam, an artist who uses nature as the inspiration for his work. He described coming across a craggy inlet on the northwest shoreline on his first visit to the small Isle of Raasay, part of the Scottish Inner Hebrides. There was something about this spot that captured his imagination, to the point that he returned many times over the course of several years. Despite the fierce winds and storms that can last for days and make conditions wild and unpredictable, he managed to set up a basic shelter close to the shoreline, where he stayed for several months at a time.

On the other side of the Atlantic, situated between the Rocky Mountains to the East and the Sierra Nevada to the West, is the Great Basin Desert in Utah. It is the largest desert in the United States, with hot summers and snowy winters, and is home to some of the oldest trees on the planet. This is where the second participant, Christi, a wilderness rites of passage guide, has taken people on retreats to this location since the late 1970s. After people go home, Christi typically stays on for a few weeks or so on her own, not to work, but to nurture her connection to land, a practice she has maintained for over thirty years.

The methodology

The primary aim of the interviews was to gain insight into people's lived experiences of being alone in nature. To achieve this, the study employed a phenomenological approach that is commonly employed by researchers seeking an in-depth understanding of individuals' experiences (Berg et al., 2006; Martiny et al., 2021; Tuffour, 2017). Semi-structured qualitative interviews were conducted, with participants encouraged to describe their experiences in detail, rather than providing abstract explanations. The line of enquiry was straightforward: asking people what happens when they spend time alone in nature and exploring their experiences in depth from there.

One of the challenges in interviewing expert subjects is that they are well placed to extract meaning from their own experience. However, a phenomenological approach aims to study the experience from the perspective of the experience, which researchers refer to as 'experience-near' (Hollway, 2009). To steer away from theoretical reflections and stay as close to lived experiences as possible, I asked people to describe specific moments and events that occurred alone in nature in detail, along with the physical sensations, thoughts and emotions they felt at the time. Using a method more formally referred to as narrative analysis, I also asked interviewees to share the images and metaphors they associated with these experiences. Overall, these simple techniques allowed for a deeper exploration of respondents' lived experiences and facilitated fluid dialogue between the interviewer and the interviewee (Matua & Van Der Wal, 2015).

Interviewing people worldwide who spend extended periods alone in remote locations faces practical challenges. For one, where should the interviews take place, and how feasible is it to travel there? Ultimately,

I travelled to meet twelve people across Europe and North America. The other eight I interviewed were online. For instance, I interviewed an artist in his studio on the Scottish mainland soon after returning from a trip to the Isle of Raasay. I spoke with a wilderness rites of passage guide online from a hotel she was staying in Utah before taking a group to the desert for several weeks. Although the advantage of in-person interviews was that I felt it was easier to build a rapport and pick up on the more subtle unspoken cues, online interviews made it possible to reach people that otherwise would be impossible to include.

The average interview lasted for two and a half hours, far longer than most studies of this kind, so I amassed over fifty hours of transcripts. Common themes and features were extrapolated from the data and cross-referenced with findings from other studies to establish an overarching organizational structure (Matua & Van Der Wal, 2015). It is often noted that the process of categorizing data and creating an overarching organizational structure relies upon the interpretation of themes and patterns. Therefore, I put several credibility checks in place to validate the analysis and findings, including an external review process by a supervisory panel.

An extraordinary embodied state

What stood out across all respondents' descriptions was a shift in state that occurs. This shift can feel gradual or sudden, but in all cases, the person is aware of a change in state occurring, as illustrated in the following account:

> There are times, usually after walking for three or so days, when I start to become very conscious of how the trees and the clouds and everything else around me seems to vibrate and move together. I get this sense that the whole landscape is pulsating with every step that I take. It's as if the land and I start to move in tune together. It feels like this painting I have been looking at turns into a vivid movie, and I am in it. I don't usually talk to people about it because it sounds a bit weird, but it's like I'm dancing with the landscape.
>
> Lucas, nature therapist, Interviewee

Analysis of the descriptions of this phenomenon falls into two categories. The first category comprises people's descriptions of the state itself, which is further categorized into four core characteristics: sense of participation, embodied experience, vivid mental imagery and time fluidity. These four characteristics are consistently present in all accounts, albeit to varying degrees, and serve to uniquely identify and differentiate the experience from that of other states. The second category pertains to the conditions necessary for this state to occur. Merely spending time in nature is insufficient for this state to occur; the experience is contingent upon the environment's physical composition, multisensory stimulation, duration of engagement and intentionality of the individual. The following section provides detailed descriptions of these eight elements.

Four core characteristics

A sense of participation

A perceptual shift takes place, in which people start to experience an embodied sense of participation with the immediate physical surroundings. Respondents repeatedly described a point when everything within their perceptual range felt animated, and they felt part of this animation. This experience of the aliveness of the environment, and one's own part within it, does not present as a distortion or alteration of reality, but rather as a heightened awareness of events.

> I notice something when I spend a lot of time in nature, and that's how everything moves. Like the trees moving or the sunlight passing over the hills, and the colours change, and I think to myself, the land is moving towards me again. The land doesn't feel static in the way things normally do. It doesn't feel separate from me. I am absolutely enveloped in it, like I am inside this invisible object. I am totally wrapped in it, a part of it. It's like this window opens up, and I realize everything is alive, and I'm part of it. But it's not this dramatic event. I just get it. I feel it.
>
> Wilderness guide, Interviewee

There are several aspects to this sense of participation. First, people begin to experience the environment as animated. This is frequently referred to as their surroundings coming alive. Second, people feel an active part of this animation rather than being passive observers. There is an energizing reciprocity between the perceiver and the environment. Third, the feeling of reciprocity between the perceiver and the environment takes on a synchronic resonance, which subjects repeatedly express using terms such as rhythmic and harmonic. As one respondent commented, 'it takes a while, but slowly you start to form this resonance to the landscape'. Overall, this sense of synchronic participation is the characteristic that led to the name 'environmental attunement', which sets this state apart from other types of nature experiences and other non-normative states.

> All the woodland near where I live is covered in this dense bracken. Some of it is almost as tall as I am, and I can quickly disappear. Sometimes when I spent time in the woods, I lie down on the ground and get up close with all sorts of stuff. I can feel tiny, almost like I am another one of the insects. You notice all kinds of things. Like recently, I noticed the breeze make this tiny leaf of a plant gently flicker. And in that second, I really sensed that leaf was alive and in tune with the wind, giving little messages to each other, and then giving messages to me. I know it's a small thing, but it felt quite profound. I just love that feeling of being tuned into that.
>
> Nature therapist, UK, Interviewee

An embodied experience

The sense of participation that individuals feel is an embodied experience. Animation of the environment and the person's involvement in this animation are multisensory. As one participant stated:

> I realize that I am not only looking, visually observing everything around me, and I start listening in a more holistic way. You start to listen with your body. I feel my senses coming alive.
>
> Artist, UK, Interviewee

Although there are variances and nuances in interviewees' individual descriptions, in general, people's accounts are remarkably similar in describing a fuller range of senses being employed than we typically rely on. For example, respondents described haptic (touch), olfactory (smell), vestibular (balance) and proprioceptive (bodily movement) sensations as coming to the foreground of their awareness. As a wilderness rites of passage guide described:

> As the light changes in the desert and it starts to get darker, it creates these obscure images that are impossible to decipher with your eyes. Your eyes can play tricks. It forces you to switch on your other senses, so you start to get a more physical, tactile feel of the space. The people who've lived in these places all their lives have this. But when I arrive in the desert, it takes me a while to switch my senses on like this.
>
> Wilderness rites of passage guide, USA, Interviewee

The experience does not rely on one or two senses over others, as in more normative everyday life, where our reliance on visual and auditory senses dominates. Instead, attunement involves multiple cross-modal sensory activities. Furthermore, individuals are aware of the whole-body sensing. Human sensory systems are constantly adapting to environmental changes. For instance, when we turn off the light in a room, our loss of sight is compensated for by our senses of touch and balance. These adjustments are automatic and unconscious and go unnoticed most of the time. However, in attunement, the perceptual shift is conscious.

The embodied nature of the experience may seem obvious, considering the dominance of this sense in respondents' accounts. This finding has several significant implications. It sets attunement apart from other types of nature experiences. As highlighted in Chapter 1, studies have shown how a purely visual stimulus, such as images or videos of nature scenes, is sufficient to produce certain physiological and cognitive outcomes (Menser et al., 2021; Mostajeran et al., 2021; Ulrich, 1981). Relaxation and restorative experiences are possible with limited perceptual involvement. However, this is not the case for attunement. This point will be examined in greater detail in the subsequent chapter.

Vivid mental imagery

The third feature that stands out in people's experience is the occurrence of vivid mental imagery. Without exception, these mental images are either images recalled from autobiographical memory or imagined autobiographical states. In other words, people picture themselves in the past or imagined situations. For example, Susana, a nature therapist living in southern Spain, described coming across a juniper tree whose branches had been contorted over time by the wind into what looked like an armchair. She climbed upon it. Suddenly, the winds picked up, and her tree-throne became an ideal shelter.

> As I sat there, held by this old tree on the side of a mountain, I kept thinking about my mum. I remember when I was a kid sitting for hours on the sofa at home while she was out at work. I never felt alone or afraid because she told me she was looking after me. I sat in that tree for ages, crying, thinking how hard she had to work to look after me. I felt safe in that tree, protected, like it was holding me, telling me it's ok.
>
> Nature therapist, Spain, Interviewee

Susana's account illustrates the intensity of the mental imagery that people can experience in attunement. External stimuli continuously activate our autobiographical memory and imagination in everyday life; a faint smell has the power to recall images of a long-forgotten event, which in turn evokes images of our fresh desires. The smell of a freshly cut apple can bring us back to our childhood at the same time as fuelling our fantasy of eating one now. This interplay between physical stimuli, memory and imagination is integral to how we perceptually engage with the surrounding world. What stands out in people's accounts of attunement is the intensity of its effect. People can feel the deepest possible sensation of an experience that happened years ago, or the intense excitement of new possibilities.

The mental imagery described in people's accounts is derived from memory recall and imagination or a combination of both. Images of memories of the past merge with images from the present and imagined. For example, in Susana's encounter with the tree, she envisioned the tree as somehow comforting her and saying it was ok. These imaginative leaps tend to take symbolic form. For example, one pilgrim who regularly walked the pilgrim's way to Santiago de Compostela in Spain recalled:

> Around 2 weeks into my walk on the Camino, there was this one day that I felt refreshed and excited. I'd had a really good night's sleep and was feeling strong and ready for the day ahead. I started walking, and after a few hours, it felt like everything was moving with me. The colours looked so vibrant, and everything felt as if it was pulsating with every step I took. The whole side of the mountain was moving with me. It reminded me of walking into the warm, familiar arms of a lover.
>
> Pilgrim, UK, Interviewee

Although these images can be extraordinary in the truest sense of that word, whether in visual, olfactory, auditory or sensory-somatic forms, they are not hallucinogenic. Mental imagery is linked to the physical stimuli in the immediate environment. In people's accounts, the delineation between 'real' and 'imagined' stimuli can feel blurred, but the relationship between the two remains intact. There is an important synergy maintained between both real and imagined stimuli, which means that distortion or dissociation from reality does not occur. The dynamic between sensation, memory and imagination is a fascinating feature of attunement. The underlying perceptual processes involved are explored in greater depth in the subsequent chapters.

Time fluidity

The fourth common theme across people's descriptions relates to their perception of time. The subjective experience of the structure and duration of time is more fluid. People describe over- and underestimates of time, in which time appears to speed up or slow down:

> I've come to realize that nature seems to have its own agenda. So, when I go into nature, I am pretty much not in control of what will happen. I lose all ordinary sense of time, and the rhythms and cycles of nature take over. There are moments when a minute can feel like an hour and when a few hours just fly by.
>
> Nature therapist, UK, Interviewee

The experience of time fluidity is common in non-normative states. For instance, when involved in an activity such as playing video games or engaging in conversation with a close friend, people can lose their sense of time and feel lost in the moment (Sinnett et al., 2020). However, attunement-related time fluidity differs from the feeling of being lost in moment-by-moment, here-and-now interactions. The past and imagined are not cut off from the immediacy of the present experience, but rather folded into the present. Images of memories from the past, for instance, can feel alive in the present, as the following account illustrates:

> A few weeks back, I was camping out in some woodland. It was getting dark, so I made a small fire to set myself up for the night. I was kindling some wood to get the fire going, and there was something about the smell of that piece of wood or the way I was chipping at it, I don't know exactly, but it took me straight back to being a kid standing inside my father's shed. And the smell of wood chippings on the floor. I started to cry, full-on crying. He passed away over 30 years ago, and I've processed those feelings long ago, but the emotions felt raw. It felt like he had just passed away only yesterday.
>
> Wilderness guide, UK, Interviewee

The interviews clearly showed that the experience of time was different from that of normative states. However, the data also indicated that this altered perception of time differs from the feeling of being lost in the moment in that the experience is not limited to the immediacy of here-and-now interactions. In attunement, the past and the possible are intertwined with the experience of here-and-now in ways that alter the feeling of time structure and duration. A nature therapist interviewed in Germany explained this phenomenon as follows:

> The more you tune into nature and are in that realm, you realize that the way we construct time is a myth created by humans. You can't stay

there all the time; you've got to pick up the kids from school and get on with your everyday life. So, time is a very useful myth, but a myth, nonetheless.

Nature Therapist, Germany, Interviewee

The study clearly shows that attunement affects the experience of time. Furthermore, the findings indicate that the perception of time is influenced by the quality of the interaction between the perceiver and the environment. Although the study falls short of understanding the underlying mechanisms, subsequent chapters draw on neuroscientific studies that help elucidate the phenomenon (Robbe, 2023).

Overall, the findings show that this experience has significant psychophysical distinctions from other types of nature experiences. Four core characteristics were identified: a sense of participation, embodied sensation, vivid mental pictures and time fluidity. While all four are present to varying degrees, the sense of participation stands out as the most pervasive and unique to the experience. The study also found that these four characteristics mutually influence each other and operate in an interdependent manner. The presence of these core characteristics and their pattern of behaviour led the study to classify the experience as a state of consciousness. Our current knowledge of states of consciousness is disparate and vague. However, the findings show that the phenomenon of environmental attunement fulfils the generally agreed criteria. The classification of environmental attunement as a state of consciousness is significant as it takes our understanding of the human-nature relationship in new directions. Chapter 3 examines the rationale for this classification and its ramifications, alongside a comparison with other unusual states.

Core conditions

The four characteristics provide us with a comprehensive understanding of what constitutes the state itself, and therefore, ways to identify and distinguish it from other states. The second category of findings captures the factors that cultivate the conditions for this state to occur. Overall, the findings clearly show that, when it comes to attunement, the quality of engagement matters. Simple exposure to nature, or superficial interaction, is insufficient. A state of attunement is contingent on a set of extrinsic and intrinsic factors that cultivate the right conditions. These comprise the physical composition of the environment, the multisensory stimulation available, the length of time and the person's overall intention. Descriptions of each factor follow.

Physical composition

Respondents accessed attunement states in a wide array of environments, ranging from the arid deserts of Arizona in the United States to the temperate oceanic shorelines of western Scotland, and the dense rainforest of the Peruvian Amazonia. One obvious common denominator across all these environments, however, was the absence of humans and traces of their presence. Regardless of whether the environment was lush with vegetation, such as the temperate Nantahala Forest in the Blue Ridge Mountains in Virginia, United States, or the dry desert valleys of the Haggar region in the Algerian Sahara, human presence was minimal or non-existent. In other words, the compositional make-up of the physical space was other-than-human. This may seem a rather obvious observation, but it provided an important inroad to the more precise qualities of environments needed for attunement.

Environments with no trace of human presence are rare, and respondents mentioned that even in the remotest of places, they stumble upon evidence of human life. One respondent mentioned noticing the patterns of treks left by Berber shepherds as they traversed the High Atlas Mountain range. A wilderness guide described the stone circles laid by Tuareg nomads in the Sahara and how his imagination was sparked by encountering these remnants of their activities. Another respondent recalled his surprising reaction to the sight of felled trees in a remote Alaskan forest. These human factors stand out in landscapes that are otherwise devoid of human life. In other settings, these types of stimuli might seem insignificant and go unnoticed, but alone in nature, even small traces can grab our attention and affect our state. As one respondent stated:

> I remember this one time in the Scottish Highlands. I'd been camping on my own for a week. The weather was all over the place. One day it would be sunny, then the next would be raining and high winds. It was pretty intense. I decided to walk over to this other valley to find better shelter, and when I got there, I heard the sound of a train's horn. It completely threw me. I had been on my own with nature for so long, in this bubble, it was a bit of a shock to hear it. For a minute, it threw me back into my everyday life.
>
> Artist, UK, Interviewee

The environmental psychology research literature documents well the distracting effect human presence can have on people's nature experiences, albeit such studies tend to reference less remote and isolated settings such as urban parks (Sullivan & Li, 2021). These findings follow in a similar vein but place an emphasis on the importance of freedom from human distractions in enabling individuals to connect with the other-than-human aspects of their surroundings. Regardless of any picturesque qualities or stereotypical ideas of nature, attunement depends upon the dominance of non-human factors within the subject's perceptual field. The physical composition of the environment must allow for these other-than-human factors to come to the forefront of our awareness.

Another salient point to note here is that many respondents' descriptions sit outside the types of natural environments that dominate contemporary research. More than half of the places people described spending time alone in, were not typically green spaces but instead, were rugged or so-called barren landscapes. For example, close to one-third of the sample recalled experiences in desert landscapes devoid of the type of vegetation we associate with nature. As one respondent illustrated:

> I was brought up on army bases, so we always moved around. But I live on a remote island now. I am drawn to the rugged coastline. I guess it's because I like the feeling of edges, like the edges of a shoreline or a desert, and what happens in those transitory spaces where shapes constantly change. Especially on the edges of deserts, there are moments when the shadows can seem almost stronger than solid forms. A shadow can appear more defined and solid than you in that light. Not everyone will like places like this, but they fascinate me.
>
> Wilderness rites of passage guide, USA, Interviewee

The key point here is that attunement states are not dependent upon the stereotypical idea of green space or the usual aesthetic judgements we apply (Wartmann & Lorimer, n.d.). What matters more is that the environment is free from human distraction, so that the person is free to engage with the other-than-human factors that make up the environmental composition. This finding is critical to our understanding of how attunement states come about, but also, more broadly, the aesthetic prejudices inherent in contemporary psychological research on the human-nature relationship that outcast certain types of environments. Chapter 4 explores this topic in greater depth.

Multisensory stimulation

Closely linked to respondents' descriptions of the physical composition of environments is the range of sensory stimulation that they provide. People's descriptions are filled not only with the sights and sounds of these places but also with the textures, smells and bodily sensations offered. These stimuli are a combination of biotic and abiotic factors. The temperature of the air, changing light or feeling of a breeze engage a person's attention as much as the sights and sounds of plant and animal life. There is a causal link between this multisensory stimulation and the embodied character of attunement. Without this range of stimuli, attunement is not an embodied experience.

Interviewees' accounts are filled with descriptions of the physical activity they partake in when alone in nature. They are moving bodies within a dynamic landscape. The types of physical activity have varying levels of exertion, from trekking up the steady inclines of the High Atlas Mountains, combing fingers through the lush, golden blades of alfalfa on the plains of Minnesota or subtly moving in response to the touch of a butterfly alighting on a shoulder. A pilgrim can walk for more than 30 km a day, whereas an ancestral healer searching for plants in the Amazonian rainforest moves as slowly as possible to avoid disturbing the mating calls of birds.

The data clearly indicates that attunement states involve some degree of movement. Individuals are not motionless observers, though these physical movements need not be overt or physically excessive and can often be quite subtle. An artist recalled camping out in the Cairngorms National Park in Scotland as follows:

> In the depths of winter, when there is not a leaf on the trees and not a hint of a breeze, you can tune into this less visible, more subtle stuff that's going on. Everything vibrates. You can't help but get drawn in and feel yourself moving inside this vibrating atmosphere.
>
> Artist, UK, Interviewee

It was not possible to determine with any degree of certainty from the original data if specific actions were more conducive to attunement than others. However, it was clear from the data that physical activity plays a role in activating multisensory stimulation. Looking out of the window at a scenic view does not activate the quality of sensory stimulation necessary to achieve a state of attunement. Similarly, a highly focused activity that demands attention and distracts from the multisensory stimuli afforded by the whole of the surroundings is not conducive to attunement states.

There is a balance to be struck between motionless observation and focused activity. Somewhere between static voyeurism and intense activity, there is a form of physical engagement that stimulates the capacity to attune. Respondents' descriptions of walking exemplify a level of physical engagement that is neither overly active, causing distractions from what is happening within one's perceptual field, nor overly passive, failing to sufficiently animate the encounter. One respondent recalled, for example:

> When I've been walking for three days or so, I get into this rhythm. Walking helps me let go of all the other stuff that's going on in my life and deepens my relationship with the land. The land is continually in flux, constantly changing, and in motion, so you have to move to get to know it and find a sense of harmony.
>
> Pilgrim, Interviewee

The participants mentioned other types of activities. For instance, several wilderness rites of passage guides describe spending three to five days in one location where the radius of their activity is no more than 50 metre. Within that space, they drum, dance or carry out small ceremonies. Several land artists describe spontaneous creative acts, such as moving rocks into a new formation or saying hello to the trees in their vicinity by touching each of their barks. However, shared by this diversity of activities is the fundamental process of a body moving in ways that engage the senses with stimuli afforded by the environment.

Time

> Nature for me is primarily being outdoors, in wild places away from human life. At first, I can feel like I am walking through the land. But then, over time, I experience becoming part of it and realizing that nature is inside of me.
>
> Nature therapist, USA, Interviewee

Attunement takes time. Temporal distancing is involved in accessing a state of attunement. It takes time to shake off thoughts and concerns, conversations, anticipations and the expectations of everyday life. As one respondent stated:

> I am so used to constantly feeling the cogs turning, in particular, because of technology and all its shiny flat surfaces. I can get easily irritated, distracted, sped up, and impatient all the time. And being alone in nature changes that. I feel myself gradually slowing down. At first, it can feel a bit odd when the cogs don't need to work so fast. Then you get used to it. It's powerful because, after about three days, I feel myself changing the more I feel in tune with the land.
>
> Artist, UK, Interviewee

All the subjects identified the role of time in attunement. For some respondents, the transition feels gradual, and they slowly notice it happening over time as if there is a gradual shift in awareness. For example, one respondent commented, 'It depends on how I am feeling and what's going on in my life, but it usually takes me at least a few days to switch off from my normal stuff and start to tune into what's happening around me.' For others, the shift felt more sudden and unexpected, as illustrated in the comment: 'I felt like I had been looking at this beautiful landscape, and then it just came alive.'

According to these data, however, it is difficult to precisely determine the amount of time required to reach a state of attunement. Nevertheless, the timeframes that participants generally reported varied between twelve hours and three days. It is impossible to evaluate with any certainty why it takes some people longer to reach a state of attunement than others, and to what degree other factors, such as childhood experiences and personal preferences, influence this period. It would be easy to assume that people with more experience of solitude in nature and those with a stronger sense of connection to a specific place may find it quicker to attune. However, when it comes to attunement, asserting the degree to which these factors have an influence at this stage is speculative and, therefore, a subject for future research.

What stands out from these findings is that the intense states of attunement described by the interviewees take significantly more time than the recommended average of twenty minutes nature exposure reported in most contemporary studies (Bowler et al., 2010; Brasche & Bischof, 2005; Ideno et al., 2017; Ohly et al., 2016). This difference in time prompts several important questions concerning both the possibility of achieving less intense states in shorter time periods, and therefore, the ability of the wider population to achieve attunement states in everyday life. To that end, Chapter 3 specifically examines the probability of attunement states operating on a continuum from low to high intensity, as well as the ways in which moments of micro-attunement may be achievable in shorter periods. Chapter 8 explores the feasibility of achieving micro-attunements in urban settings.

Chapter 9 is principally concerned with the broader societal issue of whether attunement states are accessible to the general population or limited to a privileged few. It is worth noting, however, that taking time out from an increasingly busy world to spend time alone in nature proves to be challenging even for those living far from the hustle and bustle of cities, whose livelihoods depend on their connection with nature. An ancestral healer from the Amazonian Forest commented to me:

My father and ancestors used to go much deeper into the forest away from the village than I do. My ancestors spent months on their own in the forest, communicating with the plants. These days it's harder to do that. I stay a bit closer to my family in case they need me but far enough to be away from people. To connect with the plant spirits, I must be on my own for at least 2, 3 days, maybe a week. But it's not as long as my ancestors did. We can't do that anymore.

Ancestral Healer, Peru, Interviewee

Intentionality

The people in this study had varying reasons for spending time alone in nature. For shamanic healers, being alone in the forest is an opportunity to connect with their ancestral spirits. The wilderness rites of passage guides of North America seek personal growth and transformation. Environmental artists use their time in nature to find inspiration for their work. Beneath these individual aims, however, lies a similar intention. All interviewees shared an openness and willingness to engage with the land, as wilderness rites of passage guide put it 'I always start with a sense of openness and wonder. That's the baseline.'

Wilderness rites of passage guides refer to 'mystery' or 'surrendering to the great mystery', while the land artists in the study tend to use more down-to-earth language describing being open to the land and 'listening with my whole body'. Regardless of the type of language used, in attunement, people describe being less singularly focused than in normative states, which limits the perceptual field by focusing attention. In attunement, people are open and curious about their immediate surroundings and are willing to engage with what unfolds. This sense of openness and curiosity is similar to what researchers of Attention Restoration Theory refer to as soft fascination, which involves paying attention to fascinating stimuli in a way that preserves mental space for reflection, rather than a hard fascination required in watching a film or reading a book (Basu et al., 2018).

On closer analysis of the data, however, the concept of soft fascination falls somewhat short of fully capturing an important aspect of the intentionality described in attunement states. In addition to the soft fascination towards the whole of the surrounding environment, people hold a desire to be involved and engage. Where it is possible to hold a soft fascination from the position of a passive observer, in attunement, it is not. The type of intentionality involved in attunement requires a willingness to not only absorb but also to be involved and reciprocate. This desire to be involved manifests in various ways, depending on the people involved. Nature therapists and wilderness rites of passage guides create physical manifestations of their intention, for example, by creating a threshold from wood or stones to step over as a symbol of their desire to connect with the land:

> Marking a threshold and stepping across evokes a sense of intent, the conscious, 'I am stepping into something' feeling that makes a huge difference because I become more open to everything that is happening around me. And that there's nothing that isn't right. Even if you get unhappy and depressed, that is a part of what is being offered to you by the land. And so that intention of 'I am stepping into this space' opens me to that kind of relationship.
>
> Wilderness rites of passage guide, USA, Interviewee

This involvement can also manifest in more sensitive and subtle ways, as a US-based land artist recounted:

> And I think, when I'm open enough to listen and to experience something so elemental as the land, it's like I arrive. I'm not just projecting my thoughts and ideas. Because you've got to get rid of all that and just allow the land in. I don't just impose my stuff on a landscape; there's a sensitivity and integration that needs to take place, a weathering.
>
> Land Artist, US, Interviewee

Regardless of differences in the type of physical activity, whether subtle or overt, the quality of intentionality involved in attunement remains consistent.

The existential dimension

As this initial study took a phenomenological approach to understanding what happens alone in nature, it did not set out to quantitatively assess or evaluate psychological effects. However, based on these initial findings, some general assertions can be made. As multiple studies concur that exposure to nature helps restore mental fatigue and alleviate the symptoms of stress and anxiety in the short term, common sense suggests that these general mental health and well-being factors can also be applied. However, the experience of attunement may affect the self in deeper and more meaningful ways. Like two sides of the same coin, an attunement to the nature around you seems to resonate with a deeper sense of self.

A state of environmental attunement is extraordinary in the true sense of the word because it extends beyond the typical boundaries of self-experience, where we let go and feel part of the immediate environment, allowing for a more expansive and enlivened sense of self. However, attunement states are not some grand transcendent moments filled with symbolic meaning; instead, our sense of self seems to resonate, in an embodied way, with the physical surroundings, animated by our perceptual participation. In these moments of attunement, we may come closest to feeling what the author and cultural anthropologist Joseph Campbell refers to as 'the rapture of being alive' (pp. 4–5, 1988). Although this more existential dimension to attunement was initially less empirically derived and more intuitively driven, Chapters 3, 5 and 6, situate the findings within the broader landscape of existing research and theories to foster a more robust understanding of how attunement affects the self.

Conclusion

The aim of this chapter was to outline the key findings from my original research of twenty individuals with exceptional experiences of solitude. First and foremost, the study identified a unique state that occurs alone in nature that is distinct from other types of nature experiences. The study was successful in identifying the core conditions and the core characteristics that make up this state, and that it positively affects our sense of self. It is important to acknowledge several limitations at this initial stage of research. The focus on 'expert' participants, the subjective nature of personal accounts and the lack of quantitative validation means the findings are not immediately generalizable to broader populations or to more commonplace settings. With that said, the findings were sufficient to reach three main conclusions, which provided a framework for further research.

First and foremost, attunement states are multisensory experiences, where time feels more fluid, mental imagery more vivid and the person feels an extraordinary sense of participation with their immediate surroundings. This observable pattern of effects led to the conclusion that attunement is not a singular feeling, but instead, meets the criteria of a unique state of consciousness that is identifiable and distinguishable from other states (Ciaunica & Safron, 2022; Kokoszka, 2007). The categorization of attunement as a state of consciousness has important ramifications. Chapter 3 examines the reasoning and implications of this categorization of attunement more closely. The chapter also compares attunement states to other exceptional states to better understand their underlying mechanics and behavioural patterns.

Second, the research successfully identified the factors that create the conditions for attunement to arise. It concluded that attunement states are dependent on the quality of engagement between the individual and their immediate surroundings. Simply spending time alone in nature is insufficient for a state of attunement to arise. The deep states of attunement described by the participants in the study take extended periods alone in environments with low-to-no human presence, where the individual is free to interact with the other-than-human multisensory stimuli within their perceptual range. In addition to these external environmental factors, attunement states require the person to be open and willing to actively engage with their immediate surroundings.

People's previous experiences and personal preferences influence how they engage with nature, which aligns with the findings from existing research. Multiple studies show that place attachment and place identity (the emotional and symbolic bonds that people feel towards a place) contribute to their desire and ability to feel an emotional connection to certain types of environments (Korpela & Hartig, 1996; Sobel, 1990). Some people may feel a closer connection to forests than coastlines, for example. While place attachment and place identity may affect the quality of attunement to varying degrees, they do not form part of the core conditions. In other words, it is not necessary to have an existing bond to a specific place or certain type of landscape to experience a state of attunement to that place.

The third main conclusion from this original study was that attunement states affect our sense of self in ways that are distinct from the cognitive and emotional effects of other types of nature experiences (examined in Chapter 6). Extensive research already shows that brief exposure to nature, even urban green spaces, helps alleviate the symptoms of stress, anxiety and generally restores mental and physical fatigue. However, attunement states seem to affect our sense of self in profound and existential ways. Like the two sides of the same coin, the multisensory participation that people feel with their immediate surroundings is inextricably linked to their experience of an embodied sense of self. This dynamic interplay between the perceiver and the environment, and the perceptual processes involved (examined in Chapter 5), is integral to understanding attunement states and how they affect our sense of self.

Attunement is an embodied state that relies upon multisensory stimulation from the environment and the person's perceptual interaction with these stimuli. This opens several important lines of inquiry. The first concerns the types of environments and multisensory stimuli that attunement states require. What do natural environments afford attunement states that other types of environments do not? And can less-remote, more accessible types of natural environments, such as so-called urban 'green spaces', provide such affordances? The second line of inquiry concerns attunement as an embodied process and how to develop a deeper understanding of the multisensory perceptual processes involved. Third, a closer examination of how this embodied state affects our sense of self is needed to assess any potential psychotherapeutic and mental health application. And lastly, and most importantly, I believe to the ongoing study of attunement, is to what extent attunement states are accessible to the wider population.

Although this original study focused on individuals who sought out extraordinary experiences of solitude in remote environments, the findings point to the potential universality of environmental attunement. While attunement states may have been most vividly observed by this initial study in remote and exceptional contexts, the capacity for attunement does not require any special physical or psychological skills. In fact, most people possess the innate capacities needed for attunement, suggesting that these states may be achieved in less-extreme conditions.

With that said, it is crucial to recognize that access to nature – and the willingness or ability to seek solitude in nature – is not distributed equally across society. Issues of inequality, cultural background and urbanization all shape who can potentially benefit from attunement experiences. The subsequent phases of my research focused on the applicability of attunement states to the general population. The following chapters explore whether attunement states are possible in less extreme and more accessible conditions, the barriers and the potential benefits to different population groups, and how Environmental Attunement Theory can inform contemporary discourse around the wider societal issues of mental health, urban design, and social and environmental justice.

References

Basu, A., Duvall, J., & Kaplan, R. (2018). Attention restoration theory: Exploring the role of soft fascination and mental bandwidth. *Environment and Behavior, 51*, 001391651877440. https://doi.org/10.1177/0013916518774400.

Berg, L., Skott, C., & Danielson, E. (2006). An interpretive phenomenological method for illuminating the meaning of caring relationships. *Scandinavian Journal of Caring Sciences, 20*(1), 42–50. https://doi.org/10.1111/j.1471-671 2.2006.00378.x.

Bowler, D. E., Buyung-Ali, L. M., Knight, T. M., & Pullin, A. S. (2010). A systematic review of evidence for the added benefits to health of exposure to natural environments. *BMC Public Health, 10*(1), 456. https://doi. org/10.1186/1471-2458-10-456.

Brasche, S., & Bischof, W. (2005). Daily time spent indoors in German homes –
    Baseline data for the assessment of indoor exposure of German occupants.
    International Journal of Hygiene and Environmental Health, 208(4), 247–253.
    https://doi.org/10.1016/j.ijheh.2005.03.003.

Campbell, J., & Moyers, B. (1988). *The Power of Myth* (pp. 4–5). Doubleday.

Ciaunica, A., & Safron, A. (2022). Disintegrating and reintegrating the self: (In)
    Flexible self-models in depersonalisation and psychedelic experiences. In
    C. Letheby & P. Gerrans (Eds.), *Philosophical Perspectives on Psychedelic
    Psychiatry, International Perspectives in Philosophy and Psychiatry* (Oxford,
    2024; online ed., Oxford Academic, 19 September 2024), https://doi.
    org/10.1093/oso/9780192898371.003.0004, accessed 27 July 2025.

Hammitt, W. E. (1982). Cognitive dimensions of wilderness solitude. *Environment
    and Behavior, 14*(4), 478–493. https://doi.org/10.1177/0013916582144005.

Hollway, W. (2009). Applying the 'Experience-Near' Principle To
    Research: Psychoanalytically Informed Methods1. *Journal of Social Work
    Practice, 23*(4), 461–474. https://doi.org/10.1080/02650530903375025

Ideno, Y., Hayashi, K., Abe, Y., Ueda, K., Iso, H., Noda, M., Lee, J.-S., & Suzuki,
    S. (2017). Blood pressure-lowering effect of Shinrin-yoku (forest bathing): A
    systematic review and meta-analysis. *BMC Complementary and Alternative
    Medicine, 17*(1), 409. https://doi.org/10.1186/s12906-017-1912-z.

Kokoszka, A. (2007). *States of consciousness: Models for psychology and
    psychotherapy*. Springer Science & Business Media.

Korpela, K., & Hartig, T. (1996). Restorative qualities of favorite places. *Journal
    of Environmental Psychology, 16*(3), 221–233. https://doi.org/10.1006/
    jevp.1996.0018.

Korpela, K., & Staats, H. (2014). The restorative qualities of being alone with
    nature. In *The handbook of solitude: Psychological perspectives on social
    isolation, social withdrawal, and being alone* (pp. 351–367). Wiley Blackwell.

Kull, R. (2009). *Solitude: Seeking wisdom in extremes: A year alone in the
    Patagonia Wilderness*. New World Library.

Long, C. R., Seburn, M., Averill, J. R., & More, T. A. (2003). Solitude
    experiences: varieties, settings, and individual differences. *Personality &
    Social Psychology Bulletin, 29*(5), 578–583. https://doi.org/10.1177/01461672
    03029005003.

Martiny, K. M., Toro, J., & Høffding, S. (2021). Framing a phenomenological
    mixed method: From inspiration to guidance. *Frontiers in Psychology, 12,*
    258. https://doi.org/10.3389/fpsyg.2021.602081.

Mateer, T. J. (2022). Developing connectedness to nature in urban outdoor
    settings: A potential pathway through awe, solitude, and leisure.
    Frontiers in Psychology, 13. https://www.frontiersin.org/articles/10.3389/
    fpsyg.2022.940939.

Matua, G. A., & Van Der Wal, D. M. (2015). Differentiating between descriptive
    and interpretive phenomenological research approaches. *Nurse Researcher,
    22*(6), 22–27. https://doi.org/10.7748/nr.22.6.22.e1344.

Menser, T., Baek, J., Siahaan, J., Kolman, J. M., Delgado, D., & Kash, B. (2021). Validating visual stimuli of nature images and identifying the representative characteristics. *Frontiers in Psychology, 12*. https://www.frontiersin.org/artic les/10.3389/fpsyg.2021.685815.

Mostajeran, F., Krzikawski, J., Steinicke, F., & Kühn, S. (2021). Effects of exposure to immersive videos and photo slideshows of forest and urban environments. *Scientific Reports, 11*(1), Article 1. https://doi.org/10.1038/s41 598-021-83277-y.

Naor, L., & Mayseless, O. (2020). The wilderness solo experience: A unique practice of silence and solitude for personal growth. *Frontiers in Psychology, 11*. https://www.frontiersin.org/articles/10.3389/fpsyg.2020.547067.

Ohly, H., White, M. P., Wheeler, B. W., Bethel, A., Ukoumunne, O. C., Nikolaou, V., & Garside, R. (2016). Attention restoration theory: A systematic review of the attention restoration potential of exposure to natural environments. *Journal of Toxicology and Environmental Health, Part B, 19*(7), 305–343. https://doi.org/10.1080/10937404.2016.1196155.

Robbe, D. (2023). Lost in time: Relocating the perception of duration outside the brain. *Neuroscience & Biobehavioral Reviews, 153*, 105312. https://doi. org/10.1016/j.neubiorev.2023.105312.

Sinnett, S., Jäger, J., Singer, S. M., & Antonini Philippe, R. (2020). Flow states and associated changes in spatial and temporal processing. *Frontiers in Psychology, 11*. https://www.frontiersin.org/articles/10.3389/ fpsyg.2020.00381.

Sobel, D. (1990). A place in the world: Adults' memories of childhood's special places. *Children's Environments Quarterly, 7*(4), 5–12. https://www.jstor.org/ stable/41514753.

Sullivan, W. C., & Li, D. (2021). Nature and attention. In A. R. Schutte, J. C. Torquati, & J. R. Stevens (Eds.) *Nature and psychology* (pp. 7–30). Springer Nature. https://doi.org/10.1007/978-3-030-69020-5_2.

Tuffour, I. (2017). A critical overview of interpretative phenomenological analysis: A contemporary qualitative research approach. *Journal of Healthcare Communications, 2*(4). https://doi.org/10.4172/2472-1654.100093.

Ulrich, R. S. (1981). Natural versus urban scenes: Some psychophysiological effects. *Environment and Behavior, 13*(5), 523–556. https://doi. org/10.1177/0013916581135001.

3

An exceptional state of consciousness

You realise that there are no flat surfaces in nature. Everything vibrates. Everything has this kinetic energy. I learned that when I was camping in the Scottish Highlands in winter. Because it's winter, you think things are dead, but after a few days, you tune into this vibration. You start to feel it, and the landscape comes alive when you do. It's powerful because I feel myself changing the more I tune into the land in this way.

Research Participant

This chapter builds on the empirical foundations laid out in Chapter 2 by exploring environmental attunement as a distinct and exceptional state of consciousness. Environmental attunement is an exceptional state of consciousness characterized by distinct changes in perception, cognition and emotion. This state involves a qualitative shift from normative waking consciousness, marked by altered time perception, vivid mental imagery and an embodied sense of participation in one's immediate surroundings. It is not the case that the person simply feels heightening or lessening certain aspects of their normal waking state. There is something that it is like to experience environmental attunement that is qualitatively different from other conscious states.

You may ask why this categorization is significant and question what difference it makes beyond the label. States of consciousness, encompassing everything from wakefulness to altered states such as those induced by drugs or meditation, directly impact our awareness, attention and perceptual processing. Different states of consciousness can profoundly change the way we experience the self and self in relation to the world around us. Because of this perception-altering characteristic, there is a long history in the fields of psychology and psychiatry of using non-normative states of consciousness (sometimes referred to as altered states) to facilitate deep psychological work, from hypnosis to the recent surge in research on psychedelic-assisted therapies. Categorizing environmental attunement as an exceptional state, fundamentally changes the lens through which we understand how the experience affects our self and self-and-world models, and opens new possibilities to leverage its potential to facilitate psychological growth and well-being.

Building on the findings of the previous chapter, this chapter examines attunement states within the wider landscape of exceptional states of consciousness. This chapter explores the phenomenology of environmental attunement as an exceptional state by combining theoretical and empirical perspectives. Throughout this chapter, the central claim is that the experience of attunement does not represent singular changes to cognition, perception or affect, but follows the basic structure and behaviours of non-normative states of consciousness. The chapter draws comparisons between attunement and other non-normative states, such as hallucinogenic, flow and aesthetic experiences, detailing their shared and divergent characteristics. The chapter concludes with a set of insights to further our understanding of attunement states, how they emerge, and their potential relevance and value to the general population.

The phenomenology of conscious states

Consciousness is a tricky topic to pin down. Philosophers debate whether consciousness and matter are fundamentally distinct (dualism), whether they arise entirely from physical processes in the brain (physicalism) or whether they are a fundamental feature of the universe, present in all basic physical entities (panpsychism). While neuroscientists try to work out just how the combined activity of billions of neurons, each one a tiny biological miracle, is giving rise to a conscious experience, and not just any conscious experience, your conscious experience. While scholars may struggle to determine exactly what consciousness is or how it comes about, it is generally accepted that consciousness involves awareness (Bayne & Carter, 2018; Dubrovsky, 2019; Nagel, 1974; Revonsuo, 2009; Tart, 2000). While awareness may vary in intensity from faint to acute, it constitutes the foundational layer of conscious experience (Damasio, 2010; Craig, 2002).

It is rare for awareness to be completely absent, apart from general anaesthesia or cases of deep coma. Some forms of awareness can be present, even in states of apparent unconsciousness. For example, in some forms of coma, a person may be able to hear what is happening around them, even if they are unable to respond. Lucid dreamers are aware that they are lucid dreaming. Awareness is not black and white or on and off; instead, it is a multidimensional phenomenon involving sensory, attentional and self-reflective capacities. Understanding the different layers and textures of awareness helps us to understand more complex states, such as environmental attunement, and how they emerge from and transform our everyday waking experiences.

At its most basic, awareness involves the capacity to sense or register that something is happening. Awareness is always the awareness of something, thoughts, sensations, objects or events. This basic awareness includes awareness of mental processes (thoughts, memories, ideas), bodily sensations and external stimuli or the integration of all of these. Awareness also involves the ability to direct and shift one's attention. For example, as I sit at my desk, I may shift my attention from the screen in front of me to the tree outside my window or to the warmth of the coffee in my hand and then back again to the task at hand. My intention drives attention.

Awareness can be extended to the capacity to recognize oneself as the subject of experience (self-awareness). This can manifest as basic perceptual self-awareness (e.g. knowing I am looking at the tree), a sense of agency over one's thoughts and actions (e.g. knowing I can change my attention to something else) and an awareness of continuity over time (e.g. aware that the tree reminds me of a tree I climbed as a young kid). At a relational level, self-awareness involves the awareness of others' conscious states. Often described as theory of mind, this is the ability to infer that other people have beliefs, desires and perspectives different from our own. The psychologist Abraham Maslow (1971). for instance, described self-transcendence, involving moving beyond personal concerns and connecting to something greater than oneself, such as altruism, a commitment to a higher cause, or spiritual experiences, as the highest level of human consciousness.

A shift in conscious states

We go about most everyday activities in a normal waking state when there is familiarity with our subjective experiences. This sense of familiarity enables us to register and respond to internal and external events without any additional intentional effort. In our normal state of wakefulness, levels of awareness can fluctuate from alert and attentive to distracted or minimally aware; however, they maintain a level of familiarity. Normal waking consciousness is characterized by an organized, meaningful and clear awareness of the self and environment that allows us to go about everyday life in an effective, emotionally regulated manner. This is the baseline state against which other states are compared.

At other times, out-of-the-ordinary stimuli (internal or external) can cause a shift in how we experience the world around us. These shifts can happen when we experience something new or exceptional, such as trying an unfamiliar sport that challenges our abilities, or when faced with an adverse situation, such as encountering something physically threatening. They also include states that alter our perception of present reality, such as meditative, hypnotic and hallucinogenic states. These types of exceptional or altered states are marked by qualitative changes in awareness, perception and self-experience, not merely by degree but by the structure of the experience itself.

Exceptional states are marked by changes in the presence and quality of awareness, the content and organization of experience, and the dynamic interplay between the self, perception and environment, resulting in a qualitatively different mode of experiencing the world. It is not only that we feel more acutely aware of what is happening around us; we experience a difference in our overall mental and perceptual functioning. A shift in state is not only the heightening of awareness or individual changes to singular thoughts, feelings or sensations. The shift is not just an amplification of particular sensations or feelings but a transformation of the entire structure of experience. This qualitative difference distinguishes exceptional states of consciousness from the everyday fluctuations in awareness.

In attunement, a fundamental change to the pattern of subjective experience occurs which has an overall effect on how people experience their immediate physical environment and their relationship with their surroundings. People recognize changes in their perceptual, cognitive and emotional responses (awareness) and consciously acknowledge changes that are markedly different from their normal states (self-awareness). In all reported cases, it is not simply that people became more alert or noticed more details; rather, their entire mode of experiencing their immediate environment and self in relation to that environment is transformed in a fundamental way. This is not just a matter of noticing more sounds or smells, but of experiencing the self, in an embodied way, as an active part of their surroundings. To borrow from Nagel's terminology of conscious states, 'there is something that it is like to be in a state' of attunement that is qualitatively different from another (Nagel, 1974).

People experience state transitions in different ways. For some, the shift feels gradual over time, while for others, it can be more sudden. For example, two different respondents commented: 'It's like a door opens up and suddenly I'm inside this pulsating landscape' and 'I gradually realize that everything is vibrating, and I feel part of this vibration.' The causal factors for this difference cannot be determined with certainty. These factors may be external, physiological, psychological or a combination of all three. Further research is required to understand these variances; regardless, the basic premise remains universal that people are aware of the shift in state taking place.

In a state of attunement, people become aware of perceptual changes in their immediate external environment, typically involving multisensory stimulation. As one respondent put it: 'It feels like I start listening with my whole body.' People also experience changes in their perception of time, either speeding up or slowing down, which is a common trait in other altered and exceptional states. People report vivid mental imagery in which external stimuli evoke autobiographical memories and imagined autobiographical events. The standout feature of attunement states is the embodied and animated sense of participation people experience in their surroundings. Emotional response to this sense of participation is often an intense feeling of enlivenment.

People can attach special significance or meaning to their experience. The shamans I interviewed, for instance, explained the experience as a connection to their ancestral spirits, while several wilderness rites of passage guides described events as helping to make sense of life's great mysteries. The symbolic meaning that people attach to the experience reflects the particular belief systems of different professions, geographies and cultures. Regardless of the variations in interpretations, people recognize the experience as something out of the ordinary and special.

Overall, attunement states involve distinct changes to multiple phenomenological properties that can be recognized by an individual experiencing the state. These changes represent a marked departure from the ordinary baseline of waking consciousness. We can further identify changes in specific phenomenological properties: sensations, emotions, intentions, perceptions, imagery and memory. These changes include variations in the sensory characteristics of the perceived world, shifts in bodily sensations, heightened sensory intensity, alterations in emotional responses, time perception, vivid mental imagery and feelings of involvement with the immediate environment. We can comfortably conclude that experience represents a non-normative conscious state.

Altered and exceptional states: A comparative review

One of the advantages of identifying environmental attunement as an exceptional state is the ability to better understand the phenomenon by comparing the properties and behavioural patterns of other exceptional states. This approach allows us to recognize significant distinctions between attunement and other non-normative states, not only in terms of their specific phenomenological qualities but also in the circumstances that bring them about. Where attunement states share important characteristics with so-called altered or exceptional states of consciousness they also exhibit distinctive features. The following section compares attunement with hallucinogenic, flow and aesthetic states, further pointing to the unique phenomenology of attunement.

Hallucinogenic states

I have often been asked if some people's experiences of attunement were drug-induced in any way. The question is understandable, given that the changes in sensory, temporal and spatial perceptions that people describe are commonly linked with induced altered states. Moreover, the use of psychoactive plants for ceremonial and healing purposes is a well-established aspect of the cultures of many shamans and ancestral healers that I interviewed. The shamans from the Shipibo tribes in the Peruvian Amazonian basin that I interviewed brew the leaves of the *Psychotria viridis* bush and bark of the *Banisteriopsis* vine to make the famous Ayahuasca used for healing ceremonies (Gonzalez et al., 2021).

Across the history of humanity, humans have engaged in practices to alter or escape from their familiar ways of perceiving self and the world around them. Psychoactive plants that induce hallucinations have been widely used during religious rituals of many cultures throughout the centuries to produce altered states of consciousness (Bayne & Carter, 2018). These hallucinogen-induced altered states of consciousness involve significant changes in sensory, time and space perception to the point where there is a noticeable distortion of one's familiar sense of self and ways of perceiving the world. In such cases, people voluntarily seek to distort or detach themselves from their normative state by actively engaging in behaviours designed to achieve the desired effect.

Each year, during the dry season, people from the Huichol communities who live in the Sierra Madre Mountain region in northern Mexico leave their homes to travel hundreds of miles through the northwest desert of San Luis Potosi in search of the peyote cactus (Myerhoff, 1976). On their return, shamans lead peyote ceremonies to restore the delicate balance between nature spirits and humans. Everyone in the community is involved, and even very small children can ingest plants. Peyote induces perceptual anomalies because of the plant's high mescaline content. At low concentrations, it can cause people to experience colours as more vibrant, sounds as more intense and movements as more pronounced. Objects can appear to vibrate, shift in shape or merge (Dinis-Oliveira et al., 2019). People begin to have vivid auditory, visual and haptic hallucinations at higher doses. Depending on the dosage, distortion or distancing from physical reality can occur.

The stories of the Huichol people, along with those of other cultures that employ psychoactive plants for ceremonial and healing purposes, are examples of voluntarily induced hallucinogenic states. However, such stories are at risk of presenting a glamorous image of the altered states. There are also instances of involuntary altered states of consciousness resulting from traumatic life events, severe stress exposure, depression or other physical and mental illnesses (Lysaker & Lysaker, 2002). At the more severe end are psychotic states that are associated with underlying conditions such as schizophrenia and occur when the perception of self and external reality is severely distorted by hallucinations, delusions or disorganized and disturbed thoughts. In psychosis, individuals not only face a severe loss of self-awareness and agency over how they experience themselves and the world around them but also persecutory hallucinations, visual or auditory, can cause deep distress.

Hallucinatory and psychotic states represent a departure from reality with varying degrees of severity. The descriptions of the individuals I interviewed, although they included pulsating landscapes, vibrating colours, vivid memories and imaginings, were always directly related to the stimuli provided by their immediate surroundings. In hallucinatory states, the connection between what is sensed and what is imagined becomes distorted or disappears. A severe form of dissociation occurs in psychotic states. However, in attunement, the real-time interplay between real and imagined remains intact. As one respondent put it, 'It is never only my imagination, it is my imagination and the land working closely together.' The close link between the real and imagined is at the heart of environmental attunement and is a crucial factor to consider when assessing the potential risks of attunement states among different populations.

Our understanding of the hallucinatory and psychotic states provides two important insights. First, it is crucial to assess the degree to which a person's experience is distorted or disconnected from reality. This evaluation allows us to determine the extent to which distortion causes suffering. The second important takeaway is the idea of classifying a state of consciousness as pathological by evaluating an individual's ability to change that state voluntarily. In psychotic states, self-agency is significantly reduced. In attunement, individuals may experience unusual effects, such as vivid mental imagery and time fluidity, as well as a noticeable change in the way they perceive and interact with their immediate surroundings. However, the connection to reality is maintained. Moreover, the state shift does not impede a person's ability to voluntarily change the state. In other words, environmental attunement does not hinder a person's ability to intentionally shift attention to other activities.

Whether environmental attunement can have a negative impact on vulnerable populations cannot be overlooked. The relevance and applicability of environmental attunement theory to the general population requires a comprehensive assessment of the risks across different groups. Research on the relationship between nature exposure and mental health is extensive, yet it predominantly focuses on positive outcomes. Empirical studies investigating the potential psychological risks of nature exposure are lacking, with only scant mention in meta-reviews (Jimenez et al., 2021).

This gap may be due, in part, to the broad assumption that nature is good: a cultural narrative with both benefits and concerns. However, this idealized generalization should not be conflated with the assumption that being in nature is beneficial for all. Without a deep appreciation of the complexity, distinctions and nuances across groups and settings, oversights in research are inevitable. Recognizing that being alone in nature can induce a shift in consciousness opens new avenues for understanding the human-nature relationship. It also highlights the potential risks associated with immersive experiences. Although short-term exposure to nature may be a low risk for most individuals, it is vital to consider that more immersive experiences could pose psychological risks to vulnerable groups.

Although there are significant differences between altered states that distort or separate a person from reality and attunement states that remain close to real-life, real-time events, there may be some similarities in how these states affect the self that warrant attention. Neuroscientists are increasingly speculating that psychedelic experiences, for instance, may have the ability to radically alter perceptions of selfhood in positive ways (Ciaunica & Safron, 2022). The main claim is that experiences of alternative self- and world-models may enhance the flexibility of one's perceptual and sensorimotor functions, allowing for the release of certain ingrained behaviours. This hypothesis does not necessarily apply only to altered states induced by drugs but also suggests the transformative potential of other types of exceptional states to broaden our understanding of what is possible and literally change our minds. I highlight this point here but return to it at a greater length in Chapter 5.

Flow states

The term 'altered states of consciousness' generally refers to states that take us out (temporarily) of our normal waking state. As outlined above, such alterations can be voluntarily induced (e.g. medication, psychedelics, hypnosis, meditation or other practices) or involuntary, as in the case of psychosis. These distorting or distancing effects can be pleasant or pathological, respectively. However, attunement does not involve any degree of abstraction from reality. The essential feature of attunement is a sense of reciprocity between the perceiver and external stimuli. Therefore, it is important to also compare attunement with other types of exceptional states, where no form of distancing from reality takes place. Both flow states and aesthetic states fit this category and therefore offer further insights into attunement.

The positive psychologist Mihaly Csikszentmihalyi coined the term 'flow state' (Csikszentmihalyi, 2000), to describe the state a person can experience when highly focused on an activity that positively challenges them, sometimes described as being 'in the zone'. His initial research involved interviews with experienced practitioners across different fields. Although flow is often associated with creativity, creative activities such as painting and Csikszentmihalyi's studies spanned a wide range of activities and situations, from highly physical activities such as rock-climbing to more cerebral pursuits such as playing chess.

Flow states are marked by focused concentration, intrinsic motivation, a sense of control and altered time perception (a feeling of being lost in the moment). Flow is achieved when a task is characterized by a balance between the person's skills and the demands of the challenge. In the context of learning, for example, to achieve flow, a student must engage in educational tasks that present a sufficient level of challenge. This balance ensures that the learner's skills are neither overmatched nor underutilized (Jackson, 1995). Conversely, a chess player whose opponent does not offer any surprise or challenge will not access a state of flow.

At first glance, flow and attunement share important features, both are immersive, self-driven experiences that can lead to a fluid sense of time and heightened vitality. However, the critical differences distinguish attunement from a unique state. Flow demands a focused level of concentration on an individual's activities. There is an intentional narrowing of the perceptual field, which focuses on specific stimuli and responses. As Csikszentmihalyi wrote, when describing flow in the context of dance, 'music limits the field by focusing attention' (p. 105). Attunement is less object or event orientated. The psychological energy involved is not singularly focused. Instead, the perceiver's intentionality is towards the whole of their surroundings. The perceiver holds a soft fascination towards everything within their perceptual field, and a spontaneity of response to what emerges. For example, a rock climber in flow is absorbed in the next hold and bodily movements, while a person in attunement might pause on the mountainside, becoming aware of wind, light, sound and a sense of participation in the landscape as a whole.

The second substantial difference between the two states is that attunement is embodied. Attunement is dependent on multisensory stimulation between the perceiver and the environment. As researchers discovered after Csikszentmihalyi, flow can occur in both physical and mental activities. For example, it is possible to achieve a state of flow through a wide range of mental activities such as reading a book or playing a video game. Mental activities of this type can provide the required levels of challenge responses that evoke flow (Jackson, 1995). Whereas multisensory perceptual participation is integral to the attunement experience.

Csikszentmihalyi's research showed that flow is not limited to structured activities or occupations, such as rock climbing or playing chess. Short episodes of microflow are achievable in everyday situations such as talking and joking with friends or enjoying a meal you have cooked. He concluded that flow operates along a continuum of experience, from spontaneous and unintentional microflow moments that can be achieved in everyday life to the deep flow states experienced by skilled people in structured activities. Furthermore, Csikszentmihalyi claimed that these moments of microflow are not insignificant and can help reduce stress, improve general mental health and enrich the overall quality of life.

Philosophers and cognitive scientists generally agree that all states of consciousness operate along a continuum of experience, typically from low to high intensity. The overall pattern of a state may remain constant along the continuum of experience, but its duration and intensity can change under different conditions (Ottiger et al., 2021). This continuum model offers compelling evidence that 'micro-attunements' can be cultivated in accessible settings, without requiring remote wilderness or extended isolation. Just as microflow can be achieved through everyday pastimes, micro-attunements might be possible through brief but deliberate multisensory engagements within accessible green spaces such as urban parks or small gardens.

In summary, flow research provides concrete evidence that exceptional states can be scaled to fit everyday life and provide genuine psychological value, despite their reduced intensity. The challenge lies in identifying the minimal conditions needed for micro-attunement to occur, and developing places and practices that make this multisensory engagement accessible to diverse populations in their daily environments. The general application of attunement states to everyday life is the focus throughout Part 3 of the book.

Aesthetic experiences

The experience of 'being in the zone' or 'getting lost' in the moment is not exclusive to a state of flow. Aesthetic experiences share similar effects.

Broadly, aesthetic experience is defined as occurring when an object – be it an object or event – enters the foreground of our attention and is met with fascination (Marković, 2012). While simply liking or judging the beauty of an object falls within the domain of normative experience and everyday ways of interacting with the world around us, aesthetic experiences involve an extraordinary feeling of unity with the object of fascination.

It may seem a leap to try and apprehend the phenomenon of environmental attunement through the lens of aesthetic theory. Being alone with nature cannot be further from a civilized society's art galleries and theatres. However, the philosophy of aesthetics is fundamentally concerned with how we perceive the world around us. While aesthetic preferencing is simply to like or judge the beauty of an object, and therefore falls within the domain of normative experience and everyday ways of interacting with the world around us, aesthetic experience is categorized as an exceptional state. The experience transcends the everyday through the heightened effect and symbolic meaning that it evokes.

The experimental psychologist Slobodan Markovic and colleagues at Belgrade University spent over a decade empirically researching aesthetic experience and determined three core components: fascination with an aesthetic object (which requires a high level of arousal and attention), appraisal of the symbolic reality of an object (a symbolic meaning that involves high cognitive engagement) and a strong feeling of unity with the object of fascination (emotional affect), which operate interdependently in a manner that has a global effect on the way a person perceives and engages with their surroundings (Marković, 2012). Inherent within this apprehension of aesthetic experiences is the subject–object relationship, a philosophical tradition that can be traced back to Kant, and the notion that some form of contemplative distancing is required between subject and object for any intellectual meaning-making to occur.

Artists of the 1960s and the 1970s questioned whether concepts and behaviours were more interesting than objects. Yoko Ono spoke for this new generation of artists when she famously declared that art was behaviour (Fineberg, 1995). These artists not only started to experiment with new materials and techniques, but they also reached out into the formerly untouched space of the observer to invite their active involvement. Artists such as Nancy Holt in the United States and Hamish Fulton in the UK reached out to nature, not to treat it as a neutral and objective medium to be represented on the canvas, but to be experienced. These artists reacted to the flattening of nature into scenery and immersed themselves in the environment. In this context, the constructs of subject and object seemed inappropriate and irrelevant.

Prior to this, John Dewey and Maurice Merleau-Ponty developed phenomenological models of aesthetic experiences (Dewey, 1994; Romdenh-Romluc, 2011). However, the works of philosophers such as Heburn, Carlson and Arnold Berleant from the 1960s onwards specifically re-examined the aesthetics of nature and the environment (Brady & Prior, 2020). Berleant (1995) examined the total immersion of the individual in the environment in consideration of the ways in which environmental factors impose themselves on the perceiver, and how the perceiver energizes the environment.

Berleant developed the idea of aesthetic engagement that differs from traditional models by returning aesthetics (from the Greek *aisthetikos*, 'of or for perception by the senses') to its etymological origins, stressing the primacy of sense perception. Berleant was not novel in this. John Dewey and Maurice Merleau-Ponty also stress the primacy of perception. Prior to Berleant, however, a hierarchy of senses prevailed in aesthetic theories that separated the senses, privileging vision above all others. Although pioneering, the works of Dewey, Merleau-Ponty and Gibson all retain traces of this bias. Berleant takes this further by recognizing perception as the mutual activity of all sense modalities and how experience takes on an aesthetic quality through our conscious focus on our multisensory perceptual participation.

Berleant positions the perceptual participation of the individual as central to the experience. Unlike conventional models of aesthetic experience, which privilege vision, Berleant asserts that perception is the mutual activity of all sense modalities. In Berleant's view, there is a continuum of experience from the everyday to the aesthetic. The aesthetic dimension of the experience comes from the conscious focus of our attention towards our multisensory perceptual participation. Traditional models characterize aesthetic experience as an extraordinary sense of unity between the subject and object. Berleant shifted emphasis to the multisensory perceptual participation of a person situated within the environment (Hughes & Berleant, 2023).

In doing so, Berleant redefined the aesthetic experience from being characterized as an extraordinary sense of unity that occurs between subject and object to the intentional and embodied sense of participation within a physical space. Where unity is passive, participation is active. There is a vitality to the participation that enlivens this experience. In unity, we can lose ourselves to the other in the moment. In participation, our sense of self remains both intact and energized. By emphasizing the multisensory perceptual participation between the perceiver and environment, as opposed to dualistic models, Berleant's concept of aesthetic engagement provides a philosophical framework for the study of environmental attunement to be placed within.

In terms of research, positioning attunement within this philosophical frame of reference broadens the field of enquiry beyond cognition to include both perceptual and bodily processes. In sharp contrast, for example, with the use of functional magnetic resonance imaging (fMRI) technology to study people's reactions to viewing nature images and videos, the study of environmental attunement will fall short if it does not involve embodied responses to prolonged multisensory stimulation. One of the major breakthroughs in the scientific study of environmental attunement and nature experiences more broadly will come from finding ways to bring the lab into the field, instead of attempting to bring the field into the lab. The fields of psychology and cognitive science must find ways to embrace the embodied. Arnold Berleant's work provides an impetus.

The practical challenges of researching embodied experiences should not be viewed as impediments; instead, they should be viewed as an impetus for innovative research methods. Such endeavours start by valuing the embodied experience and willingness to extend the search for human consciousness beyond cognition to include perceptual and bodily processes. Hence, the categorization of attunement as an exceptional state of consciousness of the embodied kind, and not as a purely mental state, is significant. Chapters 5 and 6 specifically explore how the recent surge of research on multisensory perception and embodied approaches within the cognitive sciences can be applied to the study of environmental attunement.

In conclusion

Attunement states are qualitatively distinct from normative waking consciousness and involve altered time perception, vivid mental imagery and embodied participation in the environment. While attunement shares some characteristics with other non-normative states, such as hallucinogenic states (which distort reality) or flow states (which narrow focus), its distinguishing feature is multisensory environmental embeddedness. What sets attunement apart is the person's perceptual participation within the multisensory environment: attunement is not simply a mental phenomenon but an embodied state grounded in lived, sensory experience.

In attunement, one experiences the self and world in profoundly different ways compared to everyday life. This is neither a transcendent or mystical escape, nor does it involve distortion or detachment from reality. Rather, attunement is defined by a new and expansive sense of self that emerges through direct reciprocal engagement with environmental stimuli.

Individuals remain anchored in the physical world, even as their perception of the self and surroundings is fundamentally transformed.

In summary, the categorization of environmental attunement as an exceptional state of consciousness is significant for four key reasons.

1. *Broadening the understanding of nature experiences*: This broadens our understanding of the effects of natural experiences beyond the well-researched cognitive benefits of passive exposure to nature environments. There is something that it is like to be in a state of attunement that is distinct from the satisfaction of climbing a tree, the feeling of awe at the top of a mountain or the feel-good factor of walking in a beautiful garden. There is a quality and texture to the experience that profoundly affects self- and self-world models.

2. *Challenging existing research parameters:* Attunement's reliance on multisensory interaction challenges conventional psychological nature research models that prioritize passive or visually dominant forms of nature engagement. By foregrounding the role of multisensory perception, attunement calls for innovative field-based research models to shed light on the complex multi-modal interplay between self and the environment. There are methodological and practical challenges to overcome, not least in how we find ways to track and capture real-time multisensory data and not solely rely on people's recollected personal accounts. However, the biggest barrier may well be psychology's persistent belief in dividing the mind from matter and humans from the rest of life – a point expanded upon in Chapter 4.

3. *Expanding the understanding of conscious states:* The central role that multisensory perceptual processing plays in attunement states suggests that conscious states may be more closely linked to perception that was previously credited. Attunement states therefore offer an understanding of exceptional states of consciousness by expanding consciousness studies beyond individual cognition to encompass environmental relationality. In so doing, environmental attunement research can contribute to a broader understanding of the phenomenology of human consciousness.

4. *Relevance to the general population:* Attunement states, like other exceptional states, exist along a continuum of intensity. While deep attunement often requires extended solitude in remote environments, this research and comparative analysis indicate that shorter, less intense forms of micro-attunement are possible in more accessible, everyday settings. Recognizing this continuum broadens the theoretical and practical significance of attunement, suggesting that its psychological

benefits are not limited to those with access to the wilderness. This insight inspired my subsequent research on how attunement can be cultivated by a wider range of people in diverse environments, a theme explored in the following chapters.

Environmental attunement is best understood as an embodied, exceptional state of consciousness that is qualitatively distinct from normative and non-normative experiences. Its reliance on multisensory participation with the environment sets it apart from hallucinogenic, flow and aesthetic states, thus offering new perspectives for research and practice. Importantly, attunement operates along a continuum, with micro-attunements accessible in everyday contexts, broadening their relevance beyond those with access to remote wilderness. This insight not only challenges existing research paradigms in psychology but also opens new possibilities for fostering well-being and ecological connections in contemporary society.

References

Bayne, T., & Carter, O. (2018). Dimensions of consciousness and the psychedelic state. *Neuroscience of Consciousness, 2018*(1). DOI: 10.1093/nc/niy008

Berleant, A. (1995). *Aesthetics of environment.* Temple University Press.

Brady, E., & Prior, J. (2020). Environmental aesthetics: A synthetic review. *People and Nature, 2*(2), 254–266. DOI:10.1002/pan3.10089

Ciaunica, A., & Safron, A. (2022). Disintegrating and reintegrating the self–(in) flexible self-models in depersonalisation and psychedelic experiences. In C. Letheby & P. Gerrans (Eds.), *Philosophical Perspectives on Psychedelic Psychiatry, International Perspectives in Philosophy and Psychiatry* (Oxford, 2024; online ed., Oxford Academic, 19 September 2024) https://doi.org/10.1093/oso/9780192898371.003.0004, accessed 27 July 2025.

Csikszentmihalyi, M. (2000). *Beyond boredom and anxiety: The experience of play in work and games.* Jossey-Bass.

Damasio, A. (2010). *Self comes to mind: Constructing the conscious brain.* Pantheon/Random House.

Dewey, J. (1994). *Experience & nature* (9th printing). Open Court.

Dinis-Oliveira, R. J., Pereira, C. L., & Dias da Silva, D. (2019). Pharmacokinetic and pharmacodynamic aspects of peyote and mescaline: Clinical and forensic repercussions. *Current Molecular Pharmacology, 12*(3), 184–194. DOI 10.2174/1874467211666181010154139

Dubrovsky, D. I. (2019). The hard problem of consciousness: Theoretical solution of its main questions. *AIMS Neuroscience, 6*(2), 85–103. DOI: 10.3934/Neuroscience.2019.2.85

Fineberg, J. D. (Ed.). (1995). *Art since 1940: Strategies of being.* Abrams.

Gonzalez, D., Cantillo, J., Perez, I., Carvalho, M., Aronovich, A., Farre, M., Feilding, A., Obiols, J. E., & Bouso, J. C. (2021). The Shipibo ceremonial use of ayahuasca to promote well-being: An observational study. *Frontiers in Pharmacology*, *12*, 623923. DOI: 10.3389/fphar.2021.623923.

Hughes, E., & Berleant, A. (2023). Aesthetic engagement as a pathway to mental health and well-being. In M. Poltrum, M. Musalek, K. Galvin, & Y. Saito (Eds.), *The Oxford handbook of mental health and contemporary western aesthetics* (1st ed.). Oxford University Press.

Jackson, S. A. (1995). Factors influencing the occurrence of flow state in elite athletes. *Journal of Applied Sport Psychology*, *7*(2), 138–166. DOI: 10.1080/10413209508406962.

Jimenez, M. P., DeVille, N. V., Elliott, E. G., Schiff, J. E., Wilt, G. E., Hart, J. E., & James, P. (2021). Associations between nature exposure and health: A review of the evidence. *International Journal of Environmental Research and Public Health*, *18*(9), 4790. DOI: 10.3390/ijerph18094790.

Lysaker, P. H., & Lysaker, J. T. (2002). Narrative structure in psychosis: Schizophrenia and disruptions in the dialogical self. *Theory & Psychology*, *12*(2), 207–220. DOI: 10.1177/0959354302012002630.

Marković, S. (2012). Components of aesthetic experience: Aesthetic fascination, aesthetic appraisal, and aesthetic emotion. *I-Perception*, *3*(1), 1–17. DOI: 10.1068/i0450aap.

Maslow, A. H. (1971). *The farther reaches of human nature*. Viking Press.

Maslow, A. H. (1993). *The farther reaches of human nature*. Arkana.

Myerhoff, B. G. (1976). *Peyote hunt: The sacred journey of the Huichol Indians*. Cornell University Press.

Nagel, T. (1974). What is it like to be a bat? *The Philosophical Review*, *83*(4), 435. DOI: 10.2307/2183914.

Ottiger, B., Van Wegen, E., Keller, K., Nef, T., Nyffeler, T., Kwakkel, G., & Vanbellingen, T. (2021). Getting into a 'flow' state: A systematic review of flow experience in neurological diseases. *Journal of NeuroEngineering and Rehabilitation*, *18*(1), 65. DOI: 10.1186/s12984-021-00864-w.

Revonsuo, A. (2009). Altered and exceptional states of consciousness. In *Encyclopedia of Consciousness* (pp. 9–21). Elsevier. DOI: 10.1016/B978-012373873-8.00002-5.

Romdenh-Romluc, K. (2011). *Routledge philosophy guidebook to Merleau-Ponty and phenomenology of perception*. Routledge.

Tart, C. T. (2000). *States of consciousness*. Iuniverse.com.

Part 2

In Theory

4

Embracing the totality of nature

Yes, though you may think me perverse, if it were proposed to me to dwell in the neighbourhood of the most beautiful garden that every human art contrived, or else of a Dismal Swamp, I should certainly decide for the swamp. How vain, then, have been all your labours, citizens, for me!

Henry David Thoreau

Thoreau's words point to an essential truth regarding environmental attunement. Even the most barren landscape, or a dismal swamp, can afford the possibility of accessing a state of attunement. Beyond the visual aesthetic of a place, when it comes to attunement, what matters is the dominance of other-than-human stimuli within a person's perceptual field. As a result, people can experience states of attunement in a wide variety of environments, including those that fall far outside our idealized images of green space or preconceptions and prejudices of what constitutes good nature. These diverse environments can have perceptual properties that stimulate attunement states.

I interviewed a renowned shaman who told me that he believed that everything that exists is alive, and everything alive is nature. Everything. Plants. Animals. Air. Stones. Humans. Thoughts. Feelings. Everything. In his worldview, a car is alive and is part of nature as a giant sycamore tree. Memories are as much nature as the sound of bees. He is not alone. This idea of nature ties all the great shamanic traditions across continents and cultures, from the Tenger shamans on the plains of Mongolia to the Shipibo ancestral healers in the Amazonian rainforests of Peru. Surprisingly, this belief underpins most modern natural sciences. In contrast, the field of psychology has a different perspective. Psychology persistently treats humans as separate from nature. Mind reigns superior over matter, and as a consequence, nature is destined to remain little more than a pleasant and therapeutic backdrop.

This chapter challenges the dominant psychological perspective that treats nature as separate from humans. The chapter critiques psychology's reliance on the principle of 'exposure to green space', arguing that it oversimplifies the diversity of environments and overlooks the embodied, multisensory character of environmental engagement. It argues that embracing the multifactorial composition of environments and human involvement can advance our understanding of the psychological significance of nature, beyond its cognitive effects. This chapter introduces a framework for evaluating environments based on their degree of human impact, which ranges from low to high. Low-human-impact (LHI) environments, where other-than-human stimuli dominate the perceptual field, have been proposed to provide unique affordances conducive to attunement states. The chapter concludes that attunement is not limited to rare or remote experiences but that micro-attunements can be achieved in more accessible environments. By broadening our understanding of where and how attunement occurs, we open new possibilities for fostering deeper connections with other-than-human life around us.

What do we mean by nature?

Up to this point, I have used the term *nature* without providing much definition or specificity, using the term in its broadest and most commonly used sense to refer to other-than-human life. Words matter, as Wittgenstein claimed: language not only describes our reality but also shapes it. In the first two decades of the twenty-first century, numerous scholars argue that the term *nature*'s common meaning as all things separate from humans is rooted in Western philosophical, cultural and political history, and that the linguistic complexities that arise in the use of the term *nature* are deeply intertwined with ideas of colonialism, power and privilege. Scholars, such as Carolyn Merchant and Timothy Morton, call for the death of nature and a new nomenclature. Timothy Morton (2009), for instance, uses this argument in his book *Ecology without Nature* to reject the idea of nature as a means to accept the interconnectedness of everything.

The idea of pristine nature as a form of heavenly paradise unsoiled by human imperfection runs deep in the human imagination—from the ancient Mesopotamian myth of the Garden of the Hesperides to the Abrahamic religions' stories of our expulsion from the Garden of Paradise. In all these myths lies a tension within the human-nature relationship, where, on the one hand, we seek to transcend the temptations of the sensual world, while, on the other, we strive to return to the garden.

Influential nineteenth-century environmentalist John Muir (2018) viewed nature as God's temple and argued that certain types of environments should be ring-fenced and protected from humankind to remain pristine and pure. Heavily influenced by the work of Muir, landscape architect Frederick Law

Olmsted lobbied for the protection of the great Yosemite National Park in the United States and helped secure an act from Congress to ensure that the land did not fall into private ownership and was devoted to popular resorts and recreation (Runte, 1990).

Although it is difficult to challenge, without some apprehensiveness, policies that protect extraordinary places such as Yosemite National Park from human impact; in contrast, writing on the history of the American wilderness, Roderick Nash (2014) claims that nature only exists as a state of mind, and the idea of wilderness as untouched nature, he argues, is an objectification of the land born out of white colonialism that, albeit idealizing, compounds a separation that ultimately ends in damage to both planet and people.

However, the seven First Nations tribes that populated the Yosemite Valley for close to 4,000 years prior to this act and their removal show us a different way: one which sought to nurture the reciprocity between humans and the rest of nature (Spence, 1999). These people did not need to protect the land from themselves; rather, they were the land. Poet and activist Paula Gunn Allen (1986) captured America's First Nations people's worldview in the following way:

> We are the land; that is the fundamental idea embedded in Native American life. The land is not really the place (separate from ourselves) where we act out the drama of our isolated destinies. It is not a means of survival, a setting for our affairs. It is rather a part of our being, dynamic, significant, real. It is our self. It is not a matter of being close to nature. The Earth is, in a very real sense, the same as our self (or selves). (pp. 191–192)

Ducharme and Couvet's influential work, 'How the diversity of human concepts of nature affects conservation of biodiversity' (2020), systematically explores how the idea of 'nature' is far from universal and has profound implications for biodiversity conservation research, policy and practice. Their analysis reviews the use of the term 'nature' across languages, scientific literature and conservation policy documents and examines how different philosophical and cultural traditions have shaped its meaning over time. Through this analysis, Ducarme and Couvet identified four main categories of meaning, each with distinct implications.

Nature as non-human material world

Nature is seen as everything that exists independently of human activity-pristine wilderness, untouched landscapes and ecosystems that are free from human influence. This is the most widely applied use of the term. Conservation in this view emphasizes preservation and minimizing human intervention. From this perspective, in the field of psychology, humans and their endeavours are separate from nature, and natural environments are in contrast to built environments.

Nature as everything

Nature is understood as everything within the universe, including processes and changes, life cycles, ecological succession and evolutionary dynamics. Humans are a part of this dynamic. This categorization is well illustrated in the words of Paula Gunn Allen. In addition, scientific theories from Darwin's evolution to quantum mechanics' discovery that the structures and processes of subatomic particles constitute the fundamental units of energy and matter reflect this worldview.

Nature as a value or ideal

In this category, nature is viewed as an ideal to be aspired to or a value to be protected, often with strong normative, aesthetic or spiritual dimensions. Conservation efforts here may focus on maintaining landscapes or species that embody this ideal, and their 'pristine' status as illustrated by the beliefs of environmentalists such as John Muir, but that creates an objectifying idealism that historians such as Roderick Nash claim provides humans with the permission to damage the earth.

Nature as fundamental character or essence

This definition focuses on the essential qualities or 'character' of a place or entity – what makes it 'natural' as opposed to artificial. In terms of environmentalism and conservation, such beliefs aim to protect the integrity or authenticity of a place, even if some human influence is present. In human psychology, this relates to the idea of an inner nature – a true or authentic self.

Ducarme and Couvet argue that these different concepts are not mutually exclusive but often lead to conflicting priorities and conservation strategies. For example, protecting 'wilderness' (category 1) may call for minimal human presence, while conserving dynamic processes (category 2) may require active intervention and management. They also highlight how these definitions are deeply rooted in cultural and philosophical traditions, and how a failure to recognize this diversity can hinder effective interdisciplinary and cross-cultural dialogue and affect research and policy strategies.

Acknowledging the plurality of 'natures' allows for more inclusive, context-sensitive policies that can accommodate diverse values and local realities and encourage dialogue rather than conflict between different conservation philosophies – a point I return to in Chapters 8 and 9.

How does psychology define nature?

The field of psychology has predominantly aligned with category 1 of Ducarme and Couvet's analysis, treating nature primarily as separate from humans and their activities. This is not surprising, as nature presents something of a conundrum to a discipline that is dedicated to understanding the workings of the human mind and associated behaviours. With the same certainty that we make the cut between mind and matter, and subject and object, nature is treated as independent of human psychology, albeit as a beautiful resource for sustenance, relaxation and rejuvenation.

In a discussion panel following a talk I gave on the role of nature in mental health in 2018, a psychologist from the audience jokingly asked if I prescribe tree-hugging to patients. While treatment efficacy was not the focus of my talk, this comment highlights mainstream psychology's struggle to acknowledge the idea of any meaningful reciprocity between humans and the rest of nature. Categorizing nature as anything other than a resource poses an existential threat. How can reciprocity exist between the human mind and a mindless tree? Consequently, nature is treated as the benign outer reality to our sophisticated inner worlds.

The argument that trees do not share the same intellectual or emotional capacity as humans misses the point. It is not that we should learn to talk to trees but rather that there is perceptual involvement between humans and the rest of life, which the field of psychology tends to ignore or give minimal credit. This is because of the accepted superiority of the mind over matter. It is difficult, or indeed threatening, for modern psychology to grasp how there can be any form of meaningful reciprocity between the human mind and mindless nature. You may talk to a tree but the tree will not talk back. However, the language of nature is the language of the body and senses – a language in which the increasingly cognition-centred world of psychology is resistant to learning.

The human-nature divide suits modern psychology as far as it allows it to hang on to the belief in the superiority of the human mind. The cognitive turn in modern psychology since the second half of the twentieth century has only consolidated the one-way attitude towards the human-nature relationship. Nature can be accepted as an influencing factor on mental health and well-being, as a 'green pill' for symptom relief or cognitive rejuvenation, but from a psychological perspective, it cannot be embraced with any real equality or sense of kinship. Arnold Berleant (1995) articulates the issue well:

> The hardest conception of all to grasp, nature as totality, is nonetheless soberly realistic, for it recognises that ultimately everything affects everything else, that humans, along with all the other things, inhabit a single interconnected realm, and that we must realise that our ultimate freedom lies not in diminishing or denying certain regions of our world in order to favour others, but in acknowledging and understanding them all. This does not confer equal value on all. It admits rather that all activities, processes, and participants that together constitute nature have an equal claim to be taken seriously. (Berleant, 1995, p. 9)

The psychological research of nature

In the context of psychological research on human relationships to nature, three major theories paved the way for four decades of study: Kaplan and Kaplan's (1989) Attention Restoration Theory, Ulrich's Stress Reduction Theory and the theory of Shinrin-yoku, or forest bathing, as is known in English. A recent volume review of over 100 contemporary psychological studies on the human-nature relationship concluded that not only have these three theories instigated substantial research follow-up, but most present-day studies stem from or are influenced by these theories. All three theories adopted the principle of exposure to green space in their research, which has set the parameters for most of the research since.

A review of psychological studies on the human-nature relationship, particularly those from cognitive, developmental and social sciences orientations, shows that exposure to green space principle is by far the most widely applied. The term 'green space' has become a useful shorthand for places where nature is contained, as opposed to human-built environments. In cities, these green spaces include parks, green roofs, vegetables and flower gardens. The greater the distance from the city, the greater the opportunities for larger areas and a variety of green spaces.

The visual characteristics of the environment are prioritized over the other perceptual qualities. These visual characteristics determine whether a space is green. For example, a crowded urban park with traffic noise and pollution can be classified as a green space, whereas an isolated rocky inlet on a shoreline with no visual vegetation is not. Emphasis is placed on the environment's visual appeal, as culturally and aesthetically defined.

Exposure to these spaces is measured in terms of time rather than the type of activity that the individual is engaged in. The studies examine changes in stress and anxiety levels and cognitive performance of participants to short periods of exposure of ten to sixty minutes, with a mean of fifteen minutes (Schutte et al., 2021, p. 19). Consequently, there has been mounting evidence since the 1980s that exposure to so-called green spaces can lower stress, restore certain mental functions and improve recovery rates after illnesses. The widely accepted conclusion is that exposure to green spaces is beneficial. For example, an extensive peer review of published articles concluded the following.

> Evidence from the literature shows that a wide variety of people benefit from exposure to green spaces. Studies have demonstrated links between green spaces and higher performance on attentional tasks among public housing residents, AIDS caregivers, cancer patients, college students, prairie restoration volunteers, and employees of large organisations. There is considerable evidence to show that exposure to a green landscape, such as a walk in an urban park or a view of a green area outside a school window, is likely to reduce symptoms of mental fatigue. (Schutte et al., 2021, pp. 21–22)

Within the last decade, prominent studies that promote the therapeutic benefits of 'exposure to green space have had an important influence on mental health practices and policies (White et al., 2019; Meredith et al., 2020; Meidenbauer et al., 2020). For instance, in 2020, the UK government agency Public Health England referenced some of these studies in its strategy statement entitled *The Green Space Framework* (2020), which focused on ways to improve access to green spaces for a rapidly growing urban population.

The green space blind spot

The adoption of the principle of exposure to green spaces has advantages, as it makes research methods more manageable and measurable. Therefore, it is relatively easy to develop and implement quantitative research methods based on short-term exposures. These methods include stress reduction studies using fMRI to study participants' brain responses to five minutes of exposure to videos of natural scenes and attention restoration studies using diary methods to capture the effects on urban workers in city parks. However, although there are advantages, the principle of exposure to green spaces is not without bias.

The word green derives from the Old Saxon word *grün*, meaning 'grass' or 'grow', and is commonly used in the English vernacular to denote something natural or belonging to nature. We use phrases such as 'green space', 'greengrocer' and 'green energy'. Oil and gas companies greenwash their logos to symbolize good intentions towards the environment. In the context of mainstream psychological research, green has been adopted to mean all things 'natural' as opposed to 'human made'. However, the association between green and nature is far from universal.

For example, the Himba tribe in northwest Namibia would not associate their experience or land with the colour green. Himba women sing as they hand mine red ochre rocks from caves that are then crushed into a powder and mixed with oils and fats for application to their hair and skin. This red mud is even used to coat single-roomed dwellings, and consequently, the entire environment takes on a red tonality. The Himba are immersed in this red-toned environment, where traces of their human presence are minimal. Mud huts hardly appear on the skyline, and a semi-nomadic lifestyle means that agricultural imprints are barely visible.

The Himba people do not perceive the land to be red. They have a unique way of perceiving colour, which has been the subject of numerous studies (Goldstein et al., 2009; Regier & Kay, 2009). They group shades together based on tonality and light density. For example, certain darker shades of blue, red, green and purple are grouped together, as are yellow and white shades; green and blue shades; and green, red and brown shades. The Himba people see shades, contrasts and hues differently from the single colours we perceive in the West. Himba can identify and describe colours with great accuracy and specificity.

This adeptness to see the world with such nuances is not unique to the Himba. Inuit people across Alaska, Canada and Greenland are also able to identify and describe extraordinary variances in colours and tones. Both the Himba and Inuit people can pick up details in the distant landscape and ignore distractions better than most modern humans. Anthropologists have discovered similar findings among the Toda peoples of Southern India and the Sans people of the Kalahari, concluding that pre-modern cultures that live close to the land literally see the world differently than modern humans.

Studies on the visual perception of pre-modern cultures highlight that the association of nature with green is far from universal. The monochromatic branding of nature by modern, predominantly Western cultures reflects cultural and aesthetic values towards nature. Our green-tinted glasses may seem benign on the surface; however, they have significant implications. In the field of psychology, the link between green space and mental health establishes the premise that greener is better, and by logical consequence, less green space is worse. Nature is limited to a specific visual aesthetic.

However, this premise negates the variety and multifactorial complexity of environments, human multisensory involvement and any psychological significance beyond their cognitive effects. For example, looking at a landscape on a digital screen has been reported to yield similar cognitive results to physically sitting in a garden (Menser et al., 2021). The embodied, multisensory engagement of the experience is sidelined, along with any psychological benefits that may come with it.

For example, there is some evidence that built environments can be more beneficial to health in certain circumstances. For example, longitudinal studies of adults over the age of fifty have shown a lower percentage of dementia in urban populations than in rural populations (Hirst et al., 2021). Other studies suggest that high-intensity sensory stimulation associated with urban environments may serve to 'train the brain' to be more focused and astute (Cassarino & Setti, 2015). Studies of this kind highlight that environments are complex, and understanding human involvement within them requires sophisticated approaches to fully understand.

Although well intentioned, the principle of exposure to green space is an oversimplified model. On one level, it promotes an appreciation of nature; on the other, it represents a deeply problematic cultural construct that denies the true complexity of environments and our engagement with them. The upshot is that Environmental Psychology researchers generally agree that our current understanding of how different types of natural environments affect humans is very limited. Determining the differences between looking at a tree from a window and being fully immersed in a forest, from a psychological perspective, for example, remains speculative.

While it is important to acknowledge that the exposure to green space principle has been instrumental in forming the volumes of research in the field for the past forty years, it has significantly enhanced our knowledge of the benefits of nature contact and positively impacted public policy and practice. We must also recognize how it restricts explorations of the psychological potency of humans' relationships with nature. This point is underscored in studies of environmental attunement. Attunement is a conscious state determined by its embodied and environmentally embedded character that sits far outside the parameters of exposure to green space. Like indigenous peoples, such as the Himba, whose perceptual engagement with their environments defies Western colour categories, attunement states demand a multisensory understanding that psychology's exposure to the green space principle overlooks.

Evaluating environments for their multifactorial composition

By treating nature as separate, the field of psychology goes against the grain, or at least lags historically behind the modern sciences. Modern biology, physics, chemistry and their subfields are based on the interconnected nature of life. The sciences, particularly the natural sciences, offer psychological research a way to adopt a more ecological approach. Environmental biology, for instance, defines environments as the dynamic activities of biotic (i.e. living and once-living organisms, including vegetation, animals and microorganisms) and abiotic (i.e. non-living physical and chemical elements, including climate, air, temperature and minerals) factors (Huang, 2005).

For example, a city has its own micro-climate, based on a unique combination of these factors. Within this system, the life and well-being of a tree are determined by the tensions and interrelationships between these environmental factors. Reciprocally, trees influence other factors that affect environmental dynamics. The multifactorial dynamics at play determine an environment's unique characteristics and overall atmosphere. Walking through a built-up part of a city, despite the human impact, you can still notice these other-than-human biotic and abiotic factors, such as light, air temperature and small patches of vegetation pushing through. Other-than-human life is present and part of the environmental composition.

A beautifully designed urban park can be teeming with trees and stunning plant life, yet the presence of humans rushing through on their way to work, the roar of the nearby traffic and the smells of city can dominate the space. Although this park may perfectly fit the description of urban green space referenced in research as beneficial to mental health and well-being (Meidenbauer et al., 2020; Meredith et al., 2020; White et al., 2019), when evaluated through a multifactorial lens, its composition is dominated by human life.

I interviewed an environmental artist at their studio in rural Pennsylvania once. It took me two days to travel there, and upon my arrival, my host suggested that I hike in some nearby woodlands to shake off my journey. The further I walked, and the sight of the studio faded from my vision, all traces of human presence left my perceptual range. Within less than twenty minutes, I felt completely alone in nature. The senses have a finite spatial range. We only hear, see, smell, touch, taste and somatically sense within a certain distance.

The factors in any given environment stimulate our sensorium within the parameters of this range. On a spectrum from low to high human impact, the Pennsylvanian woodland was at the lower end. Other-than-human factors, abiotic and abiotic, dominated my perceptual range. In this environment, free from human factors, my awareness and attention were taken up by other-than-human stimuli. My awareness and attention were not solely visually stimulated. As I moved through the woods, the sounds, smells, textures and spatial atmosphere all played a part.

One of the main conclusions of this research is that spending time alone in environments with LHI is conducive to achieving a state of attunement. Regardless of how picturesque, green or natural we perceive a specific setting as, the multisensory composition of LHI environments affords us something distinct from environments where human factors dominate our perceptual field. A beautifully planted urban park may hold visual aesthetic appeal, but the human impact within the person's perceptual range can be high due to the presence of humans, city noises, smells and so on. In contrast, an arid mountain desert, regardless of the lack of vegetation, scores low on human impact, as other-than-human factors (biotic and abiotic) still dominate the composition.

This scaling is not intended to infer any aesthetic judgement or demarcation between what nature is and what is not, but rather to determine the extent to which non-human perceptual properties dominate the environment. For example, I interviewed someone who described their experiences of attunement alone in the midst of winter on a raised bogland in Ireland. These boglands are an invaluable part of Ireland's biodiversity, as they provide habitats for rare plants and animals. But in winter, they are damp and muddy places that differ from the 'tamed nature' that appears in most studies, and that challenge any idealized image of green space. Even the most seemingly barren landscapes have perceptual properties that stimulate attunement states.

In the context of the study of environmental attunement, this scale from low to high human impact is underpinned by an appreciation of the diversity and multifactorial complexity of environments, including human presence, activity and construction. Environments are evaluated based on their multifactorial composition, ranging from LHI to high human impact (HHI). In LHI environments, non-human factors dominate the perceptual field. Human factors are dominant in the HHI environment. These factors are multisensory and not purely visual. Factors such as smell, sound and light are given equal weight. This scale determines, with greater specificity, the degree to which an environment provides the conditions necessary for attunement.

How do LHI environments cultivate attunement?

A case vignette

Irish peatlands have long served as a source of inspiration for poets, painters, writers and filmmakers. In 2019, I interviewed a land artist during his one-year art residency in Bog na Móna, a vast Irish peatland. Historically, peatlands have undergone major restoration for peat extraction over centuries. This residency formed part of an initiative to raise awareness of these extraordinary environments – shaped over millennia by water, moss and time – as vital forces, not only in terms of providing habitat for flora and fauna but also in terms of the chemical changes that play a crucial role in the global carbon cycle. During his residency, the artist spent most days on the bog from dawn to dusk, sleeping in a cabin at the bog's edge. After several months, he felt that he came to know the land.

We spent many hours together, as he described how the bogland in winter seemed timeless – its processes were slow and its movements subtle. He described how sphagnum mosses formed multicoloured carpets of yellow, brown and red. The air was damp and heavy with an earthy scent of peat and moss, tinged with the smell of decaying vegetation. The ground felt spongy underfoot, with fluctuating water levels forming pools that reflected the ever-changing weather, from a sudden drizzle to fleeting shafts of weak winter sunlight. Mists hung low over the ground and softened the landscape outline. The haunting whistle of a curlew and the occasional warble of a skylark pierced the atmosphere.

In the artist's words:

> I walk every day, not to get somewhere, just to be there. You start to notice more, especially when it is not the growing season and I do not see one other human being, not even in the distance. In winter, everything has this quiet vibration. This really has a huge effect. I can feel that I'm being changed as I'm experiencing all of this. You realise, 'I am alive.' It's really powerful, and I think what it does is, it turns into a relationship – you feel this special resonance.

This case illustrates how low-human-impact environments can uniquely afford possibilities for attunement. Psychologist James J. Gibson used the term affordances to propose that each environment offers possibilities for action. Affordances are provided by the environment to the perceiver. Different environments provide different types of affordances. For instance, a kitchen offers possibilities for actions that a garage does not. Gibson's concept of affordances is complex; however, in its broadest sense, it refers to the possibilities for action presented by an environment to the perceiver, including substances, surfaces, objects and other factors that are in close proximity.

Gibson's original concept identified affordances as primarily related to physical movements and behaviours afforded to the perceiver by a particular environment such as reaching and grasping. However, the concept was later expanded to consider how an environment affords the possibility of exercising both mental and physical abilities (Rietvel & Kiverstein, 2014). Gibson's concept of affordances provides a theoretical framework to help identify how LHI environments uniquely enable attunement.

The shift in sensory awareness

Four decades of attention restoration studies have shown that human factors within an environment have a distracting effect that can counteract any mental health benefit of being in nature. You can sit in urban parks filled with beautiful trees and still see people rushing through on their way to work; see high-rise office buildings peeking over the trees, hear nearby traffic and smell their fumes. Alongside these more obvious human factors, more subtle ones also attract our attention, such as how the park has been designed and how the quality of light is affected by pollution. These human factors, whether obvious or subtle, have a pull effect on attention, bringing us back to the happenings and expectations of everyday human life.

LHI environments offer freedom from such distractions. In doing so, they afford us the opportunity to notice and pay attention to other-than-human life within our perceptual range. It is a simple equation: freedom from human distraction enables freedom to engage with the rest of life. Free from the sensory strategies that we rely on in our everyday lives, we begin to experience the world around us and the way we engage with it as something different from usual. As such, LHI environments allow for a deeper awareness of our multisensory engagement with all other-than-human stimuli within our perceptual field.

The physiological reciprocity

In any type of environment, with every breath, we inhale particles from our surroundings. At a physiological level, parts of the external environment touch the inside of the body, and on every exhalation, the surroundings reciprocate. A network of molecules and chemical reactions interacts in such a way that it is nearly impossible to separate material entities at the microscopic level. The word 'environment' originates from the French *environ*, meaning 'to surround', to surround; yet at this molecular level, the individual is inseparable from their surroundings. The simple act of breathing in and out provides proof that we are porous beings, physiologically part of the environments we inhabit.

The practice of Shinrin-yoku, or forest bathing, as is known in the English-speaking world, involves consciously taking in the forest through the senses. There is a strong body of research dating back to the 1980s, showing that phytoncides, which are natural compounds released by trees, have anti-inflammatory, anti-oxidative and anti-microbial properties that affect physical and mental health. The research findings are striking, with systemic reviews concluding that forests reduce blood pressure and the associated anxiety and stress levels significantly more than other environments (Park et al., 2017).

Much of the physiological reciprocity involved is automatic and unconscious, yet it has tangible and observable impacts such as reduced heart rate, deeper breathing, slower bodily movements and enhanced attention. This is not restricted to forests, as studies are beginning to show that the salinity of ocean air affects blood pressure, heart rate, stress and anxiety levels. Although our knowledge is in its infancy, research on forest bathing, together with emerging studies on other types of environments, provides evidence of the physiological components of LHI environments.

The biophilic effect

The biophilia hypothesis asserts that there is a fundamental human need and propensity to affiliate with other forms of life. The theory was first introduced by German social psychologist Erich Fromm and later popularized and expanded upon by biologist Edward Osborne Wilson (Van den Born et al., 2001). Fromm approached the theory from a psychological angle (1973), while Wilson (1984) approached it from an evolutionary one. However, both agreed that biophilia forms an essential part of our desire and satisfaction with life. Wilson emphasized the necessity of nature connection for physical and mental health, framing it as a biological imperative rather than just a cultural or aesthetic preference. Fromm went so far as to claim that nature deprivation in modern societies was the root cause of many social problems that lead to psychological disorders and societal fragmentation.

Humans have evolved on the planet, just like all other animals, to have a distinctive way of life; we have carved out our own ecological niche. Alongside our advancements, this innate sense of connection to nature has remained intact, albeit in its repressed form. The biophilia hypothesis suggests that encounters with nature stimulate this weakened trait. Hence, a child can feel at ease playing in the trees at the bottom of their garden, and a young urban adult with limited nature experience can feel a profound sense of connection to a desert landscape upon their first encounter. Most significantly, the biophilia theory proposes that this innate connection remains, even if in a repressed form, and therefore can be nurtured and developed. Proving biophilia theory is challenging, but Professor Peter Kahn points out:

> It is important because if the biophilia hypothesis has merit – and I think it does – it could provide a unifying framework across numerous disciplines to investigate the human relationship with nature. (Kahn, 1999, p. 9)

In summary, LHI environments provide three basic affordances: a shift in awareness, physiological effect and activation of an innate sense of connection. Each specific LHI environment will provide additional affordances and be influenced and expanded upon by the emotional and symbolic bonds the perceiver holds towards that environment and the cultures that shape them. These bonds can affect the quality of experience and therefore influence the intensity and duration of the attunement experience. For example, a young urban adult with limited nature experiences and no particular emotional or symbolic connection to a desert or woodland landscape can benefit from the affordances they provide. It may take more time or encouragement than others, but basic affordances remain.

LHI environments and the conditions for micro-attunement

Because attunement states rely on a person's multisensory participation in their surroundings, any study of environmental attunement requires an appreciation of environments as complex multifactorial systems, in which humans play a reciprocal role. The human-impact scale assesses environments along a continuum from low to high human impact by examining the multifactorial composition of each setting, considering not only visual elements but also the full range of biotic, abiotic, human and non-human factors that contribute to the perceptual field.

Environments can be categorized by the compositional makeup of these environmental factors, rather than purely visual features. These factors provide sensory stimuli that shape a person's multisensory experience. HHI environments are characterized by the prevalence of human and human-made stimuli. These human stimuli can range from the physical presence of people to evidence of their activities such as smells, traffic noise and artificial light. In LHI environments, a combination of biotic and abiotic other-than-human stimuli dominate the perceptual field.

An LHI environment provides a unique set of affordances. The physical properties of each LHI environment have physiological effects. Freedom from human distraction brings other-than-human life to the foreground of awareness and attention. With this freedom comes the opportunity for a deeper sense of connection to this more-than-human world. LHI environments and the affordances they provide are therefore conducive to attunement states. In other words, LHI environments provide unique conditions for attunement states to arise.

Not only can the scale be used to determine with greater specificity what type of environments provide opportunities for attunement, but we can also use the scale to determine how spaces in built-up areas can provide attunement potential. The human impact scale provides a framework to assess, research and design environments in which attunement states can be cultivated. For example, urban garden designers can use the scale to design environments in which other-than-human stimuli dominate the perceptual field. Creating LHI environments within larger urban settings can provide people with opportunities for micro-attunements, the less intense yet none-the less psychologically meaningful states described in Chapter 3. The creation of LHI environments in urban areas, for example, has significant potential for public mental health and well-being, a topic discussed in detail in Chapter 8.

Conclusion

The principle of exposure to green spaces is a culturally loaded construct with an implicit aesthetic judgment that values certain types of natural environments over others, rooted in the idea of nature as separate from humans. The principle is well-intentioned and useful in terms of research methods and analysis, and it helped our understanding of the psychology of humans' relationship with nature significantly. However, the principle ignores the multifactorial dynamics of environments and human involvement. As a result, most psychological benefits and outcomes reported remain within the realm of symptom relief and restorative effects – the 'green pill effect'. Very little is known about the specific perceptual qualities of different types of natural environments and their deeper psychological effects.

Environmental Attunement Theory proposes an ecological approach that acknowledges the totality of nature, and the complexities and interdependencies within ecological systems. Within this approach, there is an appreciation that, beyond their visual or aesthetic value, environments with low human impact afford humans something unique compared to environments in which human factors dominate. They provide us with the conditions under which attunement states arise. Defining low-human-impact environments and their affordances makes it possible to look at ways to create these conditions in more generally accessible areas and, therefore, provide wider population groups with opportunities for experiences of micro-attunements.

Taking an ecological approach in no way discounts the value of visual encounters with green spaces. However, attunement states are a distinct type of nature experience that relies on multisensory participation within an ecology where other-than-human factors dominate our perceptual field. The study of environmental attunement, therefore, forces us to address the limitations of the principle of exposure to greenspace that has governed the research since the 1980s.

Environmental Attunement Theory is not alone in this view. Researchers are beginning to widen this lens. For example, since 2020, researchers at the Environmental Psychology Research Group of Surrey University in the UK have begun to distinguish between exposure to green spaces and engagement in activities in different types of natural environments. Neuropsychologists are also seeking ways to study more sensorially immersive experiences. One such advancement is the introduction of global tracking devices that marry participants' real-time capture of their experiences by using location data. This technology enables the study of longer durations in remote locations and removes some of the subjective inaccuracies of personal accounts.

New technologies present exciting opportunities; however, along with such innovations, we must consider the underlying beliefs that guide us. The real breakthrough in research, policy and practice will come from letting go of an entrenched separatist stance and embracing an ecological approach more in line with the rest of the sciences. While the linguistic use of the term nature in the vernacular as all other-than-human life is appropriate and useful, the treatment of nature as a separate entity negates the interconnected reality of a living planet.

The shaman who told me that everything is alive, and everything is nature, not only represents the beliefs of ingenious people across the globe, or the voices of scientists across various fields; wider modern society is

     Alone with Nature

starting to change its anthropocentric view. In 2008, Ecuador became the first nation in the world to legislate on behalf of water as an essential element of the existence of all living beings. In 2017, a law was passed in New Zealand that gave the Whanganui River protection as a 'spiritual and physical entity'. The Ganges and Yamuna in India, the Mutehekau Shipu River in Canada and the River Ouse in the UK have been recognized as 'living entities'. In his book, *Is the book River Alive?*, acclaimed environmental writer Robert McFarlane, plants the notion of a living ecology within the psyche of the public (Macfarlane, 2025). The tide is turning.

This Albert Einstein quote, widely attributed to a letter he wrote in 1950 to a father grieving the loss of his son, captures the challenge and the opportunity well:

> A human being is a part of the whole called by us 'the universe', a part limited in time and space. He experiences himself, his thoughts and feelings, as something separate from the rest – a kind of optical delusion of consciousness. This delusion is a kind of prison for us, restricting us to our personal desires and affections of a few persons nearest to us. Our task must be to free ourselves from this prison by widening our circle of understanding and compassion to embrace all living creatures and the whole of nature in its beauty.

For a field of study predicated on the delineation between mind and matter, and that steadfastly upholds the dualistic tradition, re-imagining everything as alive and interconnected is difficult. However, psychology must wake up to this challenge. The fantasy that we are somehow separate from nature may well be psychology's biggest blind spot. Environmental Attunement Theory prioritizes ecological reciprocity over the cartesian divide, and in doing so, offers a pathway to a deeper understanding of the human-nature relationship. Where cognition has governed the field of psychology for over half a century, Environmental Attunement Theory brings the role of multisensory perception in human experience to the forefront of our attention.

References

Allen, P. G. (1986). *The sacred hoop: Recovering the feminine in American Indian traditions* (pp. 191–192). Beacon Press.
Barbosa, O., Tratalos, J. A., Armsworth, P. R., Davies, R. G., Fuller, R. A., Johnson, P., & Gaston, K. J. (2007). Who benefits from access to green space?

A case study from Sheffield, UK. *Landscape and Urban Planning, 83*(2), 187–195. DOI: 10.1016/j.landurbplan.2007.04.004.

Berleant, A. (1995). *Aesthetics of environment.* Temple University Press.

Cassarino, M., & Setti, A. (2015). Environment as 'Brain Training': A review of geographical and physical environmental influences on cognitive ageing. *Ageing Research Reviews, 23* (September), 167–182. DOI: 10.1016/j.arr.2015.06.003.

Ducharme, F., & Couvet, D. (2020). How the diversity of human concepts of nature affects conservation of biodiversity. *Conservation Biology, 35*(3), 1019–1028.

Einstein, A. (1972, March 29). Letter to Robert S. Marcus. February 12. *The New York Times.*

Fromm, E. (1973). The anatomy of human destructiveness. Holt, Rinehart and Winston.

Goldstein, J., Davidoff, J., & Roberson, D. (2009). Knowing color terms enhances recognition: Further evidence from English and Himba. *Journal of Experimental Child Psychology, 102*(2), 219–238. DOI: 10.1016/j.jecp.2008.06.002.

Hirst, R. J., Cassarino, M., Kenny, R. A., Newell, F. N., & Setti, A. (2021). Urban and rural environments differentially shape multisensory perception in ageing. *Aging, Neuropsychology, and Cognition, 29*(2), 197–212. DOI: 10.1080/13825585.2020.1859084.

Huang, P. M. (Ed.). (2005). *Soil abiotic and biotic interactions and impact on the ecosystem and human welfare.* Science Publishers.

Kahn, P. H. (1999) *The human relationship with nature: Development and culture.* MIT Press.

Kaplan, R., & Kaplan, S. 1989. *The experience of nature: A psychological perspective.* Cambridge University Press.

Macfarlane, R. (2025). *Is a river alive?* W.W. Norton & Company.

Meidenbauer, K. L., Stenfors, C. U. D., Bratman, G. N., Gross, J. J., Schertz, K. E., Choe, K. W., & Berman, M. G. (2020). The affective benefits of nature exposure: What's nature got to do with It? *Journal of Environmental Psychology, 72* (December), 101498. DOI: 10.1016/j.jenvp.2020.101498.

Meredith, G. R., Rakow, D. A., Eldermire, E. R. B., Madsen, C. G., Shelley, S. P., & Sachs, N. A. (2020). Minimum time dose in nature to positively impact the mental health of college-aged students, and how to measure it: A scoping review. *Frontiers in Psychology, 10.* DOI: 10.3389/fpsyg.2019.02942.

Morton, T. (2009). *Ecology without nature: Rethinking environmental aesthetics.* Harvard University Press.

Muir, J. (2018). *Wilderness essays.* Peregrine Smith Books.

Nash, R. (2014). *Wilderness and the American mind.* Yale University Press.

Park, B. J., Tsunetsugu, Y., Kasetani, T., Kagawa, T., & Miyazaki, Y. (2017). Blood pressure-lowering effect of Shinrin-yoku (Forest bathing): A systematic review and meta-analysis. *BMC Complementary Medicine and Therapies, 17*(1), 409. DOI: 10.1186/s12906-017-1912-z.

Public Health England. (2020). The Green Space Framework. Lovell, R., White, M. P., Wheeler, B., Taylor, T., & Elliott, L. (2020). A rapid scoping review of health and wellbeing evidence for the Green Infrastructure Standards. European Centre for Environment and Human Health, University of Exeter Medical School. For: Natural England, Department for the Environment, Food and Rural Affairs, Public Health England, and Ministry for Housing, Communities and Local Government, England.

Regier, T., & Kay, P. (2009). Language, thought, and color: Whorf was half right. *Trends in Cognitive Sciences, 13*(10), 439–446. DOI: 10.1016/j. tics.2009.07.001.

Rietveld, E., & Kiverstein, J. (2014). A rich landscape of affordances. *Ecological Psychology, 26*(4), 325–352. DOI: 10.1080/10407413.2014.958035.

Runte, A. (1990). *Yosemite: The embattled wilderness.* University of Nebraska Press.

Schutte, A. R., Torquati, J. C., & Stevens, J. R. (Eds.). (2021). *Nature and psychology: biological, cognitive, developmental, and social pathways to well-being.* Nebraska Symposium on Motivation 67. Springer. DOI: 10.1007/978-3-030-69020-5.

Spence, M. D. (1999). *Dispossessing the wilderness: Indian removal and the making of the national parks.* Oxford University Press.

Van den Born, R. J. G., Lenders, H. J. R., De Groot, W. T., & Huijsman, E. (2001). The new biophilia: An exploration of visions of nature in Western countries. *Environmental Conservation, 28*(1), 65–75.

White, M. P., Alcock, I., Grellier, J., Wheeler, B. W., Hartig, T., Warber, S. L., Bone, A., Depledge, M. H., & Fleming, L. E. (2019). Spending at least 120 minutes a week in nature is associated with good health and wellbeing. *Scientific Reports, 9*(1), 7730. DOI: 10.1038/s41598-019-44097-3.

Wilson, E. O. (1984). *Biophilia: The human bond with other species.* Harvard University Press.

5

The restoration of the senses

The world is full of magic things,
patiently waiting for our senses
to grow sharper.

W. B. Yeats

The history of the senses in Western thought is one of misconceptions and neglect. For over two millennia, Western thinkers have treated perception as a process of input and interpretation, separating and ranking the senses based on their ability to represent the external world in the mind's eye. This mechanistic concept, rooted in the duality of mind and matter, has led to the senses being treated as subordinate to cognition – a sidelining that persists in the study of the human-nature relationship to this day. I make this claim boldly because over the past two decades, new research has revealed that our understanding of the senses to date has been based on bias rather than biology. Perception is now understood as a highly dynamic system, and our senses are far more sophisticated than previously assumed.

Building on Chapter 4's call to move beyond the visual and cognitive limitations of the 'green space' paradigm, this chapter explores the perceptual mechanisms that make environmental attunement possible. Environmental attunement constitutes an exceptional state of consciousness that cannot be adequately explained by the traditional mechanistic models of perception. By tracing the history of the senses in Western thought, examining recent scientific breakthroughs and drawing on cross-cultural and phenomenological accounts, I chart our understanding of perception from a passive, vision-dominated process to a dynamic, embodied, multisensory engagement with the world. This paradigm shift in our understanding of perception is essential for understanding how attunement states arise and their embodied and environmentally embedded character, more broadly for advancing a more ecological approach to the psychology of human-nature relationships.

The first section of the chapter examines the historical and cultural background of the senses in Western thought as the context critical to understanding the field of psychology and the cognitive sciences' apprehension of perception update. The second section explores three major strands of scientific research that radically challenge the traditional models of perception. The concluding section discusses how these new models of perception inform our understanding of environmental attunement and how studying environmental attunement reinforces the central role that multisensory perception plays in human experience.

The hierarchy of the senses

Humans have evolved to engineer the world around us expertly, to protect ourselves from danger and discomfort, and to give us more of what we need to survive. There is little denying that we rely heavily on sight and sound to navigate and manufacture the human world (Howes & Classen, 2014). Visuo-audio reliance is deeply ingrained in modern life. Text, gesture, sound and image comprise the basic components of communication (Prieur et al., 2020). The pedagogical approaches of mainstream Western education, which we have been exposed to from an early age, all prefer visuo-audio stimulation (Batson, 2009; Beacroft, 2018; Ponticorvo et al., 2019). Human-built environments are designed primarily with sight in mind. There may well be strong biological and evolutionary rationales for designing and organizing human life according to this preference, but in recent decades, scholars have begun to question the degree to which this sensory bias is universally true or culturally driven (Howes & Classen, 2014; Korsmeyer, 2015; Majid & Burenhult, 2014).

Plato argued that the material world known to us through the senses is made up of mere appearances, locating a truer, more fundamental reality as existing in the realm of forms. Aristotle rejected Plato's theory of forms by proposing the inseparability of such universal ideals from substances. For Aristotle, substance was the primary source of being. Despite his staunch empiricism, he believed intellect to be a non-bodily function that occurred in the soul. He conceived perception to be the input of stimuli through five sense organs, which he ranked according to their perceived accuracy and truth (Johansen, 2007; Slakey, 1961). Aristotle's writings in *De Anima* are an important watershed moment in Western thinking, as he paved the way for a model of perception that exists to the present day, which treats the senses as five separate and unequal sources of input.

The identification and separation of the five sensory organs may have remained consistent since Aristotle, but the ordering changed based on suspicions and beliefs of different eras (Korsmeyer, 2015). Sight and sound have not always been prioritized in all aspects of life across the centuries.

Western medieval medical practices, judicial systems and religious beliefs often gave credence to the power of touch over sight and sound (Howes & Classen, 2014; Reinarz & Schwarz, 2012). Vision was believed to be less concrete and susceptible to demonic deception and delusion, and was therefore inferior to touch (Reinarz & Schwarz, 2012). Historian Lucien Febvre suggests that it was not until the start of the sixteenth century in Europe that vision began to rise to the top (Reinarz & Schwarz, 2012).

The hierarchy of the senses that we are familiar with today, which places vision on top, took root during the Enlightenment (Howes & Classen, 2014; Korsmeyer, 2015; Reinarz & Schwarz, 2012).

Descartes paved the way by pulling up the drawbridge between mind and matter, locating the mind as a non-extended entity within the confines of the brain. The Cartesian divide further compounded the idea of a hierarchy of senses by drawing a stronger line between the body and intellect. The hugely influential Enlightenment figures, John Locke and Immanuel Kant, followed suit by conceptualizing the mind as a blank canvas to be imprinted upon and perception as the process of representing the external world. Therefore, the reliability of the input became of great importance.

In this age of reason, the so-called higher senses of sight and hearing became increasingly valued for their accuracy and predictability, and therefore, their superior intellectual value. The so-called lower senses of taste, touch and smell were perceived as ambiguous and difficult to predict, and therefore, limited in their cerebral worth. Kant famously declared smell to be so deceptive that it served little purpose. The higher senses informed the mind. The lower senses served the body. This hierarchy of the senses was embedded within Enlightenment's theories of mind.

> Kant's *Critique of Pure Reason* (1781) represents the culmination of Enlightenment philosophy, capturing the overarching duality that governed the age, with the following description of the human mind: 'This domain is an island, enclosed by nature itself with unalterable limits. It is the land of truth surrounded by a wide and stormy ocean, the native home of illusions, where many a fog bank and many a swiftly melting iceberg give the deceptive appearance of farther shores, deluding the adventurous seafarer ever anew with empty hopes, and engaging him in enterprises which he can never abandon and yet is unable to carry to completion (in Lauden, 2006).'

Kant is particularly relevant to our discourse here because he applied Enlightenment theories of mind specifically to the human-nature relationship, and his ideas went on to influence the Romantics and Western philosophy more broadly throughout the nineteenth and twentieth centuries, and I would suggest right up to the present day. Where ideas concerning nature and the sublime were already present in European philosophy, Kant's *Critique of Judgement* (1790) developed them more robustly. Kant introduced the concept of disinterestedness as a cognitively distanced observation essential to any aesthetic judgement that separates the observer from their subjective experiences or preconceptions.

This disinterestedness should not be interpreted as a lack of interest towards the object, but instead as a state in which 'One must not be in the least prepossessed in favour of the existence of a thing, but must be quite indifferent in this regard, in order to play the part of a judge in matters of taste.' According to Kant, the cognitive distancing that disinterestedness requires relies upon the higher senses, primarily vision. Through this lens of disinterestedness, the smell of dampened soil on a dew-soaked spring morning or the taste of water sipped directly from a mountain stream cannot come close to the experience of the sublime evoked by gazing upon a grand mountain vista. For Kant, no other sense modality comes close to vision. Indeed, all other senses run the risk of pulling one away from the solid ground of truth and reason.

Nor is it possible, according to Kant, for a morally good person to observe natural beauty without their reflection generating an appreciation of nature. Conversely, someone without at least one grain of moral character does not possess the capacity to hold an aesthetic appreciation for nature. Kant's aesthetic appreciation of nature inextricably links the notions of visual beauty and morality. However, in his efforts to transcend the nature experience into something of great aesthetic and moral value, Kant stripped away the embodied experience and rendered the encounter little more than a sanitized mind game.

The ideas of Kant and the Enlightenment have influenced psychology up to and including the present day. In a way, little has changed in psychology's conceptualization of perception since its Cartesian roots. Contemporary psychology's hard focus on the internal mental processes that drive human behaviour continues to treat the senses as Enlightenment thinkers did. If anything, the model of the senses as singular sources of input to internal representations has been compounded by cognitive science's mechanistic conceptualization of the brain. A meta-analysis of studies conducted over the last forty years highlighted the continued separation and ranking of the senses, with visual perception being given by far the most attention (70 per cent), followed by auditory (20 per cent), olfactory (5 per cent), haptic (2 per cent) and gustatory (>1 per cent) (Hutmacher, 2019).

The ideas of the Enlightenment are never far from contemporary psychological studies of the human-nature relationship, as illustrated by the principle of exposure to green space that dominates contemporary studies. According to this principle, the relationship is reduced to the subject's timed exposure to the object. Sensitivity and reciprocity are stripped away in favour of a sanitized version of an inherently multisensory experience. Green space is judged to equate to good nature in a measured effort to safeguard the subject from the dangers of the wild, the savage, or worse still, the boring and mundane.

However, this anaesthetizing effect is most prominent in studies that seek to measure people's cognitive responses to videos of natural scenes. Regardless of the absence of all real stimuli, where the visual stimulus is reduced to a mere digital representation, such initiatives are still categorized as nature studies. These studies may provide insights into some forms of human experience and clues to what a real encounter may evoke. However, what poor substitutes do they provide for being in nature, and what more disheartening evidence of the sidelining of the senses do we need? The ghost of Kant lives on in these laboratories.

A cultural perspective

Traditionally, the study of perception fell within the realms of philosophy and psychology. However, studying the historical and cultural formation of the senses has helped scholars identify many of the biases that exist (Howes & Classen, 2014; Korsmeyer, 2015; Reinarz & Schwarz, 2012). The cultural historian Constance Classen proposes that the Enlightenment's hierarchy of the senses not only impacted philosophy and the sciences but also fundamental concepts related to class, race, colonialism, education, gender and urbanization in the centuries that followed. The words of Swiss-born anatomist and naturist Count Albrecht von Haller (1708–1777) exemplify how the hierarchy of the senses was used to justify the separation of humans from the rest of nature and the civilized man from the savage:

> For he was destined to walk upright; he was to discover from a distance what might be his food; social life and language were designed to enlighten him about the properties of the things that appeared to him to be edible. (Corbin, 1986, p. 6)

In the centuries that followed, the higher classes, as overseers and orators of society, became the masters of sight and sound, whereas the lower classes and colonized races, who were associated with the less cerebral lower senses, were destined to work with their hands (Howes & Classen, 2014; Reinarz

& Schwarz, 2012). As a result, these ideas form part of the character of our modern age, including its profoundly classist and racist shadow.

However, cross-cultural studies help dispel many of the myths held by this hierarchy of the senses. Studies comparing the ability of different cultures to identify and describe unfamiliar smells and odours, for instance, have challenged the widely held scientific idea that smell is notoriously difficult for humans to identify and describe (Majid & Burenhult, 2014; Majid et al., 2018). In a comparative study across twenty cultures, English speakers showed a lower ability to identify and describe even the more basic odours in comparison to other cultures. In contrast, the Jahia people, a nomadic group of hunter-gatherers from the Malay Peninsula, showed a high level of proficiency in describing unfamiliar smells, as other cultures did in describing familiar colours.

The olfactory adeptness of the Jahia people is comparable to the visual adeptness of other cultures. One conclusion drawn from this study was that human olfactory adeptness is located within specific cultural contexts. It is simply not universally true that smells are difficult for all humans to identify and describe. However, it seems that there is a correlation between the value that a culture places on a specific modality and that culture's sensory adeptness.

It is easy to assume that life in a contemporary urban setting does not require a highly skilled sense of smell as is necessary in the dense forests of Malaysia. The degree to which olfactory capabilities are influenced by physical surroundings or cultural beliefs is difficult to determine. However, comparative studies help highlight a cultural dimension to sense perception that has generally been ignored until recently and demonstrate how our scientific understanding of sensory perception has been constructed through the lens of a hierarchy rooted in cultural beliefs rather than biology.

Anthropologist Paul Stoller points out that Western culture's bias towards visual observation has often led to the inappropriate interpretation of other cultures and societies (Stoller, 1989, 2010). Stoller recognized the limitations of Western culture's hierarchy of the senses firsthand when living with the Songhay people in West Africa. In a culture that perceives tastes and smells as connecting people with the place, the past and the present, and the living with the dead, conventional observational ethnographic methods proved inadequate in bridging the gap between lived experience and knowledge.

Stoller sought to embrace the sensory epistemologies of the Songhay people rather than imposing an ethnographic method that privileges text and textual analysis of visual observations. Over the course of two decades, Stoller developed an ethnographic approach that focused on aligning with the sensory strategies of the Songhay people he sought to understand. Stoller's sensory ethnography marks an important turn away from the innately dualistic and observational methods that dominated the field of anthropology, in favour of a more phenomenological acceptance of experience as multisensory and neither dominated by nor reduced to the visual.

I am familiar with the work of Stoller, as he was one of three advisors for my PhD studies and had a profound impact on how I conducted my research at the time and thereafter. Although my interviews did not follow a typical ethnographic methodology, I applied several principles of sensory ethnography to how I engaged with and captured the experiences of the people I interviewed by reframing encounters with nature from a primarily observational experience to one that is innately multisensory, embodied and extended. With many of the people I interviewed, for example, we met on the land they described, often walking there together, moving through the environment and experiencing the sensory stimuli they reference firsthand.

Even when it was not possible to interview people *in situ*, and I conducted online interviews instead, I guided the exploration of people's experiences through the associated sensations, mental imagery, memories and feelings in a reflective and collaborative manner, and with an appreciation and curiosity towards the environment and its perceptual properties. The place is treated as a living system and part of the triangular relationship alongside the interviewee and interviewer, rather than a benign presence. The sensory experience is brought to the foreground by paying attention to exploring the interviewee's experience through multisensory modalities without privileging visual observation or abstract meaning-making. Although I encourage free associations of memories, imagery and sensations, my focus always returns to the embodied experience.

An interview with a master of the senses

In 2021, I interviewed Pino, an ancestral healer from the Shipibo community, who lives on the eastern slopes of the Peruvian High Andes Mountains on the upper Ucayali River near the headwaters of the Amazon. I did not have the means to travel there at the time, so I went about setting up an online interview. It took months to organize, but with the help of a local guide and a translator, we arranged for Pino to travel from his remote village to a place down the river with access to the Internet. Once the video link was properly set up between us, we managed to talk for over two hours about his experiences of spending time alone in the forest. Although the Internet connection dropped off a few times, Pino's down-to-earth and jovial character made for a fluid and engaging dialogue.

As with many communities in western Amazonia, the Shipibo depends on plant knowledge for their daily needs, both for sustenance and medicinal and ceremonial purposes. Plant knowledge is crucial to the physical and spiritual well-being of these communities.

From a tender age, Shipibo children have been taught about the various uses of plants, including which can be harmful, healing or protective against bad forest spirits. Shipibo healers, in particular, referred to as *Onanya* (singular) or *Onanyabo* (plural), are highly revered by both Amazonian communities and scientists for their extensive knowledge (Arrévalo, 2005; Gonzalez et al., 2021). In recent years, Shipibo communities have voiced concerns regarding the appropriation of *Onanya* customs by foreigners, as well as the emergence of fraudulent shamans exploiting tourists eager to partake in some form of the renowned ayahuasca ritual native to the area. My search for genuine *Onanyabo* led me to Pino.

At the age of seven, Pino experienced the loss of sight in one eye, which he took as his destiny to become an *Onanya*, just like his father and grandfathers before him. As an integral aspect of his practice, Pino learned how to spend days and even weeks alone in the forest far from his village and family. This solitary practice has been a long-standing tradition for *Onanyabo*, enabling them to gain wisdom and forge a unique bond with plants. Pino recounted how, in the past, the *Onanyabo* would spend several months alone, deep within the forest. Although contemporary life has made it challenging to spend such extended periods away from village life, Pino emphasized that without regularly venturing into the forest alone, an *Onanya* risks losing their knowledge and spiritual connection with plants, and consequently, their ability to heal others.

Alone in the forest, plants speak directly to the senses. Each plant species communicates uniquely. Some plants need to be touched and smelt, whereas the leaves of other plants are best crushed and rubbed directly onto the skin to feel their effects. Other plants must be ingested for their effects to be sensed throughout the body. Absorbing the properties of plants in this manner, particularly those with psychotropic properties, provides the most direct physiological communication with the plant's spirit. It is only through the experience of being alone in the forest that such depth of knowledge can be acquired.

The slight changes in the rustling of leaves overhead indicate what type of birds and their predators are nearby, as well as which ancestral spirits are present. For the Shipibo, the material and spiritual realms are intertwined. The forest represents the physical face of the spirit world. By paying close attention, one can discern which spirits are present. Additionally, there is no distinction between one's inner world and the external reality. Pino's mental imagery, including any images or memories, is considered an extension of what is happening in the environment rather than an internal phenomenon. Pino's description of being alone in the forest portrays a body in motion: touching, tasting, orientating, absorbing and imagining the rest of the life of the forest. There is an interplay between sensations, memories and imaginings with the sensory stimuli offered by the surroundings.

Despite his visual impairment, Pino's exceptional skill lies in his ability to consciously adjust his sensory strategies to align with the sensory order of other-than-human society. The intentional use of whole-body sensing allows for a unique way of being with nature that differs from other types of nature experiences, such as taking a stroll through a beautiful tree-filled park, skiing down a mountain or observing a breathtaking natural scene. While not every individual I interviewed exhibited the same level of proficiency as Pino in utilizing their senses, they described a similar awareness of the sensory reciprocity between their body and the environment.

The connection between the Shipibo and Jahia peoples and the forest may seem far removed from what most people on the planet experience, but it reminds us that humans have extraordinary sensory capabilities. This adeptness is not only shaped by the physical environment in which we live but also by the cultural beliefs that underpin it. Modern society's privileging of some senses over others may have served us well in certain aspects of human development but also diminished our multisensory adeptness. At what cost to our connection with nature is difficult to quantify? The discrediting of the universality of the hierarchy of the senses marks an important turning point in our understanding of human sense perception, and how we engage with nature. But what does the science have to say?

The scientific perspective

The past twenty years have been marked by significant breakthroughs in our understanding of the mechanics of perception by cognitive scientists who have decided to take their interest beyond the brain (Berger, 2016; Buck & Axel, 1991; Shimojo & Shams, 2001; Hutto & Myin, 2017; Varela et al., 2016). As a result, the mechanistic model of perception as a one-way process of input and interpretation that prevailed for close to two millennia is being discredited and replaced with a dynamic system, within which multi-modal and cross-modal sensory activity is the norm rather than the exception. Rather than being subordinate to cognition, scientists propose the senses to be much smarter than we think and perception to be a highly collaborative process, working in a mutually influencing manner with memory and imagination (Berger, 2016; Berger & Ehrsson, 2013). This research broadly falls into three strands.

Individual modalities

The first strand of research offers new insights into sensory modalities that have been neglected previously. The more attention that these modalities receive, the more interesting and important they become. Olfactory research has also illustrated this. The Nobel Prize-winning work of researchers from Columbia University brought the scientific community's attention to the sophistication of the olfactory system by discovering that 3 per cent of genes in human DNA are dedicated to producing protein receptors attached to olfactory nerve cells. This means that a relatively small cluster of four hundred receptors in the nasal passage can discriminate between millions of smells (Buck & Axel, 1991).

The apparatus is there, but why do humans have such a sophisticated system and do we need it in a modern, sanitized world? Buck and Axel's findings have propelled a wave of olfactory research, and studies now suggest that, regardless of whether we are conscious of it, our olfactory system has a significant influence on how we think and behave towards each other (Sarafoleanu et al., 2009). Furthermore, initial research in mice suggests that rudimentary elements of memory recall processing occur in our olfactory and gustatory systems, suggesting that elements of what has typically been regarded as higher cognitive processing can occur outside the brain in the body.

As we continue to investigate, it transpires that these so-called lower senses are more intelligent and complex than historically recognized, and the line between sensation and cognition is less distinct. Researchers are also increasingly looking beyond the visual, auditory, olfactory and gustatory sensory systems, with groupings of receptors located on or near the orifices of the body, to the less localized sensory systems responsible for sensations such as touch, pain, pressure, temperature, movement, balance and vibration, with receptors located throughout the body.

For example, the proprioceptive system provides an overall sense of bodily movement and orientation with the surroundings and has receptors situated on muscles, tendons and joints inside the body (Fitzpatrick & McCloskey, 1994). The vestibular system is also located inside the body, with receptors in the inner ear, and is responsible for generating a sense of overall body balance (Lynch & Simpson, 2004). The proprioceptive and vestibular systems play a key role in coordinating and moving the body. Consider closing your eyes and then reaching your arms overhead to clap your hands. None of the famous five senses is much involved in coordinating this act.

Although vestibular and proprioceptive systems have been acknowledged for a number of decades, relatively little is known about the receptors responsible for internal sensations that are located throughout the internal organs and tissues (Critchley et al., 2004). This interoceptive system is essential for perceiving changes in the autonomous nervous system, such as awareness of changes in heart rate or breathing during physically intense activities or emotional events (Kreibig, 2010), such as feeling your heart race on the first date, the rush you feel when watching a thriller movie or the anticipation of diving into the cold sea.

Researchers have discovered that these sensations are deeply intertwined with emotional states to the extent that a dysfunction in this system may play a role in mental health conditions, such as anxiety, mood and addiction disorders (Critchley et al., 2004; Kreibig, 2010). Exemplary of the newness and significance of these discoveries was the first Interoception Summit, held by the Laureate Institute for Brain Research in November 2016 with the goal of accelerating progress in understanding the role of interoception in mental health (Khalsa et al., 2018).

Multi- and cross-modal activity

The second strand of research relates to our understanding of how different sensory modalities work together as an integrated sensorium. As noted previously, Maurice Merleau-Ponty (2012) and James J. Gibson (2014) proposed similarly integrated models of perception, suggesting that perception is generated through multisensory stimulation within a given context. Until the recent scientific renaissance of the senses, these views were marginalized by mainstream psychology's cognitive turn away from perceptual experience in the second half of the twentieth century (Pérez-Álvarez, 2018). However, evidence for the interaction among sensory modalities is growing to the extent that researchers confidently claim that cross-modal interaction is the norm rather than the exception.

Attributing the source of perception to single-sense stimuli has been oversimplified and is likely erroneous. Cortical pathways that were previously considered sensory-specific are constantly modulated by signals from other modalities (Shimojo & Shams, 2001). This multisensory integration is not restricted to the famous five, and occurs across all exteroceptive and interoceptive sensory systems (Fitzpatrick & McCloskey, 1994). Riding a bicycle is an everyday example of the complex collaboration between the proprioceptive, vestibular and visual systems (Batson, 2009; Redding, 2010). The sophistication of cross-modal integration implies that the human sensorium can operate as a highly flexible and adaptive system. Take, for instance, what happens when you turn the lights off in a room and your senses of touch, sound and balance take the centre stage. An automatic and unconscious sensorial shift occurs when systems work together to adapt to new environmental conditions (Batson 2009; Redding 2010).

Sensations, memories and imagination

The third strand of research explores the role of mental imagery in multisensory integration. Why, for instance, is it that a croissant tastes better from a brown paper bag? Researchers have begun to unpack the complex relationship between what we imagine and what we perceive in an external environment. Research suggests that perception involves the cross-modal integration of both 'real' and 'imagined' stimuli (Agnati et al., 2013; Berger, 2016; Shimojo & Shams, 2001). For example, studies have shown that what we imagine hearing (auditory mental imagery) can affect what we see (external visual stimuli).

Similarly, visual mental imagery can affect auditory perception. It is important to note that mental imagery is not limited to visual representation. It can be present in any one or a combination of sensory modalities (Berger, 2016; Nanay, 2021). Mental imagery can be visual, auditory, olfactory, gustatory or somatosensory. For example, imagining an apple can involve 'picturing' the feel of its waxy skin, the sensation of its shape in your hand, the crunching sound of your bite, its crisp fresh taste or a combination of these.

From a neurological point of view, imagination is always influenced to some degree by autobiographical memory – the organization of sensory experiences that we collect and interpret over time (Byrne, 2017; Greenberg & Rubin, 2003). Although some scholars distinguish between supposition-based mental imagery and images from memory recall (Nanay, 2021), neurological studies have suggested that delineation is less clear (Berger & Ehrsson, 2013; Damasio, 2012). In other words, images of memories from the past are never exact replays of events; there is always some imaginative component. Similarly, imagining something new relies on past experiences to varying degrees (Greenberg & Rubin, 2003; Prebble et al., 2013). Although researchers have just begun to scratch the surface of the complicated relationship between imagination, memory and sensation, it is becoming clear that perception is a product of the cross-modal integration between real, recalled and imagined stimuli (Berger, 2016; Berger & Ehrsson, 2013; Kosslyn et al., 1995). In other words, sensations, memory and imagination work together to form a perception of current events.

Redefining perception

We stand at a fascinating point in time when philosophical, anthropological and scientific communities come together to radically redefine sensory perception. This interdisciplinary lens is critical to recognize that some of the ideas we held as universally true were the product of cultural beliefs and a lack of scientific attention. The science is clear. Traditional views of the senses as isolated one-way receptors of stimuli from the external environment and perception as a process of input and interpretation are untenable. The cross-modal activity of sensory receptors is located throughout the body, and the interaction between memory and imagination reframes perception as a far more dynamic process between the perceiver and the environment. Perception is not a passive mapping of external features that recreates an external image in the mind's eye. It is an embodied process of formation that is unique to the individual circumstances and aliveness of the encounter.

The hierarchy of the senses gives credence to the idea of a top-down cognitive interpretation of bottom-up sensory stimuli, privileging the perceiver's observation of their surroundings. Redefining perception as a dynamic whole-body system fundamentally transforms our comprehension of human relationships with the environment. This erases the notion of an outer landscape represented in our inner world. A physical space is no longer a collection of objects or planes to be observed and interpreted but rather an environment that is absorbed. The idea of valuing encounters with nature that leaves behind bodily sensation by 'superimposing a pure, contemplative consciousness' (Merleau-Ponty, p. 4) seems absurd in the light of this new knowledge.

The new science of perception fundamentally supports and extends the critique advanced in Chapter 4 by demonstrating that human experience of the environment is inherently multisensory, embodied and dynamically interactive, not merely visual or cognitively mediated. This is in stark contrast to the 'exposure to green space' principle critiqued in the previous chapter that dominates existing studies. This study explains the multisensory perceptual involvement essential to attunement states and how low-human-impact environments afford opportunities for attunement states to arise that other types of environments cannot.

An environment with a low human impact affords the possibility of experiencing the fullness of the human sensorium in action. In the absence of human distractions, the entire sensorium adapts automatically and unconsciously to the presence of other-than-human stimuli. With intention and time, an embodied awareness of these adaptations occurs. Sensory happenings in the body are as significant as any emerging thoughts and memories. Mentally distancing oneself from a sensation does not add to the experience's splendour. It is by staying close to bodily sensations that we access attunement.

A week in the desert: A personal account

After interviewing someone, I like to repeatedly read the transcript from the recording over an extended period so that I can move closer to the places and sensations described, and in return, those descriptions can linger in my imagination. I have also learned that there are other ways to absorb these accounts more deeply by accompanying me in my imagination on my daily walk into the woods where I live, for instance, or the times I spend alone in remote locations. An expressive form of making sense of people's experiences comes through my own embodied experiences akin to the phenomenological research methods proposed by Max van Menen and how we make the turn from the thematic to the expressive (1997). Although such methods may be criticized for their threat to objectivity, I have come to value the embodied experience as a reflexive approach to deepening my understanding of the lived experiences of those being studied, along with text analysis and literature review. I would go so far as to say that such methods are particularly useful and relevant for studying human relationships with nature.

In January 2020, I travelled to the southernmost tip of Algeria to camp in the Tassili n'Ajjer region of Sahara, a vast plateau that straddles the borders of Algeria, Libya, Niger and Mali. The changing angle of the earth's axis every twenty thousand years transforms this region from a lush grass-covered savannah to a desert and back. However, the dry heat of the past thirteen thousand years has stripped back vegetation and eroded sandstone formations, which resemble large rock forests. The Tassili n'Ajjer region boasts not only fascinating geology but also great cultural significance, as it is home to an abundance of rock paintings dating back tens of thousands of years, which provide ancient evidence of human presence during a more fertile period in this region's past. As a result, people visit, but in general, the place lies far from any human. Local guides took me there from the oasis town of Tamanrasset some seven hundred kilometres away and helped me find a solo spot to stay there for a week.

When you travel to visit somewhere new, you have expectations not only for the place but also for yourself. These expectations have the powerful ability to drive the need to see as much as possible. A learned behaviour, perhaps. However, when one is alone in the desert for any length of time, this mercurial landscape tricks our familiar sensory strategies – the way the changing light transforms the atmosphere, the sharp shadows that cast as long as skyscrapers, the sight of heat rising from the rocks and earthy smells as intense as the spice stalls of an Algerian bazaar – all alive and dynamic as any solid entity.

The night has many layers. When darkness sucks, the atmosphere of all light sharpens any sound. When the moon rises to bathe the valley in bright silvered light, it projects rock shadows to the size of the mountains. Whirling winds strike up from the sand in seconds and circle your tent until the stillness reigns again. Sensory strategies used in everyday life are abandoned for those that fit this extraordinary other-than-human realm. You cannot but surrender to the sensory subtlety of the space demands. You can sense when changes are on their way, neither tangible nor visible; you feel that the night is about to turn into an angry dog, or the moon will rise to cast its spell. Gradually, you notice the effect of the desert on you; you feel an embodied sense of attunement to this land.

During my time in the desert, I could have maintained an observational stance and appreciated the grandeur of the rock formations, the brilliance of the setting Saharan sun, or the spectacular Milky Way stretching across the sky at night. Through such observations, I could have experienced a sense of awe at the chasm between the infinity of the universe and the finite self. Yet, the experience of spending time alone in an environment devoid of human presence, and strikingly different from my everyday life, afforded something else. My intention was one of 'being with' as opposed to 'being in', immersion as opposed to observation. This way of being with nature is in stark contrast to the disinterested Kantian observation of a sublime vista. Both types of nature experience are distinct; one may not be better or worse than the other, but the intentionality involved in each directs engagement with the environment differently.

In *The Embodied Mind: Cognitive Science and Human Experience*, Varela, Thompson and Rosch point out that intention is essential to both initiate and sustain awareness from one moment to the next, noting:

> In everyday life, our actions are so swift and automatic that we fail to recognise our intentions. However, intention comes before even voluntary action, no matter how minor, such as shifting weight from one leg to the other when tired standing up. Without intention, there could be no voluntary action. Ultimately, intention directs awareness towards a particular area, after which attention focuses them on specific aspects. (2016, p. 175)

Intentionality marks an important distinction between attunement and other types of nature experiences. In a state of environmental attunement, the intentionality of an individual directs attention to the multisensory stimulation afforded by the environment. Attunement requires the intention to engage with the whole of the surroundings in a way that allows attention to shift to various elements as and when they are presented within the perceptual field. This intentionality brings awareness of bodily sensations, guiding attention between general and specific stimuli.

Attention may shift back and forth, but the intention remains to engage with the whole surroundings. Walking through a forest, the atmosphere and mood may sit in the foreground of your attention, shift to the sound of the leaves beneath your stride and then to the unexpected breeze that chills your face. Importantly, the intention lies in the awareness of bodily sensation; it is less concerned with meaning-making and more concerned with the quality and texture of the up-close and immediate sensory experience.

Movement is a physical manifestation of our intentions. It is this physical effort to exercise intentions that helps shape our perception of the space we inhabit. Movement works to bring the perceiver in conscious contact with the environment through the senses in an interdependent and ever-emerging process. Even the most subtle gestures play their part. The moving body is not a hollow vessel that receives data from the outer world, an instrument or a means to an end; instead, it brings animation to the experience. Through movement, environments are not observed in opposition to the viewer as a composition of flat planes and objects, but an atmosphere within which one is immersed. Movement heightens our awareness of our multisensory participation with the physical surroundings, and thus is integral to experiencing an embodied sense of attunement.

In a state of attunement, the spaces in between can feel as alive as any concrete form or surface, imagination as vibrant as the real and sensations as emotional or physical. There is something that it is like to be alone with nature in this way, in terrain that has not been formed with human society in mind, which stirs our being in this extraordinary and yet familiar way. What we experience during a state of attunement does not align with any mechanistic model of perception. Instead, we experience the dynamic structure and animation of the perceived world in ways that are less possible in environments manipulated by human factors, which are primarily designed with sight and sound in mind. Recent scientific studies on the dynamics of perception go a long way to further our understanding of the perceptual processes involved in attunement. The study of environmental attunement contributes to our understanding of the primacy of perception in human experience.

In conclusion

> It is not a question of reducing human knowledge to sensation, but of assisting at the birth of this knowledge, to make it as sensible as the sensible, to recover the consciousness of rationality.
>
> – Maurice Merleau-Ponty (p. 6)

From Aristotle's famous five to the Enlightenment's divisive line between the high and low senses, and contemporary psychology's cognitive turn towards the brain for all the answers, the history of the senses is a story of misunderstanding and neglect. In the past hundred years, scholars have championed the primacy of perception in the human experience. Along with Maurice Merleau-Ponty and James Gibson, anthropologists David Howes, Paul Stoller and Sarah Pinker, cultural historian Constance Classen, psychologist Kurt Lewin and philosophers John Dewey and Arnold Berleant, all pre-empted the recent scientific breakthroughs on perception and the senses, yet their voices remain as outliers to the main thrust of Western academic thinking.

With recent scientific evidence, the tide has turned. The delineation between sensation and cognition is under scrutiny, sparking a radical rethink of the mechanistic model of input and interpretation. As a result, perception is now understood to be a dynamic system of cross-modal activity, which is influenced by memory and imagination. Where pure cognition reigned supreme in our conceptualization of human consciousness for millennia, we now appreciate that perception plays a more important and sophisticated role than previously conceived. Where we stand today, science has come a long way to support outliers' conviction of the primacy of perception in human experience.

This radical rethinking of our understanding of perception has ramifications for the psychology of the human-nature relationship. First, the idea of an outer landscape as separate from our inner world is untenable in light of this new knowledge. Such a dualistic construct negates the multisensory reciprocity between the perceiver and environment. In reality, we are continuously involved in the dynamic process of perceptual participation in any given environment. This process may happen automatically and unconsciously most of the time. However, the process becomes conscious by bringing attention to bodily sensations. The experience of being in nature is not diminished in any way by bringing our awareness to sensation. Nor does it lower intellectual, moral or aesthetic values. In contrast, sensibility brings a qualitative dimension to experience.

Arnold Berleant makes an important distinction between pure sensation and sensibility, proposing that sensibility includes a developed awareness of perceptual experience, something more like perceptual acuity (2010). To be sensefully involved in what you are experiencing as opposed to senselessly. To allow oneself to bring the sensory to the foreground of one's attention, to be intentionally in sensation, and to relish the experience as opposed to seeking to distance oneself through mindful reflection. This sensory space we inhabit is not an ocean of chaos, as Kant feared, or in opposition to his safe haven of solid walled-off ground, but instead, a place of appreciation of the sensual world and our perceptual participation within it, our first reality.

The experience of being alone in an environment with low human impact is particularly conducive to this form of sensibility. An individual is free from human distraction and is free to engage with other-than-human life. Under such conditions, with intention, our attention and actions move towards an embodied sense of attunement to the immediate physical surroundings. We recognize this as a state that is qualitatively distinct from normative states. In this state of attunement, the physical space is no longer observed in opposition to the viewer as a composition of flat surfaces and objects, but as an enveloping atmosphere within which one is immersed. By bringing the sensory reciprocity between the perceiver and the environment to the foreground of our awareness, we actualize a sense of self that is fully immersed and intimately involved with the environment.

The interdisciplinary study of the senses, coupled with evidence from the new wave of cognitive scientists, has made the traditional sidelining of the senses untenable. Not only do they highlight the cultural bias that has governed our thinking to date but they also shed light on the phenomenon of environmental attunement. These advances go a long way to explain why and how a state of attunement emerges. They make sense of an experience that could otherwise be easily labelled as mystical or transcendental. Nothing can be further from the truth. To feel an embodied state of attunement to the physical world around us is to experience the fullness of the human sensorium through action.

References

Agnati, L. F., Guidolin, D., Battistin, L., Pagnoni, G., & Fuxe, K. (2013). The neurobiology of imagination: Possible role of interaction-dominant dynamics and default mode network. *Frontiers in Psychology, 4.* https://doi.org/10.3389/fpsyg.2013.00296.

Arrévalo, G. (2005). Interview with Guillermo Arrévalo, a Shipibo urban shaman, by Roger Rumrrill. Interview by Roger Rumrrill. *Journal of*

Psychoactive Drugs, *37*(2), 203–207. https://doi.org/10.1080/02791
072.2005.10399802.

Batson, G. (2009). Update on proprioception: Considerations for dance
education. *Journal of Dance Medicine & Science: Official Publication of the
International Association for Dance Medicine & Science*, *13*(2), 35–41.

Beacroft, C. (2018). *Educating the uneducable: Deafblind education in the Soviet
Union, 1925–1960* [Doctoral thesis]. University of East Anglia. https://uea
eprints.uea.ac.uk/id/eprint/72637/

Berger, C. C. (2016). Where imagination meets sensation: Mental imagery,
perception and multisensory integration. *Inst för neurovetenskap / Dept of
Neuroscience*. http://openarchive.ki.se/xmlui/handle/10616/45157

Berger, C. C., & Ehrsson, H. H. (2013). Mental imagery changes multisensory
perception. *Current Biology*, *23*(14), 1367–1372. https://doi.org/10.1016/j.
cub.2013.06.012.

Berleant, A. (2010). *Sensibility and sense: The aesthetic transformation of the
human world*. Imprint Academic.

Buck, L., & Axel, R. (1991). A novel multigene family may encode odorant
receptors: A molecular basis for odor recognition. *Cell*, *65*(1), 175–187.
https://doi.org/10.1016/0092-8674(91)90418-X.

Byrne, J. H. (Ed.). (2017). *Learning and memory. A comprehensive reference
Volume 1*. Elsevier Academic Press.

Corbin, A. (1986). *The foul and the fragrant: Odor and the French social
imagination*. Harvard University Press.

Critchley, H. D., Wiens, S., Rotshtein, P., Ohman, A., & Dolan, R. J. (2004).
Neural systems supporting interoceptive awareness. *Nature Neuroscience*,
7(2), 189–195. https://doi.org/10.1038/nn1176

Damasio, A. (2012). *Self comes to mind: Constructing the conscious brain*.
Vintage Books.

Fitzpatrick, R., & McCloskey, D. I. (1994). Proprioceptive, visual and vestibular
thresholds for the perception of sway during standing in humans. *The
Journal of Physiology*, *478*(1), 173–186. https://doi.org/10.1113/jphysiol.1994.
sp020240.

Gibson, J. J. (2014) . *The ecological approach to visual perception: Classic edition*.
Psychology Press.

Gonzalez, D., Cantillo, J., Perez, I., Carvalho, M., Aronovich, A., Farre, M.,
Feilding, A., Obiols, J. E., & Bouso, J. C. (2021). The Shipibo ceremonial use
of ayahuasca to promote well-being: An observational study. *Frontiers in
Pharmacology*, *12*, 623923. https://doi.org/10.3389/fphar.2021.623923.

Greenberg, D. L., & Rubin, D. C. (2003). The neuropsychology of
autobiographical memory. *Cortex*, *39*(4), 687–728. https://doi.org/10.1016/
S0010-9452(08)70860-8.

Høffding, S. (2019). Review of Dan Hutto & Erik Myin, *Evolving enactivism*
(2017, MIT Press). *Philosophy*, *94*(3), 492–499. https://doi.org/10.1017/
S0031819119000044.

Howes, D., & Classen, C. (2014). *Ways of sensing: Understanding the senses in society*. Routledge.

Hutmacher, F. (2019). Why is there so much more research on vision than on any other sensory modality? *Frontiers in Psychology, 10*, 2246. https://doi.org/10.3389/fpsyg.2019.02246.

Hutto, D. D., & Myin, E. (2017). *Evolving enactivism: Basic minds meet content.* MIT Press.

Johansen, T. K. (2007). *Aristotle on the sense-organs* (Digitally printed version). Cambridge University Press.

Kant, I. (2006) . *Anthropology from a pragmatic point of view* (R. B. Louden, Ed.). Cambridge University Press.

Kant, I. (1929). Immanuel Kant's Critique of Pure Reason (Norman Kemp Smith, Trans.). New York St. Martin's Press (Macmillan). (Original work published 1781).

Kant, I. (2000). Critique of the power of judgment (P. Guyer, Ed. & P. Guyer & E. Matthews, Trans.). Cambridge University Press. (Original work published 1790).

Khalsa, S. S., Adolphs, R., Cameron, O. G., Critchley, H. D., Davenport, P. W., Feinstein, J. S., Feusner, J. D., Garfinkel, S. N., Lane, R. D., Mehling, W. E., Meuret, A. E., Nemeroff, C. B., Oppenheimer, S., Petzschner, F. H., Pollatos, O., Rhudy, J. L., Schramm, L. P., Simmons, W. K., Stein, M. B., … Zucker, N. (2018). Interoception and mental health: A roadmap. *Biological Psychiatry: Cognitive Neuroscience and Neuroimaging, 3*(6), 501–513. https://doi.org/10.1016/j.bpsc.2017.12.004.

Korsmeyer, C. (2015). The hierarchy of the senses. In *Making sense of taste* (pp. 11–37). Cornell University Press. https://www.degruyter.com/document/doi/10.7591/9780801471339-004/pdf.

Kosslyn, S. M., Behrmann, M., & Jeannerod, M. (1995). The cognitive neuroscience of mental imagery. *Neuropsychologia, 33*(11), 1335–1344. https://doi.org/10.1016/0028-3932(95)00067-D.

Kreibig, S. D. (2010). Autonomic nervous system activity in emotion: A review. *Biological Psychology, 84*(3), 394–421. https://doi.org/10.1016/j.biopsycho.2010.03.010.

Lynch, S. A., & Simpson, C. G. (2004). Sensory processing: Meeting individual needs using the seven senses. *Young Exceptional Children, 7*(4), 2–9. https://doi.org/10.1177/109625060400700401.

Majid, A., & Burenhult, N. (2014). Odors are expressible in language, as long as you speak the right language. *Cognition, 130*(2), 266–270. https://doi.org/10.1016/j.cognition.2013.11.004.

Majid, A., Roberts, S. G., Cilissen, L., Emmorey, K., Nicodemus, B., O'Grady, L., Woll, B., LeLan, B., de Sousa, H., Cansler, B. L., Shayan, S., de Vos, C., Senft, G., Enfield, N. J., Razak, R. A., Fedden, S., Tufvesson, S., Dingemanse, M., Ozturk, O., … Levinson, S. C. (2018). Differential coding of perception in the world's languages. *Proceedings of the National Academy of Sciences,* *115*(45), 11369–11376. https://doi.org/10.1073/pnas.1720419115

Merleau-Ponty, M. (2012). *Phenomenology of perception* (D. Landes, Trans.). Routledge.

Nanay, B. (2021). Unconscious mental imagery. *Philosophical Transactions of the Royal Society B: Biological Sciences, 376*(1817), 20190689. https://doi. org/10.1098/rstb.2019.0689.

Pérez-Álvarez, M. (2018). Para pensar la psicología más alla de la mente y el cerebro: un enfoque transteórico. *Papeles Del Psicólogo – Psychologist Papers, 39*(3). https://doi.org/10.23923/pap.psicol2018.2875.

Ponticorvo, M., Di Fuccio, R., Ferrara, F., Rega, A., & Miglino, O. (2019). Multisensory educational materials: Five senses to learn. In T. Di Mascio, P. Vittorini, R. Gennari, F. De la Prieta, S. Rodríguez, M. Temperini, R. Azambuja Silveira, E. Popescu, & L. Lancia (Eds.), *Methodologies and intelligent systems for technology enhanced learning,* 8th international conference (pp. 45–52). Springer International. https://doi. org/10.1007/978-3-319-98872-6_6.

Prebble, S. C., Addis, D. R., & Tippett, L. J. (2013). Autobiographical memory and sense of self. *Psychological Bulletin, 139*(4), 815–840. https://doi. org/10.1037/a0030146.

Prieur, J., Barbu, S., Blois-Heulin, C., & Lemasson, A. (2020). The origins of gestures and language: History, current advances and proposed theories. *Biological Reviews, 95*(3), 531–554. https://doi.org/10.1111/brv.12576.

Redding, E. (2010). Considerations for dance educators. *Journal of Dance Medicine & Science: Official Publication of the International Association for Dance Medicine & Science, 14*(2), 43–44.

Reinarz, J., & Schwarz, L. (2012). The senses and the enlightenment: An introduction. *Journal for Eighteenth-Century Studies, 35*(4), 465–468. https:// doi.org/10.1111/j.1754-0208.2012.00532.x.

Sarafoleanu, C., Mella, C., Georgescu, M., & Perederco, C. (2009). The importance of the olfactory sense in the human behavior and evolution. *Journal of Medicine and Life, 2*(2), 196–198. https://www.ncbi.nlm.nih.gov/ pmc/articles/PMC3018978/.

Shimojo, S., & Shams, L. (2001). Sensory modalities are not separate modalities: Plasticity and interactions. *Current Opinion in Neurobiology, 11*(4), 505–509. https://doi.org/10.3389/fpsyg.2019.02246.

Slakey, T. J. (1961). Aristotle on sense perception. *The Philosophical Review, 70*(4), 470–484. https://www.pdcnet.org/pdc/bvdb.nsf/purchase?openf orm&fp=phr&id=phr_1961_0070_0004_0470_0484.

Stoller, P. (1989). *The taste of ethnographic things: The senses in anthropology.* University of Pennsylvania Press.

Stoller, P. (2010). *Sensuous scholarship.* University of Pennsylvania Press.

van Manen, M. (1997). *Researching lived experience: Human science for an action sensitive pedagogy* (2nd ed.). The Althouse Press.

Varela, F. J., Thompson, E., & Rosch, E. (2016). *The embodied mind: Cognitive science and human experience* (Revised edition). MIT Press.

6

Environmental attunement and the embodied self

Life isn't about finding yourself. Life is about creating yourself.

George Bernard Shaw

The previous chapter presented the new science of perception that shifts our understanding from the traditional cognition-centred models to a dynamic multi-modal system. This multi-modal model of perception sheds light on the perceptual processes involved in attunement states and explains why attunement states are inherently embodied and environmentally integrated. Building on the insights from Chapter 5, this chapter focuses on understanding how attunement states affect the self. In doing so, the chapter challenges the traditional Western view of the self as a purely internal mental construct and investigates how attunement states affect our embodied sense of self.

Where is the self?

Phrases such as 'be yourself', 'I don't feel myself' and 'pull yourself together' are widely used in everyday language. While each of these phrases suggests a general understanding of the self as an all-encompassing entity, it also conveys complex ideas of selfhood regarding authenticity, integrity and cohesion. So, what exactly do we mean by the self? While concepts of selfhood vary significantly across schools of thought and cultures, Western philosophers, theologians and psychologists have traditionally depicted the self as an essentially internalized mental entity. However, this inner self has proven challenging for researchers to locate. However, there is an increasingly robust body of work in philosophy, psychology and neuroscience that suggests that the self is more physically grounded in the living body and its interactions with the environment.

This embodied approach to selfhood is a natural extension of the multisensory model of perception outlined in Chapter 5. Just as perception is now understood as a dynamic, whole-body process, the self is increasingly seen as arising from the ongoing interaction between the organism and its environment. The embodied self focuses on the interplay between our senses of bodily ownership, self-agency and continuity over time. By appreciating the psycho-physical dynamics of selfhood, the embodied self transcends the mind and body duality that underpins most modern psychology, which often leans towards pure cognition for all answers. Fresh breakthroughs in our understanding of selfhood mark a turning point in Western thinking, as scholars are beginning to reject the idea of an inner self in favour of the more empirically grounded embodied sense of self. Repositioning the self from a purely internal entity to one that is embodied sets a new direction for exploring how nature affects it. The new empirical evidence provides solid grounds for exploring how attunement states affect our embodied sense of self.

The first part of the chapter charts the historical context for the positioning of the self as internal, illustrating the connection in Western philosophical and psychological thinking between the concept of self, duality and the separation of humans from the rest of nature. In doing so, the chapter highlights how the Western inner tradition sets the frame for modern psychology's increasing orientation towards cognition and the neglect of the embodied experience. The second part of the chapter brings together new strands of research to explore how attunement states affect the embodied self, their impact on the self's senses of bodily ownership and self-agency (core self), and the sense of continuity over time (narrative self). The chapter concludes by exploring the transformative potential of attunement states to enrich and expand our embodied sense of self.

The interiority of the self

In a series of autobiographical texts written in the fourth century C.E, *Confessions* (1991), the early Christian scholar St. Augustine laid out the argument for the physical world as an outwards distraction from the search for the true self, which he positioned separate and intimately internal. For Augustine, the route to self-knowledge and spiritual awakening was an inner journey. As St. Augustine writes:

> And being thence warned to return to myself, I entered into my inward self... He who knows the Truth knows that light; he that knows it knows eternity. Love knows it' (p. 89).

Philosophers prior to Augustine, particularly Platonists, separated the material realm from the non-material. Augustine's emphasis on the interiority of the true self, however, was truly innovation and novel. Augustine's invention of the inner world was a brilliant metaphorical device that allowed him to articulate his understanding of the less tangible aspects of human experience. Over the centuries that followed, theologians and philosophers have adopted the language of the interior to understand and locate selfhood. However, Cary points out that the metaphor of the interiority of the self took on a literal meaning over the centuries that followed (Cary, 2000).

For Western medieval theologians, the physical and metaphysical realms were coextensive. The purpose of the physical realm was to serve the spiritual, and the goal of this life was to prepare for the next. Succumbing to the flesh was perceived as weak and the source of sin, whereas the inner world authentically reflected God's ideas. Focusing inward offered a means to transcend the physical and be rewarded by receiving God's grace. Rejection of the outer world yielded a more profound knowledge of our true self as a reflection of the divine, a self that resides within.

One extreme manifestation of this tradition of interiority was the practice of anchorism. Derived from the Greek word *anakhorein*, meaning to withdraw, the anchorite withdrew from society to live in a bricked-up room usually attached to a monastery (Jones, 2012). The practice originated with the early Christian desert hermits in the centuries following Augustine and evolved into an elite vocation in Europe throughout the Middle Ages. Anchorites believed that any interference from the outside world would upset their inner quests. As a thirteenth-century anchorite guide advised, 'Disturbance only enters the heart through something that has been either seen or heard, tasted or smelt, or felt externally' (Ancrene Wisse, 2000, p. 67).

Perhaps the most famous practitioner was Julian of Norwich (1343–after 1416), named after the church of St. Julian in Norwich, England, where she lived bricked up in a small cell between the ages of eighteen and thirty-eight (Jones, 2012. Her only connection with the outside world was a small hole in the wall of her cell, which allowed donations of food in and human waste out. Julian went on to write two texts, *A Vision Showed to a Devout Woman* and *A Revelation of Love* (2006), the first recorded female autobiographies in English. The central narrative in both texts is Julian's inner journey to transcend the material world and experience the divine.

The Enlightenment is often heralded as the watershed moment when mind was separated from matter, but the works of Plato, Aristotle, Augustine and the medieval theologians show us that the die was cast long before this. The philosophical idea that stands as the main pillar of Enlightenment thinking, as seen in the works of René Descartes as a precursor to the Enlightenment, through John Locke, David Hume and later Immanuel Kant, proposed that the workings of the mind are not only free from the workings of the body but that human thought is self-generated rather than a reflection of the divine.

The originality of this premise is questionable, of course, as heretics such as the Italian philosopher and astronomer Giordano Bruno (1548–1600) proposed similar ideas. But Bruno's teachings led to his burning at the stake by the Inquisition in a public square in Rome (Yates, 2002). Within half a century after Bruno's brutal execution, Enlightenment thinkers were free to voice ideas that would liberate the self from the suffocating confines of religious orthodoxy and pave the way for modern philosophy and natural science.

The overview I provide here is a broad sweep through the centuries, skipping important overlaps and distinctions between scholars' works. However, the point I want to underline is that there was a clear trajectory of the idea of the interiority of the self from the neo-Platonic writings of St. Augustine through to the Enlightenment thinkers, who provided a rationale for this immaterial and internal entity, associated with self-awareness and self-knowledge. The main claim I want to make is that this trajectory, underpinned by the continuing belief in the duality of mind and matter, provides an essential context in which to understand modern psychology's apprehension of the self.

The self in modern psychology

In a statement that could easily be mistaken for an extract from a fourth-century Augustinian text, one of the founders of modern psychology, Carl Gustav Jung, declared, 'He who looks outside dreams, he who looks inside awakes' (Jung, 1973, p. 33). Jung was not alone; most great figures of late nineteenth and early twentieth-century psychology sought to translate the long Western tradition of interiority into psychological theories. Various schools have aimed to bring clinical methods to this inner journey. The outer world was not wholly denied, but priority was given to the notion of a purer, more authentic self-entity that resides consistently within, albeit hidden, and aloof. The quest for self-awareness and self-knowledge was all too easily conflated with the idea of a more authentic 'ought-to-be' self, lying in wait to be discovered.

The focus on the internal self was further emphasized by the cognitive revolution of the 1950s, which more or less conceived of the human mind as a computer-like information processor continuously encoding and processing data. By the 1980s, this cognitive approach had dominated psychology subfields, with researchers using scientific methods to locate and examine mental processes – thoughts, feelings, memory, perception and learning – in specific regions of the brain. Advances in neuroimaging technology further fuelled this compulsion to locate these mental processes. However, the neural basis of this inner self, the elusive entity believed to hold the essential truth of who we are, is yet to be discovered.

As discussed at various points throughout preceding chapters, the interdisciplinary field of embodied cognition, which gained prominence at the beginning of the twenty-first century, represents an important move away from the cognitive revolution of the late twentieth century and its fixation on the brain. This field values experience as a source of understanding, in contrast to traditional scientific methodologies that favour objectivity, abstraction and extrapolation. When it comes to the study of the self, the field of embodied cognition is interested in the 'as is' self-experience of the entire organism, stemming from the ever-changing and emerging sensations within the body's physiology.

The concept of the inner self as an inherently intangible and internal entity is replaced by the idea of an embodied sense of self. The scientific study of the embodied sense of self looks beyond the search for self-representation in the brain by paying closer attention to the subjective experience of selfhood, which is grounded in the body's sensorimotor systems – hence, the name, the embodied sense of self. Where the inner self has proven to be empirically elusive (Damasio, 2012; Fuchs & De Jaegher, 2009; Varela et al., 2016), the embodied sense of self, on the other hand, holds up much better to scientific scrutiny (Asai et al., 2016).

Five decades of psychological studies of the human-nature relationship have yielded significant insights into the cognitive effects. Yet the reason why we still know very little about nature's role in selfhood may well be because we have been searching for an inner self that simply does not exist. The idea of finding our true self in nature is a poetic idea, but we have to separate the metaphorical from the empirical. When examining how nature affects the self, the concept of the inner self is deeply problematic because it neglects the organismic reality of the self-experience. Abstract ideas of selfhood may have some legitimacy in the confines of human society, in the meaning-making conversations between patient and analyst, and in the pages of the pop-psychology books that inspire us to find our true self. However, any attempt to understand how nature affects the self cannot be distanced from the embodied experience. To value cognition over sensory perception or to separate selfhood from bodily and perceptual processes is a dissociation from the reality of events. Recent moves away from the idea of an inner self towards the embodied sense of self mark an important turning point in the psychological study of humans' relationship with nature.

What constitutes an embodied sense of self?

Studies in the field are developing rapidly, but one study by researchers across several Japanese universities stands out, as it draws on close to forty years of existing empirical research to define what constitutes an embodied sense of self. The initial findings of the meta-analysis were used as the basis for further quantitative studies. The results were then cross-referenced against the work of leading neuroscientists in the field, including Gallagher (2000) and Damasio (2012). In conclusion, their work identified three structural components to an embodied sense of self: ownership, agency and narrative.

1. *Ownership*: Refers to your ability to feel your body and actions as your own (e.g. 'This is my hand that is moving.')
2. *Agency*: Refers to your ability to experience yourself as the agent of your actions (e.g. 'I am the one moving my hand.')
3. *Narrative*: Refers to your ability to experience yourself in continuity over time, enabling you to develop a sense of uniqueness (e.g. 'These are my hands that used to love playing the piano but not anymore.')

Ownership

Self-ownership describes the sense of owning your own body and actions, as in the statement, 'This is my hand that is moving.' For example, when you lift your hand to pick up a cup off a table, you have the physical sensation and psychological understanding that you are in control of the movement. As it remains automatic and unconscious most of the time, we take this basic sense of self for granted. However, in exceptionally rare neurological conditions, someone can experience a partial or total loss of self-ownership (Zahn et al., 2008).

Neuropsychologist Daniel Stern (1985) observed that this sense of self develops within the first two months of an infant's life. Stern proposed that the sense of ownership occurs at the first of the four stages in the infant's development of a subjective self. This provides infants with an overall sense of being in the world. Stern's observational research closely aligns with neuroscientist Antonio Damasio's (2012) hypothesis of the proto-self and the development of a coherent collection of neural patterns that map, moment-by-moment, the physical state of the organism. Both scholars differ slightly in terms of the timing of the phases and terminology. However, they broadly agree that the sense of ownership is associated with the very early, pre-verbal infant stage.

Physical sensations play a pivotal role in the development of ownership during early preverbal infancy. Materiality matters when it comes to the sense of ownership in these early formative phases. In adulthood, of course, a sense of ownership often operates at an automatic and unconscious level for most of us most of the time and is rarely called into question. However, this fundamental sense of self allows us to experience our presence in the world. How a sense of ownership is experienced through non-verbal sensory stimuli is particularly interesting in the context of being in environments with no human presence. As an embodied, non-verbal experience, being alone in nature relies on this sense of ownership.

Self-agency

Self-agency describes one's ability to make choices and decide the actions that influence events. It includes a sense of control over one's own body and intentionality of actions (Asai et al., 2016). The statement, 'I can move my hand, and I can choose how and when to move my hand in a certain way', exemplifies self-agency. Although they are similar and interrelated, ownership and agency are distinct. For example, someone may be aware that their hand is moving, but not feel responsible for moving it. In other words, they do not feel that they are causing the action. A hypnotic state is one such instance, but it can also occur as part of a neurological condition or damage. A sense of agency can operate on a broad spectrum. For example, someone may experience a disoriented sense of control over their decisions or the ability to make bodily actions. They may feel a delay or disconnect between their decision to move their arm and the action that follows. At the extreme end of the spectrum, a person may experience complete dissociation and disconnection.

This sense of being an integrated, distinct body with control over one's actions starts to develop between two and seven months when an infant's sensory-motor intelligence reaches a new level (Stern, 1985). The infant begins to experience a greater sense of control over their actions. It is worth highlighting here that this developmental process relies on interaction with multisensory stimuli from the environment, some of which come from human-to-human interactions, and others from the other-than-human physical environment: the sound of a ticking clock, the softness of their pillow, the smell of grass, the feel of the temperature of the air and so on.

In reviewing developmental studies, it remains difficult to separate the role of the caregiver from that of non-human interaction in establishing ownership and agency. Without doubt, the caregiver is a direct source of sensory stimulation. They also play a facilitating role by supporting the infant in engaging with the rest of the physical environment. However, it is important to acknowledge that sensory stimuli from the physical environment and active bodily engagement with them also play a role in developing a sense of ownership and agency. Overall, the literature tends to focus on the role of human interactions. Consequently, in terms of research and theory, less attention has been paid to the role of sensory involvement in physical space.

Ownership and agency working together

Psychologists and neuroscientists generally concur that ownership and agency work together to facilitate the capacity for immediate awareness of the sense of being both the owner and agent of one's thoughts, feelings, perceptions and actions (Zahn et al., 2008). This combination of ownership and agency constructs a sensory level of self-representation commonly referred to as 'a minimal self' (Asai et al., 2016), or by Damasio (2012) as the 'core self', which is a transient entity continuously generated through organismic encounters with stimuli. Developed in early pre-verbal developmental phases in infants (typically identified between the ages of two and seven months), it remains an essential aspect of self-experience throughout a person's life.

To put this in the context of an adult's self-experience, consider how a trained dancer pays careful attention to the movement and control of their body in a physical space. The dancer can spend months practising one particular set of movements, tirelessly trying to master control of their physical self in order to realize their intended action. From their origination in pre-verbal infancy, dancers have developed a sense of ownership and agency to a highly sophisticated level. In this respect, the term *core self* seems more appropriate than *minimal*, which could denote a lesser value. Although this core self operates automatically and unconsciously most of the time because of the familiarity and habitual nature of our actions in everyday life, this does not mean that it is any less valuable than the other aspects of selfhood. This core self is the primary source of experience of our presence in the physical world. This forms the foundation of our very being.

To feel our body as our own, to feel our intention come alive through movement – it is through this core self that we can choreograph our expression in the world. One has only to consider the absence of ownership and agency to appreciate that one's core self is a very precious thing. Any disturbance to the core self can significantly compromise the quality of life. In my training as a psychotherapist, I worked with patients who had experienced paranoid auditory hallucinations. Most of the time, people know that the voices in their heads are not real. However, at times, these voices took control and the patient lost all senses of ownership and agency, causing serious levels of distress. To this day, I often take a moment to touch the bark of trees I pass on my daily walk. Even though my touch may be fleeting, I appreciate how the sensation lingers on the surface of my fingers for a few seconds, and serves as a simple reminder of how lucky I am to be able to reach out, touch and feel.

The development of the core self relies on an organism's psychological interaction with physical stimuli. In this sense, ownership and agency are not purely dependent on human interaction. On its own, the infant blinks, kicks its legs, reaches out to grasp and realizes that it can pull an object to its mouth to bite and taste. The development of ownership and agency is directed and enhanced through human interaction, from the caregiver who entices the baby to reach for the rattle to the dance instructor who teaches the young adult how to master a move. However, there is a physiological component to the development of our senses of ownership and agency outside of our interactions with other humans. In other words, humans are not entirely social creatures. We also need to interact with the non-human physical environment to develop essential components of our sense of self.

Alone in nature, we have the opportunity to feel the full vitality of this core self in a way that is easily ignored or suppressed in everyday life. As a nature therapist commented to me, 'Sometimes when I am alone in the forest, I sit and close my eyes. This helps me to start listening with the rest of my body and notice how my whole body is interacting with the surroundings.' This heightened sensitivity in perceiving and identifying stimuli brings greater awareness of the reciprocity between one's body and physical surroundings. Feeling your heartbeat quickening in response to the sharp incline of a hill, for example, promotes the feeling of the body as your own.

Any conscious action involving bodily movement provides an opportunity to experience some degree of ownership and agency. Activities such as sports, dance, gentle yoga movements, drawing or painting all create such opportunities. Similarly, other types of nature experiences, such as gardening or walking in a park, can also stimulate the core self. However, one of the distinct ways in which a state of attunement affects our sense of self is through heightened awareness of this core self. As one respondent put it, 'My senses get stirred up, and my physical body comes alive. You can't help but notice it because it's such a strong feeling.'

Not all encounters with nature lead to an experience of attunement. It is possible to spend time alone in an environment with no human presence, and not access a state of attunement. A walk in a wood can be a rewarding and restorative experience that produces cognitive benefits, but the encounter does not always end in attunement. Similarly, it is possible to spend a few hours painting a picture, or playing a game of chess, and not experience a sense of flow. However, under the right conditions and with the right intention, the attunement states can be accessed. One distinguishing feature of attunement is that our senses of ownership and agency come to the foreground of our awareness and feel heightened. This heightened awareness not only allows for a more embodied sense of engagement with our physical surroundings than in more normative states but also has an invigorating effect.

A sense of narrative

Narrative is the third constituent of an embodied sense of self (Asai et al., 2016). A sense of narrative enables individuals to maintain a temporal sense of self, in terms of both continuity (extended over time through memory) and uniformity (personality and identity). Sensory experiences accumulate over time as autobiographical memories, constructing a narrative for the self (Damasio, 2012; Forrest, 2000). Autobiographical memory builds a systematic record of consistent properties that individuals discover about themselves, forming patterns of thoughts, emotions and behaviours. This enables individuals to understand and predict reactions to events, thus forming the genesis of personality and individual identity. This temporal dimension of the self is generally credited with establishing a unifying or cohesive sense of self (Fink, 1988).

To illustrate this, consider a scenario in which the narrative is absent. For example, imagine waking up one morning and not knowing who you are anymore. This occurs in rare conditions, such as transient global amnesia, a sudden and total loss of autobiographical memory (Greenberg & Rubin, 2003). In such instances, the conscious memories of lived experiences are temporarily erased. Partners, friends and neighbours become strangers. Food and style preferences must be rediscovered. A person's identity as a loving father or loyal colleague exists only outside of their awareness. Thus, they can no longer predict reactions to situations. Images of memories of their past and future selves have disappeared.

In such instances of temporary memory loss, individuals can experience a sense of self only moment by moment. When self-narrative is present, our sense of self extends beyond present temporal boundaries. The here-and-now experience of the self can hold far more than just the present. Aspects of autobiographical memory can be activated by similar or related events in the present, either unconsciously or consciously. Consequently, experiences in the present are shaped to varying degrees by the past. In terms of self-experience, there is more to the present than the present. The phrase 'being in the moment' is often used across various schools of thought and practices, from Gestalt therapy to Buddhist-informed mindfulness practices, to advocate temporally boundary-less ways of being. Several studies claim that being in nature supports this state of being (Farrow & Washburn, 2019). However, is it possible to ever be fully in the moment when memories and imagination have such an influence on our here-and-now?

One of the key findings of my research is that, in attunement, people experience vivid mental imagery. This mental imagery tends to autobiographical memory recall. Along with specific moments from the past, people can recall images of the self that they wished they were or could become. However, the imagery is not purely visual. They have different sensory modalities, for instance, the smell of their favourite food from childhood or the sound of a long-forgotten tune. Respondents described these images as more vivid than normative states, filled with sensations in the present moment. As one respondent commented: 'I prefer to go to the woods. I feel most at home there. Maybe that's from my childhood; I'm not sure. I am always surprised by what memories come up. Because I'm there with my whole body, you know, I can feel my skin, my feet on the earth, and there's so much potential for touch. I can feel the deepest possible sensation of an experience that happened years ago. This never ceases to surprise me. The woods seem to draw them out of me.'

Experiencing the past as alive in the present is a recurring and remarkable feature of attunement. Meditative or mindfulness practices, for example, aim to interrupt our learned patterns of thoughts and behaviours by practising letting go of an ego state that is hooked by the images of past and future selves. Suspending the past and future allows the emergent, as opposed to the habitual, to flow directly from the here-and-now experience. In contrast, there is temporal fluidity to attunement states that does not demarcate time in such a linear fashion. Although being in nature is often referred to as a meditative-like experience, and under certain conditions, I appreciate how it could be, attunement has different characteristics from these states. When we attune with nature, we are unexpectedly presented with the opportunity to experience embodied memories from the past as well as images of memories of a future or imagined self.

The vivid mental imagery that people experience in attunement, be it through autobiographical memory recall or imagination, means that these moments are not restricted to the here-and-now. Although the experience stays directly linked to the environmental stimuli, there are temporal and imaginary extensions to the immediate experience, through the interplay of real, remembered and imagined stimuli. This feature marks an important difference from a mindful state or a flow state, which stay focused on the here-and-now, and from transcendental and altered states that distance themselves from the 'as is'. A state of attunement is temporally expansive while remaining close to real-life and real-time stimuli.

In summary, attunement states provide a heightened awareness of the physicality of a body directly engaged with its surroundings and a more vivid sense of things happening between the space and self interdependently. This self-awareness extends beyond the here-and-now without losing connection to real stimuli. Overall, attunement states enhance senses of ownership and agency as well as the person's sense of continuity over time (narrative self). Because psychologists and cognitive scientists widely agree that an individual's capacity to experience an embodied sense of self is generally associated with psychological health (Asai et al., 2016; Gleason, 2005; Zahn et al., 2008), we can reasonably assume that attunement states have potential psychological value. Taking this hypothesis one step further, in specific cases, attunement may be psychologically beneficial to people experiencing disturbances in their senses of bodily ownership and agency at the level of the core self. Furthermore, accessing a state of attunement may be helpful for people to support their sense of continuity over time, where such faculties have diminished.

The cohesive self

Researchers agree that ownership, agency and narrative interact in a highly complex manner (Greenberg & Rubin, 2003; McAdams, 2013; Zahn et al., 2008). Without activation of ownership and agency through external stimuli, there can be no sensory experience. Without sensory experiences over time, autobiographical memory cannot be formed; thus, narrative is absent (Damasio, 2012; McAdams, 2013). In addition to examining the effects of attunement on the constituent parts of the embodied sense of self to better understand attunement, we must consider how attunement affects the overall self. Ownership, agency and narrative work dynamically to form an organized and organizing cohesiveness, greater than the sum of its parts, that acts as an essential unifying force.

On a spectrum from high cohesiveness to complete fragmentation, individuals with high cohesiveness can quickly recover from life's setbacks. In contrast, those with lower cohesiveness may struggle to maintain emotional stability and perceive minor setbacks as significant threats. For example, the fragile self may perceive rejection from a job interview or a first date as a devastating event, while the cohesive self can easily dust themselves off and move on from the experience. Fragility can make life's inevitable challenges feel unbearable and result in inappropriate emotional and behavioural responses. Severe fragmentation can lead to the terror of chaotic, paranoid or dissociative states. Heinz Kohut (2009), the originator of self-psychology, argued that cohesiveness provides individuals with the resources needed to navigate life's challenges, maintain psychological health and realize what he believed to be life's psychological goal: joyful, creative living. Disturbances to cohesiveness, he argued, underlie most psychopathologies.

Although the concept of the cohesive self-originated in psychoanalytic theories and later in Kohut's clinical observations of narcissistic personality types, subsequent empirical studies support this strong link between cohesion and psychological well-being (Asai et al., 2016; Gleason, 2005; Zahn et al., 2008). At present, there is a broad consensus among psychologists, psychiatrists and cognitive scientists that a healthy embodied sense of self equates to high cohesiveness and psychological health.

For instance, adverse changes to a person's embodied sense of self can affect their overall sense of cohesion. In extreme scenarios, disturbances in the embodied sense of self threaten cohesion. For example, in schizophrenia, is preceded by a loss of physical grounding and a sense of alienation from one's own body and thoughts (Lysaker et al., 2002). Body-oriented therapies such as dance, music and expressive arts therapies have proven to be highly effective in working with the embodied self in the treatment of severe cases of fragmentation, such as psychosis and dissociative identity disorder. Unlike traditional talking therapies that focus on the inner world of the patient in such cases, these body-oriented therapies place the embodied self at the front and centre of the treatment and work to transform the patient's overall bodily and neurobiological dynamics.

The efficacy of body-oriented therapies in the treatment of severe fragmentation demonstrates several salient points. First, construing the self as grounded in the body, as opposed to a purely internalized pattern of mental processes, significantly changes the approach to treatment. Second, stimulating the senses of ownership, agency and narrative through creative stimuli and bodily movement within a physical environment promotes cohesion. However, the message underlined here is that experiences that enhance the embodied sense of self are psychologically valuable to a person's overall sense of cohesion. Thus, the potential of attunement to affect cohesion is a compelling avenue for further exploration.

There is a significant gap between theory and practice. It took several years of research and development to transform creative processes into clinically valid methods used by body-oriented therapists. However, the way attunement affects the embodied sense of self points to therapeutic possibilities concerning cohesion. Whether such a treatment is potentially appropriate for severe cases or more everyday ruptures requires extensive research.

The transformative shift

To paint a scene from memory or to dance to a favourite tune calls upon the full faculties of an embodied sense of self. In each of these seemingly simple everyday occurrences, we experience a complex interplay of intention and action, sensation and affect, memory, and imagination. The painter transmits intention through hand gestures that mark the canvas. The body is inspired by music to move in response to rhythm and beats. In these moments, we do not lose our familiar sense of self or find a new one, but instead, our sense of self is enlivened in some way.

In a state of attunement, bodily senses are heightened, and memories and imagination become more vivid. Familiar temporal boundaries are replaced by a more fluid sense of time. In the interviews I conducted, people frequently described the heightened feeling of being alive. All of these features have the hallmark of an enhanced embodied experience, which can also be experienced in other types of settings and scenarios. Attunement is distinct from other types of embodied experiences; however, people experience an embodied sense of attunement to other-than-human stimuli within their perceptual range. People recognize this radical change to self- and world perception taking place, as illustrated in statements such as: 'It feels like this painting I have been looking at turns into a vivid movie and I am in it,' and 'I really feel this distinction between what I'm normally like, which is seeing things as separate, and those moments when I am totally wrapped in it.'

Although the person experiences the self, their immediate surroundings and the self in relation to those surroundings in a new and extraordinary way, attunement is not an altered state. No distancing or distortion of real events occurs, as is the case in certain transcendental and hallucinatory states that are induced by psychedelics. During attunement, no detachment occurs. On the contrary, the experience relies upon and remains in direct connection to the immediate physical surroundings. However, the familiar relationship between physical space and time changes radically. One interviewee commented: 'I start to feel like every part of my being, physical and emotional, past and present, is folded into the landscape.'

Neuroscientists Anna Ciaunica and Adam Safron claim that 'controlled acquisition of new self- and world models may enhance the plasticity of one's perceptual and sensorimotor experiences (2024).' This newly gained flexibility, they suggest, 'may allow the individual to "leave behind" certain habits and perceptual rigidities that hold him/her stuck in behavioural patterns'. Ciaunica's and Safron's hypotheses form part of their research on the clinical use of psychedelic experiences. However, the basic premise can also be applied to attunement states. Attunement's ability to transform our familiar and habitual self- and world models, albeit temporarily, points to the potential to support people in the development of a less rigid, non-flexible self and world perception.

In these moments of attunement, there is freedom from habitual ways of engaging with the world around us. We can let go of repetitive thoughts and behavioural patterns that are governed by the usual physical, social and temporal boundaries of everyday life. One interviewee commented:

> It takes me a few days to shake off the structures of my everyday routines. But slowly they dissolve, and that's when I start to notice the land's effect on me. When I'm open in that way, the place comes alive, surfaces come alive. I become part of this pulsating land, part of its beat.

The feeling of being alive

Through the sensation of intimacy with the physical world around us, we experience an extraordinary feeling of being alive. The embodied sense of attunement with our immediate physical surroundings resonates so deeply with our own sense of self that we feel alive in a way that is unavailable in everyday life. Feeling alive in this way is the embodiment of the idea that life is worth living. As such, attunement teaches us that kinship with this more-than-human world fulfils our deepest existential needs.

This feeling of being alive is produced far from human society and interpersonal bonds that most psychology theories determine to be essential to the fulfilment of the self. For many of the people I interviewed, the idea of feeling isolated when alone in nature was alien to them. They perceive themselves as bound in a special relationship with the land, a living part of the land.

We are facing a period in the history of humanity where our impact on the planet could have irreversible effects. Whether this began with the Industrial Revolution or went as far back as we started to farm the land, humans have been distancing themselves from the rest of nature for a very long time, and the vast majority of the scientific community agrees that we now stand at a tipping point. Thus, human supremacy is an erroneous excuse. In the presence of this threat, one wonders if the greatest psychological challenge facing modern humans is the devastation felt by the horror of self-imposed isolation from the rest of nature. As the environmentalist Trebbe Johnson writes, 'that awful blend of grief and responsibility roils in all of us who feel the burgeoning horror of the climate crisis' (2023, p. 69).

Trebbe told me about the time she met an old Navajo elder years back. The Navajo elder described to her his memories of being moved onto a reservation as a young boy: When he first arrived on this new land, outside the boundary of the Navajo's four sacred mountains, he asked his father how long it would take for the land to call him by his name. Perhaps attunement reminds us of a more ancient knowing that we have long forgotten that can say, 'I am nature too.'

The point I want to emphasize is that when people experience attunement, they experience an extraordinary feeling of being alive. This feeling, although difficult to pinpoint or quantify, is present when people are in a state of attunement. Like two sides of the same coin, through the aliveness of the encounter with other-than-human life comes an enlivenment of our individual sense of self. Attunement is not a merging or fusion of entities but an embodied sense of kinship with this more-than-human world that invigorates our feeling of being alive, a reminder that we are not purely social creatures but, first and foremost, ecological beings. What a gift attunement presents us with, and I hope, some further impetus to hold greater care for our more-than-human kin – a point I return to in Chapter 9.

In summation

As early as the fourth century, St. Augustine argued that the outer physical world distracts us from searching for a true self, which he viewed as an intimately interior entity. Scholars, however, have pointed out that this inner world was a literary invention (Ostenfeld, 1982), a brilliant metaphor used by Augustine to articulate the less tangible aspects of human experience. However, Augustine's notion of the inner self took hold for over seventeen centuries, influencing early Christian theology, medieval European religious practices, Enlightenment philosophy and the clinical methods of modern psychology. Even the cognitive sciences of the late twentieth century held on to the idea of the inner self.

The deep problem with this inner self is that it is empirically challenging to determine exactly what it is – or even if it exists. However, the interdisciplinary field of embodied cognition, which has been gaining traction since the turn of the twenty-first century, radically challenges the idea of interiority by proposing that the self is physically grounded in a living body. Rather than being a purely internalized mental representation, the embodied sense of self is an ever-evolving and emergent process that depends on the dynamic interaction between the organism and its environment.

Three important aspects of the embodied sense of self are relevant to our understanding of environmental attunement: First, it dissolves the Cartesian divide that has contributed to human separation from the rest of nature for millennia and that has inhibited a deeper understanding of the psychological potential of the immersive nature experience. Second, it acknowledges the central role of bodily sensations and perceptual processes in self-experiences. Third, scientists have empirically determined what constitutes an embodied sense of the self. The result of these three aspects is that the concept of the embodied sense of self offers a more relevant and empirical foundation for understanding how attunement affects the self.

In a state of attunement, we experience an embodied sense of self through ever-evolving and emergent sensations within the physiology of a body moving within an environment. In everyday life, our sense of self ebbs and flows in and out of our awareness, much like a river that disappears underground and resurfaces later. However, in attunement, this sense of self comes into the foreground through heightened multisensory stimulation. The experience enhances our bodily senses of ownership and agency (the core self). People often report their senses becoming more alive, with a heightened awareness of multisensory engagement with the stimuli within their perceptual field. Additionally, attunement strengthens a person's sense of continuity over time (the narrative self).

Even though the physical and temporal boundaries experienced during attunement are more fluid and less rigid than in everyday life, people do not lose their sense of self or experience a merging of the 'me' with the 'not-me'. Instead, through heightened awareness of the body's perceptual participation with the surroundings, people experience a sense of their own being – that they are whole (the cohesive self). The overall feeling of being alive reported by people is particularly noteworthy. Although often described as extraordinary, this phenomenon is not mystical or transcendent. Instead, it is a wholly embodied realization that life is worth living.

Not every experience of being alone in nature results in attunement, much like how not every creative activity produces a feeling of flow or every moment of silence generates a meditative state. The study of environmental attunement underlines that different types of nature experiences have varying psychological and physiological impacts. For example, brief exposure to green spaces can alleviate mental fatigue and various outdoor activities can yield physical health benefits. However, attunement impacts our sense of self in distinct ways compared with other experiences. The key point is that if we treat all nature experiences as the same, we miss out on the qualitative dimensions of the human-nature relationship and the deeper impacts they can have on the self.

I do not wish to suggest that attunement is an all-encompassing cure or magic pill for the wide array of psychological illnesses humans suffer. Environmental attunement is a unique state that only occurs under certain conditions. As such, it has distinct characteristics that affect our sense of self in specific ways, which points to its psychotherapeutic potential in certain conditions related to the self, as well as some broader mental health possibilities. While research tools that analyse longer-term immersive nature experiences and the perceptual dynamics of the embodied self in a quantifiable way may not yet exist, this does not mean that the topic should be dismissed.

Overall, attunement offers an opportunity to reap the benefits of an embodied sense of self. These enhance people's perceptual and sensorimotor processes, and to self, and self-and-world perception point to the psychotherapeutic potential of attunement states. However, translating Environmental Attunement Theory into psychotherapeutic practice is a significant challenge, as it is finding ways to cultivate attunement in modern life. However, indicators of attunement's potential value in the treatment of certain populations and in enhancing the quality of everyday life for most populations are strong.

In the first section of this book, the concept of environmental attunement is introduced, highlighting its fundamental traits and the conditions that facilitate its occurrence. It was classified as a unique state of consciousness, existing on a spectrum from extended deep states to brief moments of micro-attunement. The second section outlines the three essential principles of Environmental Attunement Theory. First, attunement states are nurtured in settings in which non-human stimuli fill an individual's perceptual field. Second, the perceptual processes involved are multi-modal, depending on the interaction between sensations, memory and imagination. Third, attunement states influence the embodied self in ways that suggest potential for therapy and well-being. Having defined what attunement states are and how they function, the third section of this book explores their applications in contemporary life, particularly in psychotherapy, urban design and everyday modern societies.

References

Ancrene Wisse. (c. 1230/2000). In B. Millett & H. W. Wiggins (Eds. & Trans.), *Ancrene Wisse: A corrected edition of the text in Cambridge, Corpus Christi College, MS 402* (p. 67). Oxford University Press. (Original work written ca. 1230).

Augustine. (1991). *Confessions* (H. Chadwick, Trans., p. 153). Oxford University Press. (Original work published ca. 397–400 CE).

Asai, T., Kanayama, N., Imaizumi, S., Koyama, S., & Kaganoi, S. (2016). Development of embodied sense of self scale (ESSS): Exploring everyday experiences induced by anomalous self-representation. *Frontiers in Psychology, 7*. https://doi.org/10.3389/fpsyg.2016.01005.

Ciaunica, A., & Safron, A. (2024). Disintegrating and reintegrating the self—(in)flexible self-models in depersonalization and psychedelic experiences. In C. Letheby & P. Gerrans (Eds.), *Philosophical perspectives on psychedelic psychiatry*, International Perspectives in Philosophy and Psychiatry (Oxford, 2024; online ed., Oxford Academic, 19 September 2024), https://doi.org/10.1093/oso/9780192898371.003.0004.

Cary, P. (2000). *Augustine's invention of the inner self: The legacy of a Christian Platonist*. Oxford University Press.

Damasio, A. (2012). *Self comes to mind: Constructing the conscious brain*. Vintage.

Farrow, M. R., & Washburn, K. (2019). A review of field experiments on the effect of forest bathing on anxiety and heart rate variability. *Global Advances in Health and Medicine, 8*(January): 2164956119848654. https://doi.org/10.1177/2164956119848654.

Fink, D. L. (1988). The core self: A developmental perspective on dissociative disorders. *Progress in the Dissociative Disorders, 1*(2), 43–47.

Forrest, D. V. (2000). Phantoms in the brain: Probing the mysteries of the human mind. *American Journal of Psychiatry, 157*(5), 841–842. https://doi.org/10.1176/appi.ajp.157.5.841.

Fuchs, T., & De Jaegher, H. (2009). Enactive intersubjectivity: Participatory sense-making and mutual incorporation. *Phenomenology and the Cognitive Sciences, 8*(4), 465–486. https://doi.org/10.1007/s11097-009-9136-4.

Gallagher, S. (2000). Philosophical conceptions of the self: Implications for cognitive science. *Trends in Cognitive Sciences, 4*(1), 14–21. https://doi.org/10.1016/S1364-6613(99)01417-5.

Gleason, D. K. (2005). *The self cohesion scale: A measure of the Kohutian concept of self cohesion* [PhD dissertation]. University of Tennessee. https://trace.tennessee.edu/utk_graddiss/4307.

Greenberg, D. L., & Rubin, D. C. (2003). The neuropsychology of autobiographical memory. *Cortex, 39*(4), 687–728. https://doi.org/10.1016/S0010-9452(08)70860-8.

Johnson, T. (2023). *Fierce consciousness: Surviving the sorrows of Earth and self*. Calliope Press.

Jones, E. A. (Ed.). (2019). *Hermits and anchorites in England, 1200–1550*. Manchester University Press.

Julian of Norwich. (2006). *The writings of Julian of Norwich: A vision showed to a devout woman and a revelation of love* (N. Watson & J. Jenkins, Eds.). Pennsylvania State University Press.

Jung, C. G. (1973). *Letters,* Volume 2: 1951–1961 (G. Adler & A. Jaffé Eds. R. F. C. Hull, Trans., p. 33). Princeton University Press.

Kohut, H. (2009). *The restoration of the self.* University of Chicago Press.

Lysaker, P. H., & Lysaker, J. T. (2002). Narrative structure in psychosis: Schizophrenia and disruptions in the dialogical self. *Theory & Psychology, 12*(2), 207–220. https://doi.org/10.1177/0959354302012002630.

McAdams, D. P. (2013). The psychological self as actor, agent, and author. *Perspectives on Psychological Science, 8*(3), 272–295.

Ostenfeld, E. N. (1982). *Forms, matter and mind: Three strands in Plato's metaphysics.* Springer Netherlands. http://public.ebookcentral.proquest.com/choice/publicfullrecord.aspx?p=3107431.

Stern, D. N. (1985). *Interpersonal world of the infant: A view from psychoanalysis and developmental psychology.* Basic Books.

Varela, F. J., Thompson, E., & Rosch, E. (2016). *The embodied mind: Cognitive science and human experience* (Revised ed.). MIT Press.

Yates, F. A. (2002). *Giordano Bruno and the Hermetic tradition* (2nd ed.). Routledge.

Zahn, R., Talazko, J., & Ebert, D. (2008). Loss of the sense of self-ownership for perceptions of objects in a case of right inferior temporal, parieto-occipital and precentral hypometabolism. *Psychopathology, 41*(6), 397–402.

Part 3

In Society

7

Environmental attunement in psychotherapy

Whenever we touch nature, we get clean. People who have got dirty through too much civilization take a walk in the woods, or a bath in the sea. They shake off the fetters and allow nature to touch them ... things are put right again.

C.G. Jung

There is an old Irish saying: 'You can take the man from the bog, but you cannot take the bog out of the man.' It serves to remind us that we may leave our familiar environment, but the beliefs and ways of our old world come with us. As evidence accumulates on the positive effects of nature exposure in reducing symptoms of anxiety, depression and stress and in enhancing overall mental health, nature-based therapies have gained traction since the turn of the twenty-first century within mainstream therapeutic practices and public health policies. However, in taking therapy outdoors, have we simply transplanted our human-centred models into a different setting? Regardless of where the therapy takes place, contemporary psychotherapy's anthropocentric models are destined to ignore the full psychological potential of humans' relationship with nature. How can Environmental Attunement Theory be used to draw nature into psychotherapeutic practice?

In this chapter, I argue that contemporary psychotherapy's human-centred models fail to fully appreciate the psychological potential of humans' relationship with nature. I explore the potential of Environmental Attunement Theory in helping psychotherapy move beyond its anthropocentric stance. Through two case studies, this chapter examines how a shift in therapeutic focus from an anthropocentric worldview to an environmental appreciation of the self within a more-than-human world provides a richer framework for the psychotherapeutic process. The first case study challenges the prevailing interpretation of nature experiences as non-reciprocal encounters. The second case study illustrates the therapeutic value of cultivating an individual's capacity to be alone with nature.

The chapter concludes that Environmental Attunement Theory can inform psychotherapeutic practice in three substantive ways: philosophical orientation, methodological approach and therapeutic outcomes. The first is to expand the field of exploration beyond the intersubjective domain of human relations to encompass relations with the rest of nature. The second is by foregrounding the role of multisensory perception in human experience and fostering greater sensory curiosity. The third is by acknowledging our kinship with this more-than-human world as an essential source of psychological growth and fulfilment in life. Building on earlier chapters, this chapter examines how these theoretical insights can transform psychotherapeutic practices, moving beyond anthropocentric models to embrace a more-than-human relational field.

More than relational beings

Modern psychology was founded on the long Western tradition of interiority. Early pioneers such as William James, Sigmund Freud and Carl Gustav Jung, maintained the positioning of the self as internal and sought to apply clinical methods to the inner journey of self-awareness and self-actualization. However, over the course of the twentieth century, a gradual shift took place within all major schools of psychoanalysis and psychotherapy, from intrapersonal, one-person psychology to interpersonal psychology. This shift was partially inspired by philosopher Edmund Husserl's theory of intersubjectivity which challenged the idea that one mind is isolated from the other. Husserl proposed that the formation of our subjective reality is deeply embedded in the relational processes between subjects. This idea – that our subjective reality is not singularly constructed but fundamentally shaped by our interactions with others – broadened the psychological focus from the individual's inner world to encompass the inner worlds of others. Thus, while selfhood remained internal, this interpersonal shift acknowledged the psychological interdependencies between these inner worlds.

The shift to intersubjectivity was further compounded by the fallout from Second World War. An estimated thirteen million children across Europe, the Soviet Union and Asia lost one or both parents due to combat, bombings, genocide, starvation and other war-related atrocities, creating substantial social challenges in terms of care and support for these orphans. In the UK alone, approximately 120,000 children were orphaned and 38,000 were placed in institutional care, where the quality of care varied widely. Witnessing the devastating impact of the lack of emotional support many of these children received, child psychiatrists, such as John Bowlby (Bowlby, 1980) and Donald Winnicott (Winnicott et al., 2017), became increasingly convinced of the importance of early emotional bonds. Their work contributed greatly to the introduction of the Children Act 1948, which recognized the damage that institutional care inflicted on many of these young children (Bell & Wilson, 2017).

John Bowlby, together with Mary Ainsworth (Bowlby, 1980), inspired extensive research in post-war Britain, and then further afield in the orphanages of Romania and war-ravaged countries such as Uganda, leading to a substantially researched and highly influential theory of attachment. The core proposition of attachment theory is that strong early bonds form the internal working model of attachment, which is essential for establishing an individual's capacity to relate to themselves and others, both in childhood and throughout adulthood. Conversely, inadequate emotional bonds in early infancy can lead to the development of an insecure attachment style, resulting in psychological and relational issues throughout one's life.

As John Bowlby (1980) wrote towards the end of his famous three-volume work *Attachment and Loss*:

> Intimate attachments to other human beings are the hub around which a person's life revolves, not only when he is an infant or a toddler or a schoolchild, but throughout his adolescence and his years of maturity as well, and on into old age. From these intimate attachments, a person draws his strength and enjoyment of life and, through what he contributes, he gives strength and enjoyment to others. These are matters about which current science and traditional wisdom are at one. (p. 442)

Attachment theory had a major influence on the trajectory from the personal to the interpersonal. As analyst and researcher David Holmes points out (Holmes, 1996), the explosion of mother–infant research in the 1960s, 70s and 80s was largely due to Ainsworth and Bowlby's original theory. As a result, attachment theory is one of the most extensively researched theories in modern psychology. Most recently, attachment theory has inspired neuroscience to study the associations and influences between human relations and neurobiology (Cozolino, 2014; Vrtička, 2017). This research has led to one of the most important discoveries in neuroscience: visuospatial neurons that mirror the actions we observe and sense in others. This mirroring system plays a vital role in the development of thought processes and behaviours from infancy.

Today, the basic assumption that humans are essentially relational beings is well established in the philosophical, psychological and neuroscientific fields. Intimate bonds between humans are widely accepted, both psychologically and neuroscientifically, as the foundation for a psychologically healthy and fulfilling sense of self. In adult life, as in childhood, the individual's capacity to form and nurture human relationships is considered the primary marker of psychological well-being. The healthier the bonds between us, the greater the propensity for meaning and fulfilment throughout life.

In contemporary psychoanalytic and psychotherapeutic practices, relational and intersubjective theories have taken centre stage, with the relationship between therapists and patients often viewed as the core agent of change in effective psychoanalysis and psychotherapy. Numerous studies assert that regardless of the differences in the various psychoanalytic and psychotherapeutic modalities, for example, it is the quality of the relationship between the patient and therapist that matters most. Patients' patterns of relating to people in their lives are projected onto the therapist. Through the dialogic process, the therapist helps the patient identify these behaviours as patterns from their past and work towards new ways of relating. In this type of growth-facilitating therapeutic relationship, neuropsychologist Allan Schore proposed that meaning is not singularly discovered but dyadically created (Schore & Schore, 2003). Therapeutic relationships form an intersubjective system of reciprocal mutual influence.

Psychology may have expanded its focus from interpersonal to intersubjective. However, the Cartesian divide that separates the subjective mind from matter remains firmly in place, negating the possibility of meaningful reciprocity with other-than-human life. When it comes to human psychological development and well-being, how can anything other-than-human stand up to the psychological potency of intimate human bonds? In this anthropocentric worldview, anything other-than-human can serve only as secondary to the intrapersonal and interpersonal dynamics of human life. The other-than-human may have some degree of influence and effect, but this can only ever be viewed as superficial, compared to the deeply formative and reparative qualities of human relations. After all, if you talk to a tree, it can never answer back. It is little wonder that, where we stand today, it is challenging, even threatening, for modern psychology to give credence to any sense of genuine intimacy or reciprocity with nature.

This focus on human relationships has yielded profound insights into psychological development; however, as established in Chapters 4–6, it also risks obscuring the role of other-than-human relationships in both shaping and ongoing development of our sense of self. As previous chapters have argued, attunement states are not a feel-good response to a picturesque backdrop, but a dynamic, co-creative process. The following case illustrates how conventional interpretations can overlook genuine reciprocity and vitality present in these encounters.

Case Vignette: Susana – Is it all a projection?

In 2018, I interviewed a nature therapist, Susana, who described an encounter she once had with a group of trees in Scotland's Cairngorms National Park. She was spending a week alone there, on the lookout for a new location to base the nature-based retreats she ran for many years. On the second day, Susana ventured out at dawn to spend the day getting to know the land, with no real agenda or mission other than that. She described her enchantment to me with the dramatic mountain ranges, vast moorlands, ancient woodlands, deep glens carved out by glaciation, all of which were bathed in an early autumn's atmosphere.

She came across a dozen or so old Juniper and Scots pine trees shaped in a near-perfect circle, with sunlight streaming onto the forest floor. Struck by the atmosphere of the spot, she sat down among them, imagining how many seasons they had lived, how much weathering they had endured, and all the shelter and nourishment they provided to the surrounding wildlife. Compelled to touch each one, Susana found herself dancing among them and began to sing out loud with pure joy. The forest felt so alive to Susana in that moment, as the dappled light, the shifting breeze, solid trees with waving branches and earthy autumn smells all seemed to dance together.

Susana's description echoed the deep states of attunement experienced by many of the people I interviewed over the years, its multisensory quality, the aliveness of the encounter and the extraordinary feeling of participation. Susana's experience reminded me, in particular, about a similar encounter described by Trebbe Johnson in her book, *Radical Joy for Hard Times* (2018). Johnson describes meeting an ancient tree and feeling compelled to adorn it with stones and objects from the surroundings as a spontaneous act to honour all that the tree had provided over the course of its life. Johnson later shared her experience with a psychologist colleague, who interpreted the event as a one-way projection and encouraged her to question what the encounter revealed about her.

The psychologist's reduction of Johnson's encounter to pure projection is striking, as it adamantly rejects any notion of reciprocity or mutual animation. Are encounters of this kind solely one-way? I decided to present a selection of accounts from my research, including Susana's, to a panel of twelve psychotherapists and psychologists. My intention was to provide a sample of these deep states of attunement and to ask my peers for their professional interpretation. The overwhelming response was that these phenomena, from a psychological perspective, were one-way: an unconscious projection of unmet, unresolved or unattainable aspects of the self. According to their hypothesis, the physical surroundings simply acted as objects that reflected back these aspects of self. In their view, Susana's deep sense of connection to the magnificent trees of the Cairngorms, revealed an unconscious need to fulfil an unacknowledged aspect of self.

The trees, they argued, served as self-objects, meaning that they were used in the service of some unconscious and unfulfilled aspects of the self. The concept of the self-object, introduced by Object Relations theorists such as Klein and Strachey (Klein & Strachey, 1997) and expanded later by Heinz Kohut in his theories of self-psychology (Kohut, 2009), holds that self-objects play an essential developmental role in early infancy. Parental self-objects fulfil the child's need to be affirmed and feel at ease. However, as the child develops, the use of the self-object stands in the way of self-autonomy and can become inhibiting and problematic if it continues into adulthood. Just as Narcissus gazed at his reflection in the water of the pond, finding nothing beyond a mirror of himself, the aim of analysis, they contended, was to bring these unmet and unresolved aspects of self from the shadows of the unconscious into conscious awareness for resolution.

Numerous psychoanalytic theorists and clinicians argue that literature and art also fulfil the role of self-objects. In art psychotherapy, for instance, the artwork created by a patient functions as a self-object, projecting and externalizing the client's inner world. The psychoanalytic art psychotherapist Joy Sheverian (1999) views the artwork as more than just a creative expression; it serves as a crucial vehicle through which the unconscious can be externalized and integrated into the conscious mind. The art-making process transforms internal conflicts into tangible forms that can be processed and understood, with the artwork serving as an essential medium for playing out transference and countertransference, not abstractly, but concretely.

The persistent need for self-objects in adulthood is commonly identified as problematic, for example, when an individual's self-esteem requires constant external validation. From a psychotherapeutic perspective, Susana's experience raised the question of whether her encounter with the trees pointed to the need to validate or resolve unacknowledged aspects of herself. Was Susana unconsciously yearning to appreciate the impact she had on the world, even if she resisted acknowledging it? Through this lens, a discussion of Susana's experience with the trees in therapy may lead to an exploration of the patient's self-esteem and self-worth.

However, this interpretation misses the essential qualities of the encounter that enlivened her sense of self. Susana's feelings of intimacy and reciprocity with her immediate surroundings could easily be conceived as a projection born from her unconscious need to be affirmed in some way, where nature objects were used in service of the self. However, this interpretation negates the vitality of the experience itself. The interpretation privileges projection over perceptual participation, cognition over sensation, the human over the non-human, and, in doing so, reduces the texture and the quality of the felt experience to a one-way process and strips away any sense of autonomy and the aliveness of the other-than-human life present.

In this state of attunement, the space between becomes as alive as the entities themselves. Physical sensations and bodily experiences are as vital and dynamic as the empathy and imagination the encounter evokes. However, the encounter is far from one-way. The unique set of affordances of this type of low-human-impact environment plays a vital role in the aliveness of the experience. If these affordances are discounted, it is easy to conceive of the human as the principal animating factor and the setting as the backdrop. However, this approach ignores the reality of the reciprocity involved. Where natural environments are commonly treated as a resource to relax and restore us, or even as a canvas that mirrors our projections, states of attunement challenge us to conceive of a less anthropocentric appreciation of nature encounters of this kind.

The challenge that attunement states present does not diminish the critical role of human bonds in psychological development during infancy, childhood and adulthood. Nor does it negate the intrapersonal and interpersonal dimensions of human experiences. We can still affirm that humans are relational beings, while expanding our view of relationality to encompass the rest of life. The point to underline here is that anthropocentric models of human experience fall short of appreciating the texture and quality of what happens alone in nature. They stripped it down to a one-sided event. Such interpretations, while grounded in established theory, reflect the anthropocentric assumptions critiqued in earlier chapters, privileging human cognition over embodied, multisensory participation with the dynamics of an environment.

Dissolving the dualities inherent in conventional accounts of the human-nature relationship, such as the division between mind and matter, subject and object, and sensation and cognition, opens the door to a richer understanding of nature encounters. By shifting our focus away from the intrapersonal and interpersonal models used to understand human dynamics to the multisensory perceptual participation involved between the perceiver and environment, we appreciate what is happening. This approach emphasizes that no feelings of intimacy or reciprocity are about the person and their projections, but are actively co-created through direct, embodied engagement with the environment. Multisensory participation fundamentally shapes the quality and depth of human relationships with nature. People are indeed capable of feeling a deep empathic resonance with other-than-human life, and that connection can be genuine and pure rather than a projection stemming from an unconscious need or longing.

Case Vignette: Jamie's loss of sense of self

The following section presents a hypothetical case study derived from a selection of real-life cases in my clinical work. While all identifying details have been removed, the core themes and insights were drawn directly from people's lived experiences. The aim of this case study is not to showcase clinical methods or demonstrate efficacy, but rather to further explore how being alone with nature can cultivate attunement and enrich our sense of self.

In Jamie's first therapy session, he expressed his struggle to hold everything together. When I asked what he meant by 'everything', he described the various aspects of his life – from feeling overwhelmed by projects at work to a growing sense of disconnection from the people around him. Jamie, who was usually resilient in the face of life's challenges, had experienced a steady increase in this feeling of overwhelm over the past few years, reaching a point where he feared that everything in his life might fall apart. This rising anxiety was unsettled enough to prompt him to seek therapy. He confessed that he felt strange and somehow not himself.

At thirty-seven, Jamie lived with his girlfriend for ten years on the outskirts of a small town in Wales. It was his girlfriend who first suggested that he came to therapy, fearing Jamie had not fully processed the grief from his father's death two years earlier. Raised in a large house in a well-to-do suburb of Glasgow, Scotland, with his parents and three much older brothers, Jamie was often described as 'lost in his own world'. His father would joke, 'Is Jamie away with the fairies at the back of the garden again?' Despite his father and brothers teasing, Jamie harboured no animosity towards them; he simply felt that they shared little in common.

Jamie's most enduring childhood memory was of playing alone in the rambling, walled-off garden at the back of the house while his mother attended to chores inside and his father and brothers played sports elsewhere. He would spend hours in imaginative play among the trees and shrubs. One of his favourite activities was lying on the ground beneath a giant oak tree, observing the world up close. In our sessions, he would recall in vivid detail the texture and hues of the earth and the sensation of the ground against his skin, how he loved to notice subtle changes in temperature, guess the different smells carried by the breeze, or imagine himself as a dragonfly hovering over his neighbours' gardens.

These memories stood in stark contrast to his family life, where he often felt out of tune with the boisterous behaviour of his older brothers. However, it was not that Jamie shunned the company of family and friends; he enjoyed playing with other local children. Yet, it was in the solitude of the garden or nearby fields that he felt most at home. Jamie spoke with pride about the dens he built and would laugh about the times his mother sent his brothers to fetch him back from his adventures but couldn't find him.

He felt a natural kinship with the other-than-human world, which was endlessly stimulating and creative. His love of being alone in nature continued throughout his life. In St Andrews, Scotland, where he attended university, he walked for hours to find time alone in the field. After graduating, he took up a graduate position at a technology firm on the outskirts of Cardiff and Wales. Edged on the Garn Ridge, with views over the Glamorgan Valley, he found a home with rolling hills and rugged coastlines to explore on his daily walks – so integral to his daily life. His environment was not simply the backdrop to his ruminations. Sometimes he felt lost in thought while crossing the valleys, but he was mainly enchanted by his surroundings. For Jamie, this time alone in nature was his most reliable source of comfort, a space where he knew he could let go of the struggles of the day.

Jamie is not unique in this; studies of adolescents and young adults report that favourite places help clear the mind, foster relaxation and even 'provide the courage to be themselves' (Korpela& Staats, 2014; Solitude, p. 356). This is not to say that Jamie did not enjoy the company of others; he was a sensitive man attuned to the warmth and concerns of others, nurturing close relationships with a few people while generally avoiding larger social gatherings.

The expectation of conforming to social norms and being sufficiently similar to others was never a primary concern for Jamie. Although thoughtful and sensitive to the needs of others, Jamie's sense of self was not defined by social expectations, and his preference for being outside social groups did not negatively impact his self-esteem. However, his father's death prompted him to question his identity, sparking existential concern that he had not previously experienced. During one session, for example, Jamie remarked, /I don't know if I've been hiding from people all my life or if I'm just more comfortable being alone in the woods.'

Although Jamie and his father were never close, his father's death stirred unexpected feelings. His father was known to outsiders as gregarious and 'the life of the party', but was often argumentative within the family. Their relationship had always been distant and utilitarian, and as a consequence, Jamie felt that he could not fully grieve a father whose bond lacked emotional depth. Instead, he found himself mourning a father he wished he had – a figure who could have offered warmth, understanding and validation as he was growing up, rather than unpredictability and distance.

The loss of his father triggered him to wonder why his father showed him so little interest and whether this neglect lay at the root of his ambivalence towards social relations. He questioned whether his long-standing preference for solitude, which was always a comforting and familiar space, was a character flaw. He scrutinized his decisions, such as choosing to walk five miles to and from work each day instead of using that time to meet friends and colleagues. His reflections took on a darker tone, raising critical questions about whether his enduring preference for solitude was a form of creative adaptation or maladaptive response to early emotional neglect.

What emerged in Jamie's case is not a simple narrative of grief but a deeper existential unease instigated by his father's death. The reverberations that another person's death creates within us are not always feelings of grief or loss towards the other; sometimes, those reverberations stir something else. Jamie began to perceive his essential aloneness – something he had lived with comfortably throughout his life – as a failure to relate to the world, causing an insecurity he had never felt before. The familiar comfort of being alone in nature, this once loyal and trusted space, now seemed to signal something amiss. Jamie's self-questioning, initially a natural response to a significant life event, evolved into a profound source of discomfort.

Jamie's case illustrates the complexity of solitude as both a fulfilling space and a source of discomfort and distress. For most of Jamie's life, solitude was seldom lonely, and being alone in nature, in particular, was a sensorially engaging experience. Spending time alone in nature fulfilled Jamie, whereas many of his social interactions were unstimulating. For most of his life, Jamie felt that his sense of self was less defined by social norms and less congruent with the rest of society. However, events cast Jamie's desire to be alone in nature under a negative light. Instead, he began to experience what Irvin Yalom describes as an 'existential isolation' – a more fundamental sense of isolation from essential aspects of our perceived world that can arise when forced to face the reality and proximity of death.

Solitude and being alone 'with' nature

The Handbook of Solitude (Coplan & Bowker, 2014) offers the first comprehensive compilation of psychological research on the construct of solitude, distinguishing between different types of solitude, each with unique psychological underpinnings, benefits and potential risks. An overarching message is that not all solitudes are equal. The evidence is clear that while solitude can have detrimental effects on mental health, it can also be a deeply restorative and enriching experience when experienced in healthy forms.

One of the critical distinctions of solitude drawn from this comprehensive review is the beneficial type of solitude, often voluntary and self-imposed. Studies have shown how this type of solitude can provide space for self-reflection, creativity, mental restoration and emotional regulation. For example, individuals who intentionally seek solitude may benefit from reduced stress, heightened self-awareness and enhanced creativity. Positive solitude allows for a deeper sense of connection with the self, fostering greater sense of autonomy and cohesion. It is typically associated with feelings of empowerment and self-discovery, in which individuals actively choose to retreat from social interactions for psychological and emotional nourishment.

In contrast, a detrimental type of solitude or loneliness, typically involuntary, is often characterized by feelings of social isolation, withdrawal and depression. Individuals who experience this form of solitude may feel isolated, disconnected from human life, and excluded from meaningful social relationships. This type of solitude can stem from life circumstances, such as losing loved ones, social anxiety or other factors beyond an individual's control. The propensity for such feelings can also stem from attachment patterns developed through early emotional bonds. Potential issues associated with negative solitude include increased risks of depression, anxiety and other mental health concerns. Chronic social isolation is identified as a risk factor for general mental health, cognitive decline and physical health issues.

Solitude can also be experienced differently, depending on situational factors, life stages, and the social and cultural meanings of different settings. For instance, solitude can be beneficial for children and adolescents as they develop a sense of identity, as private space 'provides children and adolescents with tangible signs that they are unique and different' (Coplan & Bowker, 2014, p. 354). Spending time alone in hiding places offers freedom from immediate social demand. Similarly, familiar favourite spaces help promote positive emotional outcomes and emotional self-regulation.

However, extended periods of solitude can become problematic if they evolve into social withdrawal, particularly during transitional or challenging periods. Similarly, solitude may be valued during intense work or creative endeavours but may lead to isolation if it becomes a habitual way of avoiding social interactions. The salient message here is that solitude is complex and nuanced and not inherently good or bad. Our understanding of the developmental role of being alone remains scant, particularly our knowledge of what happens when we spend extended or repeated periods alone in nature. As Korpela and Staats (2014) point out, longitudinal studies on the effects of solitary retreats on nature are non-existent, and our empirical apprehension of the qualitative dimension of such experiences, which may be the most important, is negligible.

As I briefly mentioned in Chapter 1, Donald Winnicott's article, 'The Capacity to Be Alone (1990) stands out in an ocean of psychological literature on the importance of human bonds. In this article, Winnicott argues that infants reach a developmental stage, roughly between eighteen and twenty-four months, where they begin to develop their capacity and interest in being alone without direct attention from the mother. As Winnicott states, 'the capacity to be alone is a highly sophisticated phenomenon and has many contributory factors'. Initially, it begins with the experience of being alone, while in the presence of another, typically, the primary caregiver. As Winnicott states, 'although many types of experience go to the establishment of the capacity to be alone, there is one that is basic, and without a sufficiency of it the capacity to be alone does not come about; this experience is that of being alone, as an infant and small child, in the presence of mother.'

Over time, the infant develops the capacity to be alone without the presence of another through the internalization of a reliable and attentive caregiver. This internalized experience of emotional and physical containment, or 'good-enough mothering', as Winnicott terms it, forms the foundation of the child's capacity to be alone in the absence of their primary caregiver. The infant learns to be content without stimuli and responses from another, avoiding feelings of anxiety or isolation. Winnicott explains this early autonomy and self-sufficiency as the genesis of the essential psychological resources needed not only to be at peace when alone throughout life, but also to be a source of self-reflection, creative thinking and personal growth.

Winnicott's article appears in the last chapter of his book, *The Maturational Processes and the Facilitating Environment: Studies in the Theory of Emotional Development*. Published towards the end of his career, shortly before his death in 1971, the book is a collection of his most influential essays exploring the role of interpersonal relationships in children's psychological development. After a long and celebrated career championing human relations, particularly that of the mother in forming the type of facilitating environment essential to the healthy development of the infant, it is extraordinary that Winnicott should conclude with the capacity to be alone.

Winnicott's ideas overlap with Bowlby and Ainsworth's attachment theory, which posits that early emotional bonds act as a secure base from which the infant gains confidence in exploring. Both theories infer an internalized working model of relating to the world around us based on these initial bonds. Winnicott's theory differs in two ways. First, it identifies the early experiences of being alone as significant for the emotional maturation of the self, claiming a quality of aloneness essential to selfhood. Second, it specifically refers to a child's exploration of the world without other humans. Second, Winnicott's theory aligns with the work of British psychiatrist and psychoanalyst Anthony Storr, author of *Solitude* (1989).

Originally titled School of Genius, after historian Edward Gibbon's claim that solitude is the 'school of genius', the book *Solitude* provides a compelling counterargument to the contemporary psychological assumption that humans are primarily relational beings. As Storr states, 'In the field of psychotherapy, current wisdom assumes that intimate personal relationships are the chief, if not the only, source of human happiness. However, the lives of creative individuals often seem to contradict this assumption. Many of the world's greatest thinkers and artists have not formed close personal ties. Much human pleasure and fulfilment as well as creative achievement come from solitude. Not everyone who lives alone is pathological or necessarily unhappy.' For both Winnicott and Storr, choosing to be alone is not a retreat from the world but a vital space for the self to flourish.

Through case studies and historical examples, from philosophers and artists to scientists, Storr expands upon Winnicott's intuition that the capacity to be alone is crucial for developing creativity, self-awareness and psychological well-being later in life. Storr builds on Winnicott's ideas by demonstrating that solitude can be a creative force. Both thinkers suggest that the capacity to be alone is foundational to psychological health, although Storr extended this to argue that solitude is also a prerequisite for achieving the highest forms of creative expression. In Storr's view, conscious solitude is not an act of withdrawing from life, but instead choosing to engage with it on a deeper level, exploring free from the constraints of societal norms, beliefs and prejudices.

There is further synergy between Storr and Winnicott's work in their definitions of creativity and the role it plays in achieving a sense of agency and fulfilment in life. This form of creativity is not necessarily that of a professional artist or confined to conventional artistic endeavours, but a form of self-expression that allows individuals to articulate their experiences of being alive, finding ways to understand and express the less tangible aspects of the human condition – its joys and struggles – and to experiment with new ways of being and engaging in the world. As Winnicott writes, 'In creative living, you or I find that everything we do strengthens the feeling that we are alive, that we are ourselves' (pp. 39–44).

The psychological 'truth' of our age may well be that humans are essentially social creatures, with an inherent need for belonging so deep in all of us that it sets the mould for our way of existing in the world. Winnicott, Storr and some more recent studies stand out by challenging this position, proposing that the experience of being alone enriches our perception of the self and world. They converge on the claim that consciously and intentionally retreating from society is an essential part of self-actualization and creative living, and therefore, echo the Augustinian idea of the inner journey to some degree.

While it is feasible to be alone in nature while being lost in one's thoughts, to be 'alone with nature' is a different proposition. One is a retreat from human society to one's own concerns, the other is an active engagement with one's surroundings, to hold wonder and curiosity towards everything within one's perceptual field, and to be spontaneous and creative in response to those stimuli. The central proposition of Environmental Attunement Theory is not one of isolation but instead that being alone with nature is the pathway to attunement.

It is in this quality of 'being alone with' nature that is essential to attunement, whether the deep states achieved by spending extended periods in remote locations or the more frequent micro-attunements, such as those Jamie experienced in his daily walks. Jamie's desire to be alone was a desire to be in relationship with the natural world around him. His bond with nature held qualities beyond the restorative effects of exposure to nature. Whether this connection to nature was on par with or a substitute for human relations in Jamie's life is inconsequential. Rather than comparing or casting his capacity to be alone with nature as a form of social avoidance or anxiety in therapy, it was acknowledged and appreciated as meaningful and fulfilling. Jamie's relationship with other-than-human life was folded into the therapeutic process and granted the same attention and privilege as human relations.

Bringing therapy outdoors

While solitude may not be actively promoted, contemporary therapy has increasingly sought to incorporate nature and the outdoors into its practice. Nature-based therapy is a broad category that encompasses various approaches that integrate natural settings and activities into existing therapeutic practices and models. Nature-based therapies have increasingly gained traction in mainstream therapy practices and public health policies, primarily for two reasons. The first is the growing recognition in the mental health field of the benefits of contact with nature in reducing symptoms of anxiety, depression and stress, as well as in promoting overall mental health. Second, there is an overwhelming need to find solutions to the increasing mental health burden. This category can be grouped according to geographical and cultural influences.

Wilderness Therapy has roots in North American traditions, such as vision quests and wilderness youth camps (Fredrickson & Anderson, 1999; Naor & Mayseless, 2020; Talbot & Kaplan, 1986). It typically involves multiday expeditions in natural settings, combining clinical intervention with the challenges of the wilderness. These programmes are often designed for adolescents and young adults struggling with behavioural, emotional or substance abuse issues. Participants engage in outdoor survival tasks, group therapy and individual counselling, building self-esteem, problem-solving and social skills. Similarly, *Adventure Therapy* integrates physical activities like hiking, rock climbing, kayaking or ropes courses with therapeutic processes, and has been used with at-risk youth, trauma survivors and individuals seeking to build resilience and leadership skills.

Ecotherapy (or Nature Therapy) stems from ecopsychology and its guiding principle that the health of the planet is inextricably linked to the psychological health of humanity and the individual (Buzzell & Chalquist, 2009; Lobo et al., 2018). Ecotherapy encompasses a wide range of therapeutic practices aimed at reconnecting individuals with the natural world, such as mindful walks in nature, nature meditation and outdoor arts-based activities. Although ecotherapy has broad mental health applications, it is most closely associated with treating emotional distress caused by climate change and human-driven environmental damage, referred to by authors such as Trebbe Johnson (Johnson, 2018) and Johanna Macy as 'climate grief' (Kaza, 2020), or by Glenn Albrecht as 'solastalgia' (Albrecht, 2019).

Forest Bathing (Shinrin-Yoku), which originated in Japan in the 1980s, involves spending fifteen to sixty minutes focusing on the sights, sounds and smells of the forest environment to promote relaxation and reduce stress (Farrow & Washburn, 2019; Park et al., 2010). It is a meditative practice that encourages individuals to slow down, focus on their senses and immerse themselves in a forest environment, which has been shown to lower cortisol levels, improve mood and boost overall well-being. Its popularity in the West is largely due to a substantial body of research from Japanese universities and its alignment with well-established mindfulness movements.

Other nature-based therapies, such as *Environmental Arts Therapy* and *Horticultural Therapy*, have roots in public mental health services. Environmental Arts Therapy, pioneered by Ian Siddons Heginworth (Heginworth, 2008), involves the therapeutic use of natural materials, locations, themes and seasonal cycles. Horticultural Therapy employs gardening and plant-based activities as therapeutic tools and is used in diverse settings such as hospitals, rehabilitation centres, prisons and community gardens. It has proven to be effective for individuals with conditions such as depression, anxiety, dementia and PTSD.

These examples highlight the diversity of practices under the umbrella of nature-based therapies and their wide range of mental health applications from trauma and addiction to developmental challenges and existential concerns. However, research on the efficacy of some of these therapies across diverse populations remains in its infancy. Public health policies in the UK, for example, are increasingly advocating nature-based mental health initiatives, both in terms of improving access to natural spaces and funding programmes that incorporate nature-based practices. As these therapies advance, theoretical, ethical and regulatory considerations will become more prominent along with the need for professional training, which will further energize research and development.

In all of these practices, nature is used as the therapeutic setting, albeit with varying degrees of physical activity and interaction. The interaction between the individual and the setting is either directly facilitated by the therapist or conducted under their guidance or supervision. The therapeutic work extends beyond the traditional dyadic therapist–client relationship, forming a triangular relationship between therapist, client and environment. In addition to the cognitive, affective and physical benefits associated with exposure to nature, Jordan argues that natural settings transcend the limitations of the conventional consulting room by creating opportunities for clients to engage with their emotions and trauma in an embodied and experiential manner (Jordan, 2015). Similarly, Ian Siddons Heginworth describes how natural settings and their elements can be actively used as a medium to explore, interpret and resolve thoughts and feelings.

Drawing the more-than-human in

Psychotherapeutic work with Jamie remained within the boundaries of the conventional therapeutic space. We held weekly hour-long sessions in a private and comfortable consulting room, maintaining the physical and temporal boundaries that have become synonymous with professional and ethical practice. In conventional talking therapies, this space provides the containment necessary to explore the client's inner world and the intersubjective space between the patient and the therapist. I never met Jamie outside this space, nor did I directly observe or facilitate his encounters with nature. Our work remained indoors. Jamie's experiences of being alone with nature were self-directed.

The process shared the same therapeutic aim as it would in traditional talking therapy: to help Jamie better understand himself and his relationship to the world around him through an exploration of life experiences – past, present and imagined. The dialogic process employed in the consulting room was a reflexive exploration of his life experiences. However, unlike traditional talking therapies, there was an intentional focus on Jamie's experience of other-than-human life. Although the psychotherapeutic work remained within the conventional containment of the physical space and structured time, the field of enquiry was broader than intrapersonal and interpersonal dynamics. While we did not use nature as a setting or medium in this process, Jamie's relationship with nature was given space and credence. While most contemporary nature-based therapies transfer human-centred practices and theories to outdoor settings, Jamie brought nature into the therapy room.

We examined the significance he gave to his father's death, how this loss unsettled his familiar sense of self, and forced him to question his relational patterns. Through this process, he began to feel at ease with himself once more, was less concerned with his differences from others and was deeply appreciative of the qualities and textures of his day-to-day life that came from his connection to nature. It is not that every time Jamie was alone with nature he experienced some grand epiphany or life-enhancing meaning. Nor was his connection to nature a magical solution to all his psychological concerns. However, Jamie's relationship with the natural world brought special qualities to his experience of being alive.

This qualitative dimension was not defined by his possessions, achievements or social connections but through his sensory involvement with other-than-human life. This sensitivity found its fullest expression in moments of attunement and the embodied realization that he, too, is part of nature. As Jamie commented:

> I love how everything moves. Like the leaves on the trees and the sunlight passing through them. Nothing feels static or separate in the way things normally do. It's like everything is singing and dancing and making their presence felt. I get totally wrapped up in it, part of it. It's when I feel my most alive. (Interview extract)

Alone with nature, Jamie rediscovered a freeing energy in experiencing himself and the world around him differently from the rest of his life. He could 'let go' of his insecurities and any thoughts of low self-worth. Feelings of isolation from society were replaced with a deep appreciation for his connection to the nature around him. The therapeutic process supported Jamie in acknowledging and cultivating his relationship with the more-than-human world. In doing so, he became less fixated on life events that led to self-doubt and self-criticism of his social differences. Jamie developed a deeper appreciation of his non-human relations as a valid and integral part of his sense of self. There was more to his life and experience of being alive than human relations. This embodied knowledge helped Jamie find a greater balance across various dimensions of his life.

In conclusion: How Environmental Attunement Theory informs psychotherapy

The emphasis on interpersonal relationships in human development and the impact of intersubjectivity on psychological theory, research and practice has often stigmatized aloneness and sidelined the potential of human-nature relationships. While nature is widely accepted as beneficial for mild symptom relief, cognitive functioning and general well-being, the qualitative dimension of the human-nature relationship remains undervalued. Nature-based therapies that impose human-centred models on human-nature relationships may be justified in doing so, and evidence shows that they can achieve positive outcomes.

However, such approaches inevitably fail to fully embrace how nature affects one's sense of self. Human-centred theories and techniques have been applied to nature-based therapies; however, these anthropocentric models do not fully explain the behaviour of the reality under study. They do not represent the wholeness of events. Bringing people into nature has benefits; however, perhaps the next advancement in nature-based therapies may be best served by taking a less anthropocentric stance and integrating an ecological worldview. This is where Environmental Attunement Theory can best inform psychotherapeutic practice by expanding the field of exploration beyond the intersubjective to encompass this more-than-human world.

Environmental attunement values and encourages multisensory engagement with the natural world, which serves as an invigorating and vital component of one's sense of self. Environmental attunement can influence psychotherapeutic practice in three substantive ways: philosophical orientation, methodological approach, and therapeutic outcomes. As discussed throughout this book, intersubjectivity theory, and its dualistic underpinnings, sets the frame for most psychotherapies. In contrast, Environmental Attunement Theory is phenomenologically informed and primarily concerned with the nature of first-person experience and how the world is perceived by the individual. Phenomenal properties are not conceived as pure projections in service of the self but rather as animations of real-life reciprocity.

The second way in which Environmental Attunement Theory informs psychotherapeutic practice is through methodology and methods. The overarching methodological approach expands the field of exploration beyond the intersubjective by encouraging the therapist to draw attention to the person's perceptual participation in this more-than-human world. This fosters fresh curiosity and perceptual sensibilities towards the entirety of life. The sensory experience is prioritized, or at the very least, given equal credence to abstract meaning-making. While phenomenologically informed therapies such as Gestalt and Person-centred therapies also value and prioritize the lived experience, environmental attunement distinguishes itself by intentionally expanding the scope of exploration beyond humans to include the rest of life.

The most significant methodological difference from conventional nature-based therapies is that the process does not require replacing the indoor setting with an outdoor setting. The therapist does not need to play a facilitating role in the person's relationship with nature nor do they provide direct guidance or education. Applying Environmental Attunement Theory in therapy does not require specialized techniques to train therapists to facilitate attunement experiences. The therapist holds an appreciation that there is more to life than our relationships with other humans. They expand the field of inquiry beyond the intrapersonal and interpersonal to include the broader environment without seeking to apply anthropocentric models to interpret encounters with nature.

In this expanded space, other-than-human life is acknowledged and appreciated as an intrinsic part of a person's relational dynamics. Human relationships are not seen as the sole source of life fulfilment. Nor are the mind and the body, the human and the other-than-human, treated as separate and independent. This does not devalue human relations, but encourages the cultivation of the capacity to be alone with nature as bringing an additional dimension to the development and fulfilment of the self. Cultivating the capacity to be alone with nature is the pathway to attunement and the embodied realization that we are part of nature. This pathway is a conscious and intentional act that does not need to be instructed or observed by a therapist, but simply encouraged so that each person can find their own way.

In terms of therapeutic outcomes, psychotherapy informed by Environmental Attunement Theory may well be particularly applicable to conditions related to the self. The indicators are there that attunement states' ability to offer an alternative self-and-world model may help people to let go of unhelpful habitual patterns and encourage curiosity and creativity. These states may help restore a person's overall sense of self when recovering from difficult life events, and re-establish self-agency, resilience and self-esteem. At the more existential level, nurturing our capacity to attune to this more-than-human world may well provide the embodied realization that life is worth living.

Environmental Attunement Theory invites conventional psychotherapy to consider the possibility that there is more to our psychological life than other people. Expanding psychotherapy's focus beyond human relationships to include our embodied connections with a more-than-human world presents fresh opportunities for psychological growth and fulfilment. In practical terms, this boils down to cultivating the capacity to be alone with nature as a pathway to attunement. However, for most people today, opportunities for attunement are increasingly shaped by the realities of urban life. The next chapter examines how contemporary urban spaces, despite their physical limitations and social complexities, can weave opportunities for environmental attunement into the fabric of urban living.

References

Albrecht, G. (2019). *Earth emotions: New words for a new world*. Cornell University Press.

Bell, M., & Wilson, K. (2017). *The practitioner's guide to working with families*. Palgrave Macmillan.

Bowlby, J. (1980). *Attachment and loss*. Vol. 3: Loss, sadness and depression. Hogarth Press.

Buzzell, L. & Chalquist, C. (Eds.). (2009). *Ecotherapy: Healing with nature in mind*. Sierra Club Books; Distributed by Publishers Group West.

Coplan, R. J., & Bowker, J. C. (2014). *The handbook of solitude: Psychological perspectives on social isolation, social withdrawal, and being alone*. Wiley Blackwell.

Cozolino, L. J. (2014). *The neuroscience of human relationships: Attachment and the developing social brain* (2nd ed.). W.W. Norton & Company.

Farrow, M. R., & Washburn, K. (2019). A review of field experiments on the effect of forest bathing on anxiety and heart rate variability. *Global Advances in Health and Medicine, 8*, 2164956119848654. https://doi.org/10.1177/21649 56119848654.

Fredrickson, L. M., & Anderson, D. H. (1999). A qualitative exploration of the wilderness experience as a source of spiritual inspiration. *Journal of Environmental Psychology, 19*(1), 21–39. https://doi.org/10.1006/jevp.1998.0110.

Heginworth, I. S. (2008). *Environmental arts therapy and the Tree of life*. Spirit's Rest Books.

Holmes, J. (1996). *Attachment, intimacy, autonomy: Using attachment theory in adult psychotherapy*. J. Aronson.

Johnson, T. (2018). *Radical joy for hard times: Finding meaning and making beauty in Earth's broken places*. North Atlantic Books.

Jordan, M. (2015). *Nature and therapy: Understanding counselling and psychotherapy in outdoor spaces* (Dual First). Routledge, Taylor & Francis Group.

Kaza, S. (Ed.) (2020). *A wild love for the world: Joanna Macy and the work of our time* (1st ed.). Shambhala.

Klein, M., & Strachey, A. (1997). *The psycho-analysis of children*. Vintage.

Kohut, H. (2009). *The analysis of the self: A systematic approach to the psychoanalytic treatment of narcissistic personality disorders*. The University of Chicago Press.

Korpela, K., & Staats, H. (2014). The restorative qualities of being alone with nature. In *The handbook of solitude: Psychological perspectives on social isolation, social withdrawal, and being alone* (pp. 351–367). Wiley Blackwell.

Lobo, L., Heras-Escribano, M., & Travieso, D. (2018). The history and philosophy of ecological psychology. *Frontiers in Psychology*, 9. https://www.frontiersin.org/articles/10.3389/fpsyg.2018.02228.

Naor, L., & Mayseless, O. (2020). The wilderness solo experience: A unique practice of silence and solitude for personal growth. *Frontiers in Psychology*, *11*. https://www.frontiersin.org/articles/10.3389/fpsyg.2020.547067.

Park, B. J., Tsunetsugu, Y., Kasetani, T., Kagawa, T., & Miyazaki, Y. (2010). The physiological effects of Shinrin-yoku (taking in the forest atmosphere or forest bathing): Evidence from field experiments in 24 forests across Japan. *Environmental Health and Preventive Medicine*, *15*(1), 18–26. https://doi.org/10.1007/s12199-009-0086-9.

Parliament of the United Kingdom. (1948). Children Act 1948 (11 & 12 Geo. 6 c. 43). https://www.legislation.gov.uk/id/ukpga/Geo6/11-12/43

Schaverien, J. (1999). *The revealing image: Analytical art psychotherapy in theory and practice*. Jessica Kingsley Publishers.

Schore, A. N., & Schore, A. N. (2003). *Affect regulation & the repair of the self* (1st ed.). W.W. Norton.

Storr, A. (1989). *Solitude*. Flamingo.

Talbot, J. F., & Kaplan, S. (1986). Perspectives on wilderness: Re-examining the value of extended wilderness experiences. *Journal of Environmental Psychology*, *6*(3), 177–188. https://doi.org/10.1016/S0272-4944(86)80021-4.

Vrtička, P. (2017). The social neuroscience of attachment. In A. Ibáñez, L. Sedeño, & A. M. García (Eds.), *Neuroscience and social science: The missing link* (pp. 95–119). Springer International Publishing. https://doi.org/10.1007/978-3-319-68421-5_5.

Winnicott, D. W. (1990). *The maturational processes and the facilitating environment: Studies in the theory of emotional development* (Repr.). Karnac [u.a.].

Winnicott, D. W., Caldwell, L., Robinson, H. T., Adès, R., & Kabesh, A. T. (2017). *The collected works of D. W. Winnicott*. The Winnicott Trust.

8

Environmental attunement in the city

In his 1862 essay entitled '*Walking*', Henry David Thoreau wrote, 'I can easily walk ten, fifteen, twenty, or any number of miles, starting from my door, without passing by any house or crossing a road except where the fox and the mink do: first along a river, then a brook, and finally through the meadow and the woodside.' Since then, the global population has increased fivefold, compelling humanity to exchange the horizon for the skyline. The United Nations anticipates that the proportion of the global population residing in urban areas will increase from 55 per cent to over 70 per cent by 2050 (United Nations, 2019). For the world's richest countries, the rate of growth will be steady, while in some parts of the world, urbanization will mushroom. For example, the population of Mongolia's capital city, Ulaanbaatar, skyrocketed from 500,000 to 1.5 million between 2001 and 2020 (Cui et al., 2019).

Cities have consumed fields and forests, manipulating environments to such an extent that the sort of access to nature described by Thoreau is fast becoming a distant memory in the history of humanity. Instead of trying to find an ever-disappearing nature, the challenge facing humanity is to allow for all of nature in our increasingly expanding cities. Yet, even in cities, the earth persists beneath the concrete. Urban environments are teeming with biotic and abiotic life forms beyond humans. Nature prevails, but maybe not as previously imagined, prompting us to continuously reimagine and reinvent the possibilities for humans' relationship to nature. This chapter explores the principles of environmental attunement in the city, its application to modern urban design, and its contribution to the emerging interdisciplinary discourse of a more-than-human city.

Broadly speaking, urban green space refers to any area within a city that is predominantly made up of 'soft surfaces' like soil, grass, shrubs and trees (Swanwick et al., 2003). These spaces are diverse and range from city parks and planted public squares to city farms, rooftop grasslands, private gardens, sports fields, environmental art projects and mini-agricultural sites. The benefits of urban green spaces on overall well-being have been extensively documented and linked to a broad spectrum of health benefits, from mental health benefits to better pregnancy outcomes (Dzhambov et al., 2014), improved child development and morbidity rates (de Keijzer et al., 2016).

The forms of these spaces are diverse. Biotic and abiotic factors, from vegetation and wildlife to the local weather and climate, along with structural elements such as the positioning within the built environment, all have their influence. Additionally, the designs of these spaces are imbued with the cultural and socioeconomic dynamics of their respective cities, which in turn shape the thoughts, feelings and behaviours that determine how people interact with them. The term 'urban green space' (UGS) is contentious for numerous reasons, many of which I elaborate on in Chapter 4, but in short, not least because its wie-ranging application renders it insufficiently comprehensive. However, it remains unclear which categories and features of UGS provide particular benefits to specific groups.

My initial research on being alone in nature was of people who spend extended periods in remote locations. This is how I first identified deep states of attunement, what sets them apart from other types of nature experiences and how they come about. However, the types of people and environments that I first researched are far removed from everyday modern life. In a world where most people live in built-up environments with no access to the type of nature described by the participants in my early research, I questioned the universality of my findings. I began to research the possibility of people accessing attunement in less extreme, more accessible conditions, and if a form of attunement was achievable through the nature available in a city.

This chapter situates Environmental Attunement Theory in the context of contemporary Urban Green Space design. This chapter explores how UGS affords opportunities for urban dwellers to experience micro-attunements, the less intense, more momentary attunement states described in Chapter 3. This chapter identifies the features of UGS that foster the conditions under which these micro-attunements occur. The chapter concludes by proposing ways in which the principles of Environment Attunement Theory can be used in interdisciplinary discourses on the future of our cities and the well-being of their citizens,

Attunement in the built environment

Scholars sometimes refer to the term attunement in relation to people's feelings towards a particular architectural space or atmosphere (Bille &

Schwabe, 2023). When discussing attunement in the city, it is important to distinguish between the use of the term in its more generic form and the embodied state of consciousness identified through my work. The term 'attunement' derives from the Middle English word 'atune', meaning 'to tune' or 'adjust'. Its origins trace back to Old French 'atuner', from Latin 'ad' (to) and 'tonare' (to thunder or make a sound) (de Gaynesford, 2017). Over time, the term has evolved beyond literal tuning to encompass figurative uses across disciplines, denoting harmony or resonance in relationships. While architectural theory uses attunement in this figurative way to describe an emotional connection with the mood or atmosphere of a place, the term environmental attunement refers to a specific state of consciousness identifiable by its unique behavioural pattern.

Architectural theorists, Bille and Schwabe (2023), use the term attunement when discussing how built environments can shape both individual and collective emotions, bringing the term closer to a shared experience. As cited in their 2023 publication, *The Atmospheric City*:

> This field of research has marked a shift in architectural and wider urban theory from a preoccupation with what the built environment 'does' to a preoccupation with what it feels like, not simply as subjective experience but as something designed and collectively felt. (p. 9)

The architectural scholar Pérez-Gómez (2016) uses a term similar to encompassing personal and collective moods or atmospheres of communal spaces, but links attunement closer to Martin Heidegger's interpretation of the German word *Stimmung. Einstimmung,* referring to the process of entering a mood, is commonly translated as attunement, although this is not a direct translation.

Architectural scholars' figurative use of the term attunement and the adoption of the translation of Heidegger's *Stimmung* and *Einstimmung* as attunement are distinct from the use of attunement as a psychological term. Despite similarities, the psychological use of the term environmental attunement denotes a unique state of consciousness characterized by specific effects, while architectural attunement refers more broadly to relationships between personal and collective moods within a built environment. This point is emphasized here for two reasons. The first is that this chapter explicitly explores attunement states in urban environments, as distinct from the more figurative use of the term used in architectural texts. Second, this distinction is critical for interdisciplinary discussions of human relationships with both natural and built environments.

Micro-attunements

The principle that states of consciousness operate along a continuum of experience was adopted by Mihaly Csikszentmihalyi in the early stages of his research on flow states. Csikszentmihalyi and his team of researchers identified that people can experience a version of flow during less structured and more trivial activities than originally believed (Csikszentmihalyi, 2000). He concluded that moments of microflow follow the same behavioural pattern as deep flow states and are still intrinsically rewarding and beneficial. Flow researchers in the decades that followed demonstrated that while successfully learning a new dance can evoke a deep state of flow, everyday activities such as cooking a different meal or focusing attention on reading a challenging book can also evoke a flow state governed by the same pattern of effects, albeit less intense and sustained (Jackson, 1995; Ottiger et al., 2021; Privette, 1983).

With an increased interest in psychedelic states and their psychotherapeutic potential, philosophers of consciousness and neuroscientists have reached a broad consensus that altered and exceptional states of consciousness operate along this continuum. This stream of research is particularly important for the study of environmental attunement because it supports the hypothesis of micro-attunements and, with that, the possibility that states of micro-attunement can be achieved in less extreme, more everyday settings than those required for deep states of attunement. The interviews and secondary research I conducted following the original study overwhelmingly pointed to this being the case.

The people I interviewed who spent time alone in different types of natural environments included those living in urban settings and using the city's gardens, parks, canal walkways, rooftops and allotments. They described a more subtle and fleeting, yet similarly distinctive, unusual states, and like their more intense counterpart, these micro-attunements are identifiable by heightened multisensory awareness, vivid mental imagery, fluidity of time and an embodied sense of resonance with the other-than-human stimuli within their perceptual field. These micro-attunements also appear to affect a person's overall sense of self, enhancing their embodied awareness of their presence in the world and evoking an invigorating feeling of being alive.

These micro-states still require time and space away from human distractions in environments where other-than-human stimuli populate the person's perceptual field, but to a much lesser degree than in deeper states of attunement. It is possible that the conditions required for micro-attunements are available in urban settings. However, they are not accessible in all types of urban green space. Not every city park can provide the same set of affordances as low-human-impact environments typically found in remote locations. The first section of this chapter explores urban green space design to make distinctions across various types. This sets the context for the second section which presents a hypothetical case study to examine the specific characteristics of urban green spaces that offer pathways for attunement.

Defining urban green space

As previously mentioned, the term urban green space is problematic because it relies on categorizing nature as separate from humans while reducing it to recognizable vegetative forms. In reality, the interaction between biotic and abiotic factors shapes every environment. Distinguishing where other-than-human life ends and human life begins is not straightforward in such multifactorial compositions. For example, shopping malls contain both biotic and abiotic life, and the presence of planting can transform certain sections into areas that might be defined as green spaces. Using the amount of visible vegetation as the primary criterion to define urban green space is, at best, vague, and, at worst, ignorant of the physiological realities.

In a review of over hundred prominent research articles on urban green space, less than half of the studies provided a clear definition of the term, though many implied one (Knobel et al., 2019). Among these, the most general interpretation referred to a vegetated variant of open space, including city parks, communal gardens, courtyards, urban farms and forests. These interpretations typically describe land use as focused on human needs sustained by human intervention. Researchers emphasize that such broad definitions potentially limit our ability to distinguish key differences, draw insights from diverse contexts or synthesize results effectively. While urban green space remains useful as a linguistic shorthand, we should aim for context-specific definitions within Environmental Attunement Theory rather than relying on broad generalizations. Where historically, the term may have been appropriate, today's urban green space designers are engaging with complex urban issues, and as a consequence, creating increasingly sophisticated solutions.

Paris, France's capital city, is an interesting example with a long history of urban green space design. In 1564, Queen Catherine de Medici commissioned the gardens of the Tuileries Palace in the city centre, drawing on the Renaissance styles she admired from her upbringing in Florence. These designs, in turn, hark back to the gardens, courtyards and promenades of the Roman villas. A century after Catherine's endeavours, King Louis XIV remodelled the gardens into a formal style popular during his reign, aiming to reflect the political power of his rule. Although initially reserved for royalty and elites, the gardens opened to the public in the late nineteenth century, allowing everyone to enjoy the majestic space. Today, the gardens remain largely intact and serve as a respite from city life, where the city's inhabitants and visitors can walk, socialize or simply observe their surroundings in a very similar fashion to previous generations.

Along these historical gardens, since the turn of the twenty-first century, Paris has prioritized its urban green space design to address the pressing environmental needs of the city. The city has planted over twenty thousand trees and has added 62 hectares of green space. Additionally, certain vehicles, such as buses and trucks manufactured before 2001, vehicles manufactured before 1997 and motorcycles manufactured before 2000, have been banned from entering the city. Paris also issued a 'license to green', encouraging citizens to plant in their available spaces. By 2040, the city plans to create green spaces in more than eight hundred schools. These efforts have made Paris one of the world's leading cities in terms of environmental pollution.

In comparison, in Mexico City, air pollution ranks as the eighth most common cause of death, accounting for 5.9 per cent of the fatalities. With urban development putting pressure on ground-level spaces, the city has taken advantage of rooftops to create green infrastructure. At Bosque de Chapultepec, one of Mexico City's largest parks, circular single-story offices in botanical gardens are planted with resilient stonecrops. This vegetation withstands the local climate, while producing oxygen and filtering out carbon dioxide and heavy metals. These green roofs regulate office temperatures, absorb rainfall and assist in keeping buildings dry. In addition, local hospitals use rooftops to help patients convalesce.

Five design pathways

The ambitions of Paris and Mexico illustrate how contemporary urban green space design in the first half of the twenty-first century increasingly falls within the wider context of 'nature-based solutions', which work to address environmental challenges such as climate change mitigation and biodiversity protection, in conjunction with social issues such as ensuring human well-being. These solutions are driven by growing evidence of how nature affects public health and by increasing awareness of environmental challenges (Frumkin et al., 2017; Taylor & Hochuli, 2017). Nature-based strategies emphasize that incorporating urban green spaces is a sustainable and practical approach to fostering psychological well-being while also addressing environmental issues such as air, noise and light pollution, as well as social concerns such as economic discrimination, crime and social exclusion. Researchers from the School of Environment and Life Sciences at the University of Salford, UK have pointed out:

> Greener environments can foster belonging, equity, trust, and relationships across generations and cultures to prevent exclusion, marginalization, and violence. These environments encourage outdoor social interaction, improving community cohesion, which in turn helps address social issues like crime. Community cohesion is especially vital in multicultural areas, as it enables intergenerational social bonds. (Carter et al., 2015)

The High Line in New York City, a 1.5-mile-long public park constructed on a disused elevated railway, was designed collaboratively with various stakeholders to address the health, social and environmental concerns of the city. In addition to a great example of multifunctional design, it exemplifies another major influence on contemporary urban green space design: the rewilding movement. The High Line's aesthetic reflects the natural cycles of life, creating different moods and atmospheres that evoke feelings of being in a wild space. The head designer Piet Oudolf commented on how he gained inspiration from the self-seeded landscape that grew wild for twenty-five years after the trains stopped running (Millington 2015).

Rewilding advocates allow green spaces to evolve naturally, enabling ecological processes to reclaim and reshape the environment without human intervention. Rewilding redefines nature's role in cities, making it an integral part of the urban ecosystem, while reconnecting city dwellers with natural life cycles. There is, however, a difference between a naturalist or 'non-manicured' planting aesthetic, and rewilding as a regenerative methodology. In scientific circles, rewilding dates back to the 1990s Wildlands Project in the United States, which aimed to create wilderness corridors untouched by human activity. This project promoted natural vegetation and wildlife regeneration through the phasing out of human intervention, such as farming, mining and logging.

Some environmental scientists, such as Dolly Jørgensen, have argued that loose interpretations of rewilding may be unproductive or even harmful (Jørgensen, 2015; Lehmann, 2021). On a philosophical level, advocating for untouched nature perpetuates the divide between humans and the environment, potentially leading to environmental neglect. From a historical perspective, Roderick Nash (Nash & Miller, 2014), in his history of the American wilderness, suggests that the very notion of wilderness is a fantasy and a by-product of Euro-American colonialism. On a practical level, some rewilding critics call for nature-based solutions to accept human involvement in ecosystems and encourage collaborative participation in environmental stewardship. The idea of rewilding in the city may well be more fantasy than a viable strategy, but it has attracted sufficient interest for it to be considered a design pathway in itself.

In summary, contemporary urban green spaces are not confined to a single function or a traditional interpretation. Instead, they offer multiple opportunities to enhance city life, which I summarize in the following five design pathways.

1. Restorative: Enhancing mental and physical restoration, alleviating anxiety and stress, and promoting physical well-being.
2. Social fostering of social engagement, community interaction and cohesion.
3. Environmental mitigation of air pollution, noise and heat, while boosting biodiversity and microbial presence.
4. Aesthetic: Elevating the overall visual appeal, ambiance and sensory sophistication of urban areas.
5. Rewilding: Regeneration of spaces, biodiversity and ecological processes to thrive without human intervention.

What distinguishes these five pathways from those in past centuries is a new understanding of the mental health and well-being benefits of nature, as well as an increased focus on addressing the environmental challenges that cities face. While urban green space design in previous centuries did not ignore these benefits, they have a more pressing influence on contemporary design intentions. With new evidence that increased urban biodiversity not only improves environmental conditions but also positively influences mental and physical health outcomes, both directly and indirectly, these pathways are not mutually exclusive. For example, a single space can be designed to promote health benefits and positive environmental impacts simultaneously. Similarly, designated rewilding spaces can form part of an urban park scheme designed for social interactions.

The central question in this chapter is whether these pathways provide opportunities for attunement states to occur. Attunement is intrinsically rewarding – something done for its own sake without the need for external rewards or validation. It is experienced for the intrinsic satisfaction it provides without relying on external outcomes for any larger purpose. Attunement states are self-contained. The physical conditions that attunement requires revolve around the freedom from human distraction in order to engage with other-than-human stimuli. Therefore, simple exposure to green spaces is insufficient. Attunement requires time and space away from human life to experience the multisensory stimulation of other-than-human life. Therefore, many urban green spaces fall short of providing the quality of nature contact needed for attunement. Human impact has the potential to dominate each of these design pathways, with the possible exception of rewilding initiatives.

The following section presents a hypothetical case study that examines how Environmental Attunement Theory can be applied within the context of contemporary urban green space design. This case study is based on a synthesis of in-depth interviews I conducted with adult residents of the Barbican Centre, a large, post-Second World War multifunctional complex located in Central London, UK. The insights and themes from these interviews were cross-referenced with findings from related studies to assess the feasibility of achieving micro-attunements in this particular urban setting.

Where brutalism meets the woodland's edge: A case study

When I interviewed Sally, a 71-year-old resident at the Barbican Centre in Central London, she told me, 'I can lose myself in the gardens here. I feel miles away from everyone.' Although she had lived in an apartment on the 23rd floor of one of the three residential towers since 1989, it was not until the restrictions put in place during the COVID-19 pandemic, between 2020 and 2022, that the green spaces of the Barbican became an integral part of her daily routine. 'The Barbican gardens are a bit of a secret', she said. 'There are gardens hidden in gardens. Most of the public who come to visit the Centre don't even know about them.'

The Barbican Centre in London stands as a remarkable example of post-Second World War urban regeneration and architectural aspiration. On 29 December 1940, German Luftwaffe mounted an extensive bombing raid on London, destroying most of the houses and streets in this area. The City of London Corporation spent over a decade following the war conceiving an ambitious scheme for the site's redevelopment. The architectural practice of Chamberlin, Powell and Bon received the commission in the 1950s to construct a multipurpose complex addressing the social and private housing shortage, serving as a principal venue for the performing arts, and accommodating a public library, art gallery and various educational facilities. The project eventually broke ground in the early 1960s (Alison et al., 2014).

The site has a rich and layered history, from Roman occupation to the rebuilding of the city after the Great Fire of 1666 and the building boom of the Victorian era. However, the design of the scheme sought to look to the future rather than take its reference from the past. The architects employed a Brutalist style, a modernist form of architecture that developed mainly in post-war Europe between 1945 and 1970. Characterized by monolithic structures brought together as a whole in asymmetric compositions, architects used reinforced concrete as the primary construction material, harnessing its sculptural qualities to create striking forms and innovative structural solutions, such as overhanging balconies and protruding elements.

Although brutalism is often criticized for its seemingly austere and cold aesthetics, it reflects the original architects' vision of creating an urban sanctuary. As architectural historians have pointed out, the ethical principles of brutalism are often overlooked because of their distinct visual aesthetics. Tower blocks and terraced buildings are arranged around elevated walkways and gardens. This elevated urbanism segregates foot traffic from vehicles by establishing a system of raised walkways, known as podiums, that links various parts of the complex and cultivates a sense of community while creating an atmosphere of calmness in contrast to the surrounding city.

It is this layered and complex composition of spaces and forms that provides the Barbican with the opportunity to mix green spaces. Landscaping comprises an array of gardens, terraces and water elements, from expansive open areas featuring lawns, woodland trees and aquatic landscaping to a selection of smaller communal gardens accessible only to residents, and more intimate green spaces hidden from the public. Jules Waite, from the London Wildlife Trust, described one such garden, named the wildlife garden at the Barbican, to me as 'a secret within a secret'.

Renovations to the Barbican gardens

From the balcony of her 22nd-floor apartment, Sally witnessed the renovation of green spaces stretching across the elevated podiums that run throughout the Barbican complex. The previous planting scheme consisted of a more traditional mix of lawns, flower beds, trees and shrubs, all of which required relatively high maintenance and irrigation levels. City planners saw refurbishment as an opportunity to improve landscaping by creating a series of distinctive atmospheric green spaces for the public and residents to enjoy. The next generation of landscapers worked with the unique microclimate of the Barbican, creating biodiverse, climate-resistant green spaces for flora and fauna to thrive.

The new designs were led by Nigel Dunnett, Professor of Planting and Vegetation Technology at the University of Sheffield, who has a particular interest in ecologically diverse small-scale green spaces in dense urban environments. His concept embraces sustainable urban greening principles and focuses on biodiversity, water conservation and resilience to fluctuating weather conditions. Planting was carefully matched to microclimatic environmental conditions to minimize artificial irrigation needs, support urban temperature regulation and enhance plant performance (Russo, 2023).

The diversity of plant species, colours, heights and structures exemplifies many of the pathways of contemporary urban green space design, fusing ecological sustainability, social concerns and aesthetic considerations against the striking Brutalist architecture. Short lawns previously maintained for visual appeal that required considerable maintenance and water were replaced with urban meadows. This design introduces a new aesthetic sensibility that appreciates nature's organic forms and seasonal changes. Unlike conventional urban green spaces, which prefer summer annual plants for their visual appeal, the scheme allows perennial plants to self-seed before dying back in winter. Neat pruning and maintenance have been replaced by the desire to respect and witness the cycle of life. As one resident commented, 'I began to feel more aware of the seasons living here.'

Dunnett describes his approach as establishing 'a multi-layered and dynamic habitat ... an ecological oasis within the heart of the city'. Trees, such as birch (*Betula pendula*) and rowan (*Sorbus aucuparia*), form the upper canopy. Inspired by the natural woodland edge, an atmospheric understory of shade-tolerant shrubs, such as hazel (*Corylus avellana*) and hawthorn (*Crataegus monogyna*), flourishes. Ferns and shade-loving perennials, including varieties of *Geranium* species, provide texture and support to various urban wildlife, emulating the intricate layers of a natural woodland ecosystem. This life at the woodland's edge is not a process of rewilding; the design principles may be similar, but the intent is different.

The gardens of the Barbican embody the spirit of the centre's original architects, with their vision for the future rather than a return to the past. This is a human and non-human habitat – a symbiotic collaboration between humans and other-than-human life. The deliberate fusion of humans and nature at the Barbican is done in such a way that the individual's perceptual field is filled with care and sensitivity towards the other-than-human atmosphere created. It is not that the person's attention is focused on a few natural elements; rather, spaces within the Barbican allow one's surroundings as a whole to convey an other-than-human feel.

The Wildlife Garden at Barbican, for instance, is not left to grow wild, although the name might suggest otherwise. It is actively managed to support biodiversity and habitats of over three hundred wildlife species. The garden also features solitary spaces for residents, tucked away at the end of pathways and between dense plant clusters. These intentionally designed solitary spaces allow residents to spend time alone with their surrounding nature undisturbed by human activity. The wildlife garden is one such private green space Sally regularly visits, commenting: 'You can spend 45 minutes or an hour there and come across nobody else. It really is like entering another world.'

The Wildlife Garden in the Barbican Centre challenges the conventional rules of urban green space design. The garden appears unkempt, with no apparent order, and contains what could be described as 'ugly' or 'messy' elements, such as piles of rotting grass. The sounds, smells and temperatures are distinct from those of the surrounding spaces. The mastery of this scheme lies in creating unexpected encounters with other-than-human life. In this space, sensory experiences, such as smell and touch, provide immersion, allowing a sense of being part of an extraordinary environment.

Alone with nature by design

The gardens at the Barbican work on several levels, offering a variety of functions that enhance the quality of life for the visiting public, residents and the wider ecology. The wide-open podium spaces bridge residential and communal buildings, populated by swathes of naturalistic planting that stretch to the distant London skyline. The variety of gardens offers opportunities for residents to meet and interact – whether picnicking in the summer under large oaks or finding a tranquil corner among tall grasses and shrubs – to meet and talk at the end of the day. Hidden spaces tucked between dense plantings provide residents with respite from the constant stimulation of urban life. In this way, these spaces mirror the multifunctional designs of contemporary urban green spaces across the world, from the High Line in Manhattan, New York, to roof gardens in Mexico City. What stands out as exceptional about the Barbican gardens is the intentionally designed pockets of privacy throughout the scheme.

The green space at the Barbican Centre values aloneness as a positive and rewarding experience, encouraged and supported by design. The pockets of privacy provided allow residents the opportunity to feel safe and at ease and to take the time to appreciate and engage with other-than-human life. There is a level of sophistication in design that distinguishes aloneness from loneliness. In the Wild Garden, in particular, the variety of multisensory stimulation from other-than-human life creates an unexpected and spontaneous quality that transforms the experience from one of simply being alone in a green space to being alone with the non-human ecology surrounding you. In doing so, the garden provides the essential aloneness and quality of contact with nature required by attunement states.

The Barbican garden design can be situated in a broader academic debate about the tension between individualistic and community needs in society, and the cultural and societal biases towards aloneness. The Barbican scheme demonstrates how aloneness as a positive experience can be considered and encouraged through design. Although contemporary urban design has radically changed since the turn of the twenty-first century to address the social and environmental concerns of the modern city, aloneness is seldom part of the design criteria. It is more the case that contemporary urban green spaces aim to eliminate aloneness by enhancing social interactions through design. Increasingly, policymakers, developers, architects, artists, community organizations and designers work together to combat through social interactions. Consequently, the opportunity to be alone with nature in the city, as a positive experience, is neglected or ignored in contemporary schemes and seldom the topic of research.

As discussed in Chapter 7, the experience of being alone is often stigmatized, or even pathologized, and rarely is its positive virtue valued and encouraged. For example, some studies claim that exposure to social activity can have an adverse effect and exacerbate feelings of loneliness in certain circumstances (Astell-Burt et al, 2022). This does not suggest that initiatives to combat loneliness through socially designed green spaces are not beneficial or enhance the value of city life. Evidence for the detrimental effects of loneliness on public health is incontestable, and studies clearly show that time in urban green spaces helps alleviate negative effects.

The point to underline is that, in the context of such a culturally complex understanding of aloneness, it is striking that designers of the gardens at the Barbican Centre have intentionally created opportunities for residents to be alone with nature. On a crisp spring morning or a hazy autumnal evening, one can find a space among the Barbican's Brutalist concrete forms that provides a level of intimacy between the solo self and nature, which is rare in urban settings. Such opportunities may exist in people's private urban gardens or vegetable growing allotments on the fringes of a city, but seldom in such inner city areas that are accessible to the general public.

While the Barbican gardens offer a rare urban experience of solitude within such a densely populated setting, this intentional design to foster aloneness mirrors the Zen garden or 'karesansui' in Japan. In both, the encounter between nature and the individual is cultivated purposefully. In Zen gardens, this concept is taken further. Dating as far back as the fourteenth century, the Karesansui, which are typically situated inside the grounds of temples, embody the principles and practices of Zen Buddhism and are designed to facilitate monks' meditations (Saito, 1985). The choice and composition of natural elements simplify and symbolize nature. Raked gravel represents flowing water, while carefully placed rocks evoke islands or mountains. Encouraging the visitor's reflections on the finite and the infinite, the individual and the universal, the invisible spaces, and tensions that exist between each element are made present.

Describing the Ryoan-ji Garden in Kyoto (the Temple of the Dragon at Peace), after its restoration in 1950, artist Isamu Naguchi wrote, 'One feels that the rocks were not just placed there, that they grew out of the earth (the major portion buried), their weight is connected to the earth, and yet perhaps for this very reason they seem to float like the peaks of mountains. Here is the immaculate universe swept clean' (Walker, 2017).

The Japanese Zen garden brings us into close contact with the relationship between self and nature, as a meditative device that seeks to dissolve that which lies between. While the Barbican gardens are similar in offering a more intimate connection between self and nature, there are significant differences as well. The Barbican spaces offer a more active and immersive experience. There is a sense of participation and aliveness to be gained in one's direct involvement with the immediate surroundings, rather than simply through one's contemplative observation. There is a spontaneity and creativity between stimuli and response that brings the encounter to life.

Prior to the refurbishments of the Barbican green spaces, Sally found the gardens visually appealing and enjoyed looking at them from her balcony, but rarely spent much time visiting them, except while walking through on her way to somewhere else. After the refurbishments, she started to use the spaces more to meet with friends and fellow residents and availed of the new seating areas. When the COVID-19 pandemic struck in 2020 and social distancing restrictions were imposed on Londoners, Sally was motivated to use the gardens on a more regular basis, to the point where spending up to one hour a day on her own in the gardens became part of her daily routine.

As Sally described:

> I got used to spending time alone there and started to appreciate the gardens. I've become a lot more sensitive to things, like if it's going to rain, or if the temperature is about to drop. And it's not like it's the same every day. There's always something new and unexpected that happens. Like the other day, when I was in the Wild garden, two herons landed on the pond and started fishing for frogs. I get so involved in this other world. It's a very strong feeling and I get totally absorbed. It stirs up all sorts of emotions and memories. When I come away from the wild garden especially, I sometimes have a little shake to remind me that I'm back in the city.

The Barbican gardens provide both the capacity to be alone and the quality of contact with other-than-human life, essential to attunement states.

These micro-states may be less intense and prolonged than the deep states of attunement that people experience through extended periods alone in remote locations. Nonetheless, micro-attunements are characterized by the same pattern of effects and can affect our sense of self in similar, albeit less intense, ways. In addition, it should not be overlooked that these micro-states of attunement may alleviate the feelings of loneliness that people experience in cities by enhancing their feelings of kinship with other-than-human life.

The green spaces at the Barbican Centre do not represent an attempt to return to the wild, although naturalistic planting and unmanicured visual aesthetics may suggest. These spaces exist through human design and survive through human management. They rely on human stewardship, which accepts our responsibility to help other-than-human life thrive in urban settings. However, what makes Barbican gardens stand out in terms of the psychology of environmental attunement is the intention of the design – an intentionality that goes against the tide of contemporary societal and cultural norms by valuing the space and time to be alone with nature, with the appreciation that it is a relationship that requires and deserves nurturing. Opportunities to be alone with nature are intentionally and skilfully incorporated into this concrete Brutalist scheme. The Barbican demonstrates that attunement states can be accessed in designed urban ecosystems.

As a result, the Barbican gardens represent a new turn in urban green space design that embraces the cycles of the seasons rather than prioritizing the full blooms of summer plants. It values the sensuality and surprise of biodiversity over any formality and control of planting. It goes beyond most contemporary design principles to value solo encounters with a wider ecology as an integral part of city life. The Barbican gardens point to specific types of urban green spaces where moments of micro attunement are possible. In doing so, the Barbican gardens offer a new pathway for contemporary urban green space design to pursue by illustrating how urban green spaces can cultivate our capacity to spend time alone with nature in the city and experience moments of attunement in a safe and unthreatening way.

Over the course of my research at the Barbican gardens, in particular by speaking with residents, I have grown increasingly confident that urban green spaces of the future can afford urban dwellers opportunities to experience micro-states of attunement, and their benefits. However, I want to acknowledge the limitations of my research, including the small sample sizes and subjectivity of my methods and interpretations. My intention, therefore, is not to offer concrete conclusions, but rather for Environmental Attunement Theory to stimulate interdisciplinary discourse, not only in the field of psychology but also among urban planners, designers, architects and communities on ways to enhance the quality of urban dwellers' relationships with nature. While the Barbican Centre exemplifies how intentional design can foster states of micro-attunement, the next frontier lies in scaling these principles to the city as a whole.

Towards the more-than-human smart city

As argued in Chapter 4, any meaningful urban future must transcend a separatist anthropocentric stance. Looking to the future, given the projections for global population growth and urbanization, it is all too easy to have a dystopian view for life on the planet. How can we sustain such an imbalance between humans and other-than-human life? However, humans' ability to imagine something different may be our greatest hope. Recent scholarship has called for radical reimagining of cities, moving beyond technocratic and anthropocentric models to prioritize multispecies justice, ecological cohabitation and the agency of non-human actors (Heitlinger et al., 2024). Research on biodiversity-sensitive urban design demonstrates how interdisciplinary methods and digital technologies can support the flourishing of both human and nonhuman city dwellers.

The concept of a more-than-human smart city represents a radical reimagining of urban life – one that moves beyond the traditional, human-centred smart city to embrace the complex interdependencies between humans, animals, plants, microbes and the built environment. Rather than designing cities solely for human efficiency and convenience, the more-than-human smart city seeks to create urban spaces where multiple species can thrive and where digital technologies are harnessed not only for human benefit but also to support the flourishing of entire urban ecosystems. This approach recognizes that cities are not just social or technological systems, but living multispecies assemblages whose health and resilience depend on the well-being of all their inhabitants.

Rather than returning to a lost paradise, or luddite proposal of a planet rewilded, the idea of the smart more-than-human city embraces new technology, and how data, sensors and digital infrastructure can be used to make visible the needs and experiences of non-human urban dwellers-foxes, trees, soil microbes and pollinators. This includes innovative approaches to the collection of urban data that can help understand a city from the perspective of a worm, nettle plant or wind. Technology can help us capture, understand and respond to the signs and requirements of non-human life and foster urban environments in which the needs of all species are considered in planning and governance.

Achieving this utopian vision depends on creative, interdisciplinary collaboration. Addressing the complex dynamics of multispecies urban settings cannot be achieved in any single field. Instead, more-than-human cities of the future must be shaped by collaborative teams that bring together technologists, ecologists, artists, architects, policymakers, psychologists, mental health experts and community members, each contributing their unique perspectives and expertise. Only through such interdisciplinary efforts can we begin to imagine and build inclusive cities for all life forms.

The more-than-human smart city advances many central arguments within the Environmental Attunement Theory. Rather than treating nature as a backdrop for human benefit, it takes on an ecological democracy that embraces the interdependence of all living entities. It champions the central claim of Environmental Attunement Theory that there is more to life than humans.

The smart more-than-human city presents a future vision of urban life where human attunement to the wider ecological community can be valued and cultivated. In contrast to the anthropocentric stance that dominates modern psychology, Environmental Attunement Theory contributes a psychological perspective that aligns to the values and principles of this vision of the future.

Conclusion

Chapter 8 expands on the core principles of Environmental Attunement Theory presented in previous chapters by demonstrating that attunement states are not exclusive to remote locations but are also accessible within consciously designed low-human-impact urban spaces. In Chapter 3, attunement is presented as a spectrum, ranging from deep, immersive states experienced during prolonged periods in remote low-human-impact locations to more subtle, fleeting 'micro-attunements' that can occur in everyday contexts. This chapter builds on this framework by exploring how urban green spaces, when intentionally designed to minimize human distractions and maximize multisensory engagement with other-than-human life, can foster micro-attunement states for city dwellers.

The Barbican Centre gardens demonstrate how features such as biodiversity, multisensory stimulation and freedom from the distraction of human activities can be achieved at the heart of a bustling city. While these urban experiences may not evoke the same intensity or duration of attunement states as those found in remote settings, they follow the same underlying pattern: heightened sensory awareness, embodied sense of resonance with the environment and invigorating feeling of being alive. Designing spaces for environmental attunement does not negate the need for other types of nature experiences in the city, such as public parks for social interactions and community vegetable plots. There are many different forms of nature experience that benefit humans and their wider ecology in various ways. It is important to recognize that attunement states represent a distinct and valuable form of nature experience, offering pathways to enhance self-awareness, mental health and well-being.

The more-than-human smart city presents an exciting future for humans' relationship with nature by embracing ecological democracy and the interdependency of all living entities. The more-than-human smart city offers a vision of urban life where attunement to the broader ecological community can be valued and cultivated. Such initiatives show the potential for the psychology of environmental attunement to contribute to interdisciplinary discourse that seeks to move beyond green space towards cohabitation. The vast majority of people on this planet, however, can no longer walk outside their front door and find themselves alone in the kind of nature our ancestors did or engage with consciously crafted biodiverse urban spaces like those at the Barbican Centre. Access to nature is increasingly a pressing issue, particularly for underprivileged and marginalized communities. Access to nature and social justice are inextricably linked. Discussions of environmental attunement psychology and its applications must acknowledge these societal challenges to remain meaningful. The next and final chapter is dedicated to this cause.

References

Alison, J., Ferrari, A., Kenyon, N., Saumarez Smith, O., Dixon, T., Leigh, M., Meades, J., Parry, E., & Westwood, V. (2014). *Barbican: Life, history, architecture*. Barbican Art Gallery.

Astell-Burt, T., Hartig, T., Putra, I G. N. E., Walsan, R., Dendup, T., & Feng, X. (2022). Green space and loneliness: A systematic review with theoretical and methodological guidance for future research. *Science of The Total Environment 847* (15 November): 157521. https://doi.org/10.1016/j.scitot env.2022.157521.

Bille, M., & Schwabe, S. (2023). *The atmospheric city*. Routledge.

Carter, J. G., Cavan, G., Connelly, A., Guy, S., Handley, J., & Kazmierczak, A. (2015). Climate change and the city: Building capacity for urban adaptation. *Progress in Planning, 95*, 1–66. https://doi.org/10.1016/j.progr ess.2013.08.001.

Csikszentmihalyi, M. (2000). *Beyond boredom and anxiety* (pp. 231). Jossey-Bass.

Cui, D., Wu, D., Liu, J., Xiao, Y., Yembuu, B., & Adiya, Z. (2019). Understanding urbanization and its impact on the livelihood levels of urban residents in Ulaanbaatar, Mongolia. *Growth and Change, 50*(2), 745–774. https://doi.org/10.1111/grow.12285.

de Gaynesford, M. (2017). Introduction: What is attunement? In M. de Gaynesford (Ed.), *The rift in the lute: Attuning poetry and philosophy.* Oxford University Press. https://doi.org/10.1093/acprof:oso/9780198797265.003.0001.

de Keijzer, C., Gascon, M., Nieuwenhuijsen, M. J., & Dadvand, P. (2016). Long-term green space exposure and cognition across the life course: A systematic review. *Current Environmental Health Reports, 3*(4), 468–477. https://doi.org/10.1007/s40572-016-0116-x.

Dzhambov, A. M., Dimitrova, D. D., & Dimitrakova, E. D. (2014). Association between residential greenness and birth weight: Systematic review and meta-analysis. *Urban Forestry & Urban Greening, 13*(4), 621–629. https://doi.org/10.1016/j.ufug.2014.09.004.

Frumkin, H., Bratman, G. N., Breslow, S. J., Cochran, B., Kahn, J. P. H., Lawler, J. J., Levin, P. S., Tandon, P. S., Varanasi, U., Wolf, K. L., & Wood, S. A. (2017). Nature contact and human health: A research agenda. *Environmental Health Perspectives, 125*(7), 075001. https://doi.org/10.1289/EHP1663.

Jackson, S. A. (1995). Factors influencing the occurrence of flow state in elite athletes. *Journal of Applied Sport Psychology, 7*(2), 138–166. https://doi.org/10.1080/10413209508406962.

Jørgensen, D. (2015). Rethinking rewilding. *Geoforum, 65*, 482–488. https://doi.org/10.1016/j.geoforum.2014.11.016.

Heitlinger, S., Foth, M., & Clarke, R. (2024). *Designing more-than-human smart cities: Beyond sustainability, towards cohabitation.* Oxford University Press.

Knobel, P., Dadvand, P., & Maneja-Zaragoza, R. (2019). A systematic review of multi-dimensional quality assessment tools for urban green spaces. *Health & Place, 59*, 102198. https://doi.org/10.1016/j.healthplace.2019.102198.

Lehmann, S. (2021). Growing biodiverse urban futures: Renaturalization and rewilding as strategies to strengthen urban resilience. *Sustainability, 13*(5), Article 5. https://doi.org/10.3390/su13052932.

Millington, N. (2015). From urban scar to 'park in the sky': Terrain vague, urban design, and the remaking of New York City's High Line Park. *Environment and Planning A: Economy and Space, 47*(11), 2324–2338. https://doi.org/10.1177/0308518X15599294.

Nash, R., & Miller, C. (2014). *Wilderness and the American mind* (5th ed.). Yale University Press.

Ottiger, B., Van Wegen, E., Keller, K., Nef, T., Nyffeler, T., Kwakkel, G., & Vanbellingen, T. (2021). Getting into a 'Flow' state: A systematic review of flow experience in neurological diseases. *Journal of NeuroEngineering and Rehabilitation, 18*(1), 65. https://doi.org/10.1186/s12984-021-00864-w.

Pérez-Gómez, A. (2016). *Attunement: Architectural meaning after the crisis of modern science.* The MIT Press.

Privette, G. (1983). Peak experience, peak performance, and flow: A comparative analysis of positive human experiences. *Journal of Personality and Social Psychology, 45*(6), 1361–1368. https://doi.org/10.1037/0022-3514.45.6.1361.

Russo, A. (2023). Transforming contemporary public urban spaces with planting design. Shifting from monocultural planting blocks to naturalistic plant communities. *Ri-Vista. Research for Landscape Architecture, 21*(2), Article 2. https://doi.org/10.36253/rv-14888.

Saito, Y. (1985). The Japanese appreciation of nature. *The British Journal of Aesthetics, 25*(3), 239–251. https://doi.org/10.1093/bjaesthetics/25.3.239.

Swanwick, C., Dunnett, N., & Woolley, H. (2003). Nature, role and value of green space in towns and cities: An overview. *Built Environment (1978–), 29*(2), 94–106. https://www.jstor.org/stable/23288809.

Taylor, L., & Hochuli, D. F. (2017). Defining greenspace: Multiple uses across multiple disciplines. *Landscape and Urban Planning, 158,* 25–38. https://doi.org/10.1016/j.landurbplan.2016.09.024.

United Nations. (2019). Department of Economic and Social Affairs, Population Division. World Urbanization Prospects: The 2018 Revision (ST/ESA/SER.A/420).

Walker, S. (2017). *The Japanese garden.* Phaidon.

9

Environmental attunement in an equitable society

> I wouldn't call myself a nature person. I don't know the names of plants, or birds, or any of that stuff. But I can listen to the sound of the rain for hours. I love to run my hand across the bark of a tree I'm walking passed – I like the tingling sensation it leaves on my skin. Or those moments when you can feel the change of season in the atmosphere.
>
> Research Participant

The primary goal of Environmental Attunement Theory is to bring people into a deeper relationship with this more-than-human world. However, it would be remiss not to point out the chasm that this theory attempts to bridge. Attunement states arise through the intentional practice of spending time alone in low-human-impact environments. However, this seemingly simple practice is more readily accessible to the privileged in our society. Where we stand today, access to nature in modern society is far from equal. Significant disparities exist across social groups in terms of opportunities for access and quality of engagement with nature.

Leah Thomas coined the term 'Intersectional Environmentalism' to describe the inextricable link between environmentalism, privilege and power, and simultaneously that the fight for the planet lies in tandem with the fight for civil rights; in fact, that one cannot exist without the other (Thomas, 2022). The evidence is clear. Studies have repeatedly shown that it is the most under-represented and underprivileged in society who are the most adversely affected by environmental injustices (Colley et al., 2022; Rigolon, 2016; Rigolon et al., 2018; Wu et al., 2022).

The aim of this final chapter is to position Environmental Attunement Theory in the context of the growing disparity in access to quality engagement with nature across different social groups. The chapter highlights how this 'nature gap' in modern society disproportionately affects people across lines of socioeconomic status, gender, sexuality and race. This chapter looks at how the nature gap is not just a matter of proximity or individual choice but is profoundly shaped by complex social issues and deep-rooted cultural narratives. The final section of the chapter concludes with reflections on how the psychology of environmental attunement can be used to inform nature-based strategies for addressing both environmental and social injustices.

The nature gap

As discussed in Chapter 8, greater biodiversity in cities improves air quality, reduces noise and helps moderate temperatures in our cities, while urban green spaces are known to provide significant mental health benefits, thereby improving the quality of human life. A healthy society has equitable access to a safe and biodiverse nature. Yet, are twice as likely as men to report safety as a barrier to spending time in urban parks (Kalms, 2019). Queer people's historical migration to urban areas to avoid social isolation in rural life has been at the expense of their relationship with nature. Racial and economic inequalities mean that low-income and minority communities are more likely to live near green spaces that are polluted, poorly maintained and unsafe, whereas affluent neighbourhoods enjoy cleaner, safer and more biodiverse spaces.

The gender divide

> I'm not the outdoorsy type. I'd never go on a hiking or camping holiday. But I love to lie down on the grass and just close my eyes. Soak in all the smells and feel the earth's temperature on my body. I love to listen to the sounds of the birds and sing along. On a rainy day, I'll go for a walk in my local park and squelch around in the mud when nobody's watching.
>
> Jeanette, London Resident.

The clearest disparity exists across gender. Although proximity to green space may be equal for men and women, in reality, men are much more likely to spend time alone in nature (Colley et al., 2022; Richardson & Mitchell, 2010). In broad terms, men generally visit natural environments more and experience better health benefits from living in proximity to green spaces than do women. Women report, at twice the rate of men, that safety is a barrier to spending time in these spaces and for good reason. The UK's capital city, London, for instance, has a relatively high proportion of green space per capita compared to other global capitals. Almost half of all London residents live within a five-minute walking distance of a park. However, incidents of harassment and threats in these urban green spaces are significantly higher for women.

As the quote above highlights, alongside the very real threats to safety that exist, there are social and cultural dimensions to consider to people's willingness and motivate to be alone with nature. I interviewed Jeanette, a 33-year-old female London resident, as part of an initiative exploring people in the mental health professions' experiences of nature in the city. When I interviewed Jeanette, she was about to graduate as a psychotherapist. Her urban life was busy, and moments alone outdoors were limited. She did not identify as the 'outdoorsy' type, even though she clearly enjoyed an intimate relationship with the biotic and abiotic stimuli the city had to offer. There was a sensory texture and quality to her experiences that afforded her joy.

The image of the male in nature is imprinted on Western imagination in a saintly or heroic form. Every child brought up in the Christian tradition learned of Jesus's forty days alone in the desert. Images of St. Jerome in the wilderness and St. Francis of Assisi, blessing animals, proliferated western art. Romantic poets and artists perpetuate the grandiose image of man in nature. William Wordsworth captured his wild imaginings as he strode across England's Lake District. While the German Romantic painter Caspar David Friedrich created the iconic image of the lone male figure on a mountain ridge, surveying with sublimity the entirety of nature laid out before him.

In the new world, the work of great American nature writers such as Henry David Thoreau in *Walden* and John Muir in *The Yosemite* was instrumental in formulating the American image of the great outdoors, as observed through the eyes of the privileged, self-labelled civilized male. The potency of such works on the American psyche cannot be overemphasized, as they directly influence policies that remain intact today regarding several of America's national parks (Runte, 1990).

Eco-feminist thinkers argue that the same patriarchal structures involved in the treatment of nature as separate and subordinate can also be found in the oppression of women as they stem from the same ideologies of domination. In her seminal work *The Death of Nature*, eco-feminist writer Carolyn Merchant argues that this shared oppression can be traced back to the Enlightenment and Industrial Revolution, when the ecologically oriented, female-centred image of nature was replaced by a mechanistic, patriarchal order organized around the exploitation of natural resources (Merchant, 1989). While the Enlightenment undoubtedly marks a turning point, I would argue that the archetypal imagery was established long before. Where the image of the male in nature takes on a saintly or heroic form, the female image is split between the wicked or the virginal.

In the creation myth of Adam and Eve, for example, Eve's betrayal of a promise made to God casts man out of the Garden of Eden. The medieval French play *Le Jeu d'Adam et Eve*, performed by members of the public across towns and villages in thirteenth-century France, captures the contempt her actions caused.

Oh, evil woman full of treason.
Forever contrary to reason.
Bringing no man good in any season.
Our children's children to the end of time
Will feel the cruel whiplash of your crime.

(Quoted by Kraus, p. 44).

Throughout Western folklore, a herbalist spinster who lives outside the village or holds special powers over plants and animals is cast as a witch. For example, in German folklore, the Gingerbread Witch lives deep in the forest in a house made of sweets to lure children to death. In contrast, the adolescent girl in the story of Little Red Riding Hood dares to venture into the forest on her own, to either be eaten by the wolf or saved by a woodsman or hunter, depending on the version of the tale. Whether sorceress or object of seduction, the fate of the woman alone in nature lies in the hands of the men who seek to rescue or destroy her.

Re-imagining the image of woman in nature

The work of eco-feminist artists in the late 1960s and the 1970s challenged these traditional representations of women in nature based on the core belief that both women and nature have been subjected to male patriarchal oppression because of their shared reproductive capabilities. The work of artist Ana Mendieta, born in Cuba in 1948, is an important illustration of the re-imagining of women in nature that took place. After moving from orphanage to orphanage, she escaped the Cuban Revolution in 1961 and moved to the United States (Blocker & Mendieta, 1999). Mendieta is not a painter of nature. She did not represent the landscape through the medium. Instead, using her body, Mendieta imprinted her silhouette in mud, blood or other natural materials, creating powerful embodied statements about the lost connection between earth and female identity. Her work is the immersion of the feminine in the original source. As Mendieta explains:

My work is grounded in the belief in a Universal Energy which runs through everything – from insect to man, from man to spectre, from spectre to plant, from plant to galaxy. My works are the irrigation veins of the Universal fluid. Through them ascend the ancestral sap, the original beliefs, the primordial accumulations, the unconscious thoughts that animate the world. (in Blocker & Mendieta, p. 34).

Her work emerged at a time when artists were exploring whether concepts and behaviour were more interesting than objects, leading to new and innovative art practices. Artists not only incorporated new materials and techniques but also began to extend their art into formerly untouched spaces and environments. By immersing herself within the land, the traditional separation between subject and art object and the honoured tradition of contemplative appreciation of a beautiful nature scene were deliberately breached. Mendieta subverts the conventional distancing between artist and subject, observer and nature, pristine and soiled, and presents an alternative archetypal image of woman as one element within this universal energy. Mendieta work strives for a land 'unbaptized', free from the patriarchal structures of power and female oppression and the domination of nature that stem from Judeo-Christian traditions (p. 131).

In Britain, the eco-feminist women of Greenham Common in the 1970s and the 1980s embodied a similar radical fusion of environmental and feminist activism. Resonating with Mendieta's earth-body performances, these women used their bodies and collective creativity to protest the nuclear militarism and patriarchal systems. At their peace camp, they wove webs of yarn into the military base's fences – a symbolic act linking the exploitation of nature to the oppression of women – and performed rituals such as keening (mourning future victims of nuclear war), asserting care and reciprocity as political tools. Like Mendieta, they sought to reclaim the feminine as inseparable from ecological cycles, rejecting man's domination of nature for embodied engagement with the land.

The queer divide

Jeanette moved to London in 2013, aged nineteen, from her home in a 'new town' just over an hour's train ride away from the city. Built for commuters in the late 1960s, the small town on the edge of the agricultural land had little to offer its youth. Although she had a close relationship with her parents and older brother, she always felt that she would have to move. In particular, as a young lesbian woman, Jeanette knew that her hometown could never offer her a sense of community and belonging. Jeanette's move to the city follows a well-trodden path in queer life. Research studies since the 1970s have clearly shown that lesbian and gay people have significantly higher levels of internal migration to urban environments than heterosexual populations.

Studies examining the mental health and well-being of young lesbian and gay people in rural or semi-rural and urban areas concur that these groups experience significantly lower self-esteem, life satisfaction and social support than their urban counterparts. These groups are more likely to experience psychological distress, conceal sexual orientation and face stigma-related challenges. Although no substantial research exists on rural transgender and gender non-conforming people, existing reports point to similar insights.

Generations of young queer adults left their homes for the city in search of identity, acceptance, belonging and often basic self-preservation. In 1972, Queer culture commentator Wittman described Gay migration to San Francisco:

> We have fled from every part of the nation, and like refugees elsewhere, we came not because it was so great here, but because it was so bad there. By the tens of thousands, we have fled small towns where to be ourselves would be to endanger our jobs and any hope of a decent life … and we have formed a ghetto out of self-protection. (Wittman, 1972, p. 330–339; Mortimer-Sandilands & Erickson, 2010, p. 265).

Since the 1970s, laws and attitudes towards sexual minority groups in most Western countries have shifted dramatically, and social activities have been extensively commercialized. Consequently, cities are widely accepted to be queer-friendly, in that they are safer and more inclusive than their rural, semi-rural and suburban counterparts, and provide greater social, professional and health opportunities. Contemporary queer culture is characterized as essentially metropolitan, heavily coded by nightlife, music and fashion. Implicit within the coding of queer culture as cosmopolitan is a turning away from nature – not necessarily a direct rejection of nature, but a suspicion towards the Western heteronormative construct of nature that has traditionally alienated and vilified the queer as 'unnatural'.

In recent years, for instance, proponents of Queer theory, have criticized the eco-feminist movement for maintaining a dualistic gender worldview that ignores the possibility of a graduated spectrum between masculinity and femininity. Queer theory has influenced environmental studies to consider gender and sexuality as separate but interrelated social constructs that do not conform to binary sex categories. This influence of Queer's theory on eco-criticism has created a subcategory of queer ecology, which has integrated concepts such as the deconstruction of binaries and the fluidity of sex and gender identity, to subvert how cultural narratives framed within heteronormative perspectives have shaped our understanding of nature.

Leading scholars in the field, such as Catriona Mortimer-Sandilands, propose that the conceptualization of so-called pristine nature, for instance, sets up the argument for the 'not-natural' as sinful, as has been the case with the prejudicing of queer sexuality as 'unnatural' and therefore 'sinful'

(Mortimer-Sandilands & Erickson, 2010). Urban green spaces can be considered 'heteronormative' in the sense that these spaces reflect the heteronormative hierarchies of property and propriety that exist in wider society (Berlant & Warner, 1998, p. 548). Whereas the desert is queer not just insofar as it is 'ugly', for example, but also because it fails to meet heterosexual standards of (re)productivity and usefulness (Seymour, p. 166-167).

The argument proposed by queer theorists that gender and sexuality are socially constructed, rather than biological, has led some authors to argue that queer theory is, at its core, biologically illiterate and indeed biophobic (Garrard, 2010). Such rejection of the materiality of life harks back to the basic division of mind from matter, a division that resonates through the structures of power and oppression that queer theory seeks to dismantle. As Foster and Kerr pointed out, queer ecology theorists aim to reconcile queer theory with ecology by eradicating the biophobia of the former and promoting a type of biophilia where nature is understood as queer (Foster & Kerr, 2024). Where queer ecology may draw on aspects of nature for self-validation, the question remains whether queer ecology can support queer people in cultivating meaningful relationships with more-than-human life.

Queer initiatives at the grass roots

The US-based organization Queer Nature provides an interesting empirical case. The organization supports LGBTQ2I+ people in reclaiming their connection to the land by teaching practical skills such as wildlife tracking, trailing, learning bird language and behaviour, and situational awareness. The organization emphasizes the importance of queer people cultivating a sense of belonging to nature, while advocating for environmental stewardship, as its founders write:

> Queer Nature is a nature-based/naturalist education project focusing on LGBTQ2I+ learners in the ecological arts and sciences. We recognize that many people have, for various reasons, not had easy access to outdoor pursuits. We envision and implement ecological awareness and outdoor self-efficacy skills as vital – and often overlooked – parts of resilience-building for populations who have been silenced, marginalized, and even represented as 'unnatural', as demonstrated throughout our history by offering sanctuary for the marginalized and the outsiders of society.

Queer Nature follows in the American tradition of wilderness camps by offering skills-based outdoor experiences. Like classic wilderness programs, Queer Nature's curriculum includes practical skills, such as wildlife tracking, bird language and bushcraft, creating opportunities for participants to build confidence and a sense of belonging in natural settings. However, Queer Nature's approach represents a significant departure from conventional models. Queer Nature is explicitly designed for LGBTQ2+ participants and those historically marginalized from mainstream outdoor narratives. Rather than emphasizing adventure, challenge and personal achievement, their approach is grounded in the belief that nature is a living, more-than-human community with which participants can cultivate kinship and healing. Being with nature is framed as a pathway to belonging and co-liberation with land.

Although some scholars have criticized queer ecology theories as conceptually vague and removed from biophysical reality, there is always a gap between theory and reality. In efforts by ecological queer theorists to prove that nature is queer, for instance, Garrard claims that we may just find that nature is not as queer as some queer theorists may hope. As Environmental Psychologist Peter H. Kahn points out 'Life is not literature, and mischief occurs when postmodernists think it is' (Kahn, 2001, p. 200). The grassroots work of Queer Nature, however, demonstrates that it is possible to break strong cultural narratives that say 'queers are not outdoorsy' and engage these subgroups in nature experiences. Their work also demonstrates a move away from transactional forms of nature contact towards something more immersive and profound. It is these deeper, embodied and reciprocal forms of engagement from which states of attunement emerge. Here, we see the opportunities for Environmental Attunement Theory to inform the design of work of this kind and, in turn, how such practices can be used to advance the theory.

The racial divide

An analysis of forty-nine empirical studies across major cities in developed countries showed striking racial inequities in the quality of nature contact in terms of biodiversity, maintenance and safety (Colley et al., 2022). Where the data evidence inequality, people of colour's lived experiences of nature must be understood within the broader context of a history of migration, oppression and racism. In the United States, for instance, until the late nineteenth century, 90 per cent of Black Americans resided in the rural South. Throughout the twentieth century, a significant demographic shift occurred, with the African American population relocating from a rural to an urban environment. By the turn of the twenty-first century, most of the population had settled in large urban centres, resulting in a disconnection from the nature that some African American history scholars suggest served to reinforce a white patriarchal agenda.

Rooted in the histories of slavery, land dispossession and environmental racism, African American environmental studies highlight the historical and ongoing impact of environmental racism, which disproportionately affects communities of colour, and how racialized communities are excluded from environmental privileges and subjected to environmental harm. African American history scholar, Dungy underscores how this population's experiences of, and relationships with, nature are often intertwined with legacies of violence, exploitation and exclusion. In her anthology of four centuries of African American nature poetry, Dungy wrote:

> Many black writers simply do not look at their environment from the same perspective as Anglo-American writers, who discourse with the natural world. The pastoral as diversion, a construction of a culture that dreams, through landscape and animal life, of a certain luxury or innocence, is less prevalent. Rather, in a great deal of African American poetry, we see poems written from the perspective of the worker in the field … The poems describe moss, rivers, trees, dirt, caves, dogs, fields: elements of an environment steeped in a legacy of violence, forced labor, torture, and death. (Dungy, 2009)

Far less recorded than in the United States are British Black people's experiences and attitudes towards a relationship with nature. When I interviewed Jeanette, she told me how her grandparents were part of the Windrush generation of migrants to the UK. When the Windrush streamliner docked in England's Tilbury in 1948, it carried hundreds of hopeful Caribbean men and women in search of work and a better quality of life. Coming from Jamaica, Trinidad, Barbados and other islands, they arrived in post-war England to encounter an unfamiliar climate, cramped urban housing and a society that often seemed indifferent or hostile. For two generations, Jeanette's family resided in London in a racially diverse part of the city's east end. She was two years old when her family moved to their new home on the edge of a small commuter village that was predominantly inhabited by a white population.

Jeanette's experiences share similarities with those of authors Ollie Olanipekun and Nadeem Perera. In their book *Outsiders: The Outside is Yours* (Perera & Olanipekun, 2022), the authors describe their experiences as Black men growing up in the UK. Nadeem Perera shares his personal account as someone born in the UK of both Jamaican and Sri Lankan heritage. Moving from East London, where the majority of his classmates were Black, to the county of Essex, adjacent to the capital, where his new schoolmates were white, he struggled to find anyone with whom to identify. He ended up leaving school at age fourteen, as Perera comments.

> In my youthful naivety, I thought that there was something wrong with me. Why don't I fit in? Why is there no place for me? I thought that my life and its terrible circumstances had ruined me to the point where I could not fit into society. As far as I was concerned, I had no future and the world couldn't have cared less. (p. 84)

He began socializing with a group of local boys in a nearby woodland, engaging in activities such as cycling, creating bonfires and relaxing, without the constraints typically imposed by educational institutions or home environments. Despite his urban upbringing and cultural background, which made the forest setting unfamiliar, he gradually acclimatized to it. He gained knowledge from the Essex boys who were well-versed in the area, understood where to light fires and discovered secluded spots away from authority figures. This information had been passed down through generations, from older siblings and those who came before them.

As Perera points out, Black boys who grow up in East London 'don't do nature'. However, he had been exposed to part of a semi-rural subculture that allowed him to feel comfortable enough to adopt the practice of heading out on his own into nearby fields and forests, where he learned that he could feel free from social expectations and judgments, and where a whole spectrum of emotions and memories could pass through without feeling stuck or consumed by his feelings:

> I didn't choose the bird life, the bird life chose me … My sex, gender, race, physical ability, or religion played no part in the woodpecker's decision to land six feet from me and go about its business. Nature at this moment was reminding me that I deserved the best from life at a time when I had almost forgotten such a truth. (p. 95)

The book describes how their mutual love for birdwatching brought them together to form an outdoor initiative entitled *Flock Together*, aimed at combating the underrepresentation of people of colour in nature in the UK. What started as a walk in a local park close to where they lived has grown into an international movement centred on community and activism through nature. Through their relationship with nature, Perera and Olanipekun describe how they transcended societal expectations and realized an ever-present possibility for every living human being – beyond race, gender, sexuality, religious beliefs and economic status – that we are all born free and equal to exist as part of this more-than-human world. The work of Perera and Olanipekun not only emphasizes inclusivity in nature but also an inclusive nature by encouraging people to explore the nature of urban environments, outside of formal parks and designated green spaces, highlighting the potential for collective action to reshape perceptions of what constitutes nature and who belongs there.

Future research

American psychologist Heinz Kohut predicted that the greatest psychological challenge of our age towards the end of the twentieth century would be the crumbling self (Kohut, 2009). His words may not be far from realized. The World Health Organization's annual *World Mental Health Report* documents rising mental health issues and concerns about the growing burden of global mental health. An emptiness seems to pervade our modern age, which is difficult to diagnose or categorize as a type of mental illness. However, the effects are as devastating as those of a life that is half-lived. To this extent, I have come to believe that attunement states offer something vital to the development and fulfilment of the self. Attunement states may be, at times, as potent as deep human friendships and loves that shape our experience of being alive. This all leads to the central claim of Environmental Attunement Theory – that cultivating the capacity to be alone with nature, in environments where other-than-human stimuli populate the perceptual field, is the pathway to attunement. Yet, as this chapter argues, these states are inaccessible to a significant proportion of the population.

The 'nature gap' is profoundly shaped by intersecting systems of power, privilege and exclusion. Attunement states – while I may claim they are a fundamental right for human flourishing – where we stand today is far from being universally accessible. Their accessibility is mediated by a complex web of historical and cultural narratives and socioeconomic systems that favour the privileged in our societies. However, the transformative work of grassroots organizations such as Queer Nature and Flock Together illustrates that it is possible to move beyond the transactional 'exposure to nature' paradigm critiqued throughout this book, to one of inclusion, reciprocity and more-than-human belonging. These initiatives also show us that the democratization of opportunities for environmental attunement is a matter of environmental and social justice.

Future research on environmental attunement must be intentionally designed to address the barriers identified in this chapter. For this theory to contribute meaningfully to modern society, efforts must be integrated to address current disparities in equitable connections to nature. This means that the social and cultural factors that influence people's ability and willingness to spend time alone in nature must play a part in any research formulation. Understanding Environmental Attunement Theory in this context, is essential to ensure the theory is not translated into an elite practice accessible to a privileged few, but instead, used as an inclusive framework that seeks to enhance the psychological health and well-being of all, alongside the flourishing of more-than-human communities.

As we strive for social justice and work to eliminate disparities in equitable engagement with nature, we must simultaneously pursue ecological justice, of which humans are an interdependent and vital part. The field of psychology will advance best by acknowledging its partial responsibility for this mission and by taking steps towards accepting the totality of nature. This chapter cannot, in any way, attempt to resolve the complex social and cultural issues that feed the nature gap in today's societies. It would nonetheless be negligent not to raise awareness and foster due concern about the inequities that stand in the way of every human being's ability to nurture their relationship with nature and their capacity to experience attunement states.

While my original study targeted an exceptional group of people with extensive experience of solitude in nature, moving forward with more interdisciplinary approaches that include diverse population groups will greatly advance the cause. Given these persistent disparities, future research on environmental attunement must be intentionally designed to address the intersectional and structural barriers identified in this chapter. Only by prioritizing the lived experiences of marginalized groups and collaborating with grassroots initiatives can we develop strategies that democratize access to attunement states.

This is where the connection between theory and practice can be an energizing force by placing people's lived experience at the forefront and centre of any research and theory. Theory can inform practice, but so too can practice inform theory, as illustrated by grassroots organizations such as Queer Nature in the United States and Flock Together in the UK. Practical initiatives that create conditions and encourage people who typically do not spend time alone with nature will teach us a lot. Future research on environmental attunement will benefit both people and the planet most by working in equitable collaboration with as diverse groups and places as possible.

By directly addressing the inequities mapped in this chapter, future research could transform environmental attunement from an elite or accidental experience into a universal resource for psychological and community well-being. Practice-based studies designed and executed in partnership with diverse groups across various environments represent an exciting way forward. This work lays the foundation for a more just and ecologically connected society, one in which the benefits of attunement are accessible to all, and the field of psychology fully embraces its role in fostering both social and ecological belonging.

It may appear constructive to quantify the human-nature relationship in an effort to produce formulas for better physical and mental health. Nonetheless, it is paradoxical, and perhaps self-defeating, to measure and analyse the human-nature relationship in this way. Just as creative potential is erased by the format of an IQ score, and the beauty of human individuality is lost in the coding of personality tests, we cannot sacrifice the profundity of the human-nature relationship to the measurable and its pseudo-advantages. Environmental Attunement Theory presents a challenge to the field of psychology to reconsider moving beyond the parameters of measuring the cognitive effects of exposure to green space, and in doing so, to stop helping perpetuate the anaesthetizing forces that have gained momentum in our modern age. Instead of treating nature as a form of medicine, our focus must shift to the experience of being in nature as an autotelic act, one that requires no goal or outcome beyond the cultivation of the relationship itself.

It cannot be overemphasized that environmental attunement research is in its earliest phases. All we know at this point is what people say about when these states occur, and in a more general way, how attunement states affect our sense of self at a psycho-physiological level. The present research, notwithstanding its limitations in terms of method and reach, attempts to show that descriptions of the phenomenon, based on personal accounts, can be effectively collected and analysed systematically and referenced against related studies from the fields of psychology and cognitive sciences. As detailed in Chapters 3 to 6, existing studies in the field of embodied cognition and other non-normative states of consciousness, for instance, are particularly illuminating.

This chapter has shown that the promise of environmental attunement will only be realized when the field confronts deep-seated inequities that shape who can access and benefit from meaningful engagement with the more-than-human world. The proposed research agenda is not just a scholarly exercise but a necessary step towards social and ecological justice. By forging stronger links between theory, practice and advocacy, we can ensure that attunement becomes a universal possibility rather than a privilege for the few. This will undoubtedly require interdisciplinary effort, as exemplified by the design initiative for the more-than-human smart city discussed in Chapter 8.

A conclusion in four parts

Environmental attunement in summary

Attunement states emerge from the experience of engaging with other-than-human multisensory stimuli. These states are distinct from normative states through a recognizable pattern of heightened multisensory awareness, vivid mental imagery, fluid sense of time and their defining feature of an embodied feeling of participation with the surroundings. In other words, these states represent more than a feeling. These defining features set attunement states apart from other types of exceptional states of consciousness (e.g. meditative, hallucinatory and flow states) and other types of nature experiences, such as taking a break in a city park, gardening with friends in a community garden, taking some time to gaze at a beautiful natural scene, cycling through a forest, hiking a steep mountain, and so on.

Distinct from other types of nature experiences, attunement states require specific internal and external factors. Intention plays a big part, and the person's willingness to hold soft fascination towards the whole of their surroundings, such as Jeanette's choice to lie on the grass and soak in her surroundings. Attunements require continuous adaptive response to the environment. These movements are not necessarily overt, but enable sensory stimulation. Attunement is uniquely facilitated by low-human-impact environments, in which non-human factors dominate the perceptual field. These environments do not need to be vast or conform to any specific type of visual aesthetics. They can range from remote locations described in Chapter 2 by the participants in my original study to intentionally designed spaces that afford human-free multisensory stimulation, such as the Barbican gardens described in Chapter 8. Together, the identifiable behavioural patterns of attunement states and conditional factors create a framework that bridges psychological processes and environmental design.

Paramount to the understanding of attunement states is the involvement of multisensory reciprocity. By bringing the multisensory reciprocity between the perceiver and the environment to the forefront of our awareness, we experience a sense of self that is more fully immersed and intimately involved with our surroundings. Attunement states impact our embodied sense of self – enhancing bodily senses of ownership and agency, and produce an overall feeling of enlivenment. We can appreciate the experience for its own sake, rather than as some form of medicine or treatment per se, because we feel fulfilled by the quality of engagement.

Significantly, these states do not require special skills or aptitudes. Furthermore, analysis from studies of other exceptional states of consciousness suggests that these attunement states follow the same behavioural pattern, operating along a continuum, from deep prolonged states to less intense more transient micro-states. Ultimately, cultivating the capacity to be alone in environments with low human impact is the royal road to attunement. Although a counter-cultural proposition, the psychology of environmental attunement may play a role in helping people live more creative, fulfilling lives.

The power of the outlier experience

There exists a paradox in researching solitary encounters with nature in that it sheds light on some of the most deeply held beliefs in human society. Adam Grant, Wharton School of the University of Pennsylvania, who has extensively researched human creativity and innovation, describes how outlier experiences – unusual, intense or highly unique events – can reveal essential insights that challenge our assumptions and force us to rethink norms (Grant, 2017). Grant argues that outlier experiences help us question whether our everyday assumptions are accurate or simply habitual, encouraging us to re-examine how we approach familiar situations. Nonconformists drive change and innovation by challenging norms and by introducing new ideas.

The level of perceptual participation involved in attunement states brings into question the traditional delineation psychology makes between sensation and cognition, and with that, the idea that cognition is the central system in self-experiences. As detailed in Chapters 5 and 6, these findings align with the principle tenets of the interdisciplinary field of *Embodied Cognition* and, more specifically, with the new science of perception that redefines perception as a dynamic system of multi-modal and cross-modal activity that works interdependently with memory and imagination.

Attunement states challenge us, therefore, to look beyond the cognitive effects of short-term exposure to green spaces and explore how our full sensory involvement within dynamic environments affects our embodied sense of self. Therefore, future studies on attunement states will advance our psychological understanding of human experience in two substantive ways. First, in our understanding of the role of multisensorial perceptual processes in self-experiences. Attunement states help us think beyond cognition to the multisensory perceptual processes involved. Second, in our understanding of how different types of environments, and our relationship towards them, affect our embodied sense of self.

Environmental Attunement Theory not only advances our understanding of a specific phenomenon but also offers a challenging perspective on the beliefs that drive contemporary human-nature research, policy and practice. Where traditionally, psychology has insisted upon the intersubjective human field as the sole source of our psychological fulfilment, attunement states show a psychological value beyond human relations. They show us that there is more to the human-nature relationship than its green-pill effect, and point us to a deeper existential dimension. In this respect, one of Environmental Attunement Theory's greatest contributions to the field of psychology, as I see it, is to bring into question the field of psychology's basic assumption that humans are somehow separate and superior to the rest of life. By challenging this basic assumption, the field of psychology can move towards addressing some of the social and environmental injustices discussed in this chapter.

From social to ecological belonging

People may be leading satisfactory lives, doing meaningful work, and having fulfilling relationships, yet they can be deprived of any real sense of attunement to the more-than-human world they inhabit. Such deprivation may go unnoticed by the individual. How does one go about noticing or addressing the effects of the loss of something that we consciously do not miss? To experience a state of attunement is to feel in a whole-bodied way that life is worth living. As Joseph Campbell phrases it, this is 'to actually feel the rapture of being alive'. How can our sense of self ever feel whole or complete without experiencing this sense of attunement to the rest of life around us?

The modern human has come to believe that our reality is first and foremost socially constructed. Not only our world, our sense-making and our sense of self are believed to be determined through our interactions with other humans. We have forgotten that we are ecological beings, and that our experience of the world is first and foremost embodied. Even before we are born, the foetus's experience is based upon bodily temperatures, tastes and movements. The world we try to make sense of is a more-than-human one.

How could we assert such a separation from the rest of nature and expect no price to pay for human fulfilment? That is a loss that the field of psychology must bear part of the blame for. Too firmly has it been asserted that our psychological development and mental health are attached solely to human relations. While these connections are important, we have overly relied on our relationship with others as the sole source of our identity, mental health and fulfilment in life. The focus has been on intersubjective realities, navigating the boundaries between the 'me' and the 'not me', and the search for happiness through others, without considering the degree to which we have lost our embodied sense of belonging to this more-than-human world.

The capacity to be alone with nature is cultivated despite, rather than because of, any societal endorsement.

Humanity has reached a point in time where we are faced with the very real threat to life as we know it, as interrelated environmental issues such as deforestation, extreme weather conditions and marine pollution are beginning to have a tangible impact on human habitats, food sources and population displacement. The fantasy of separation, and our perceived superiority, which has served to advance humanity in many ways, has now turned to threaten our very own existence. We talk of the planet as being at risk, but it is our own existence that is under question. If push comes to shove, Earth will survive in some shape or form. We will not. It is not that humans need to save nature, but that we must re-establish our connection to nature to survive. The crises we face as a species are as much a psychological issue as they are political or economic, in that they can only be wholeheartedly addressed if we can accept that we are part of nature and that this planet we inhabit does not exist to serve us.

Where it is widely accepted that the quality of interpersonal relationships is directly linked to the development and maintenance of a healthy sense of self, there has been limited research and attention given to this qualitative dimension of our connection to the natural world. The chief claim of Environmental Attunement Theory is that when it comes to our connection to nature, the quality of the relationship matters. Exposure to green space may offer relaxation and restoration; however, attunement states – whether the deep states gained through extended periods in remote locations or the micro-states achievable in more everyday settings – positively affect the individual's overall sense of self and provide an embodied sense of belonging to this more-than-human world. The ambition for the study of environmental attunement, therefore, must be to help advance humanity through a deeper understanding and respect for our relationship with nature.

My research to date is one small step in making such an ambition real in the psychological sense, by identifying and labelling a specific type of nature experience that affects our sense of self. More specifically, I have attempted to provide a framework for this state and offer working hypotheses for future research. The core conditions and characteristics of environmental attunement provide a basis to begin translating theory into practice. However, the greatest contribution of Environmental Attunement Theory to the field of psychology may well be to help rethink psychology's belief that we are solely social creatures and to consider our shared identity as ecological beings. Amidst escalating environmental issues, it is hard to fathom how meaningful, sustainable change is possible without such reckoning.

The person who cultivates the capacity to spend time alone with nature learns how to experience attunement, and in doing so, becomes both deeply enriched and connected with the rest of life around them. To choose a life with environmental attunement is to lift the dull cloud that descends upon us from the overwhelming and desensitization of everyday modern life. The task is not easy and is bristling with the problems of cultural biases and social injustices; yet, the impetus for action is greatly propelled by the environmental crisis we face. One way or another, if humans are to go on, we must radically rethink our relationship with the rest of nature. If we reach a point where people deliberately choose to cultivate their capacity to attune to this more-than-human world, there is hope.

A call to action – Moving beyond the current paradigm

This book began with two questions: What happens when we spend time alone with nature and why does it matter? The answer to the first was an exceptional state of consciousness that enhances our embodied sense of self. The answer to the second came in the form of a call to action for a fundamental shift in the field of psychology's approach to both research and practice. First and foremost, Environmental Attunement Theory calls for the field of psychology to accept the interconnectedness of life and the multifactorial dynamics of the environments we design and inhabit. Second, Environmental Attunement Theory adds to the growing number of voices calling to replace the dualistic frameworks that have prioritized pure cognition with an acknowledgement of the role multisensory perception plays in human experience. Third, it is a call to broaden our focus beyond the intersubjective domain of humans as the sole source of human flourishing, with an appreciation for our relationship with the rest of life as psychologically significant.

As this chapter has argued, advancing the theory in any meaningful way can only be propelled by grappling with the environmental and societal issues that we face. In practical terms, this means that it is time for the field of psychology to move away from measuring the cognitive effects of time-based exposure to green space and instead deepen our understanding of the multisensory dynamics of different environments and human involvement within them. It is time to address the nature gap by reaching out to understand and incorporate the voices of the minorities and marginalized within our society. Together, through interdisciplinary collaborations, we can replace an anthropocentric vision of the future, with one flourishing through cohabitation within a more-than-human world.

References

Berlant, L., & Warner, M. (1998). Sex in public. *Critical Inquiry, 24*(2), 547–566. https://doi.org/10.1086/448884.

Blocker, J., & Mendieta, A. (1999). *Where is Ana Mendieta?: Identity, performativity, and exile.* Duke University Press.

Colley, K., Irvine, K. N., & Currie, M. (2022). Who benefits from nature? A quantitative intersectional perspective on inequalities in contact with nature and the gender gap outdoors. *Landscape and Urban Planning, 223,* 104420. https://doi.org/10.1016/j.landurbplan.2022.104420.

Dungy, C. T. (2009). *Black nature: Four centuries of African American nature poetry.* University of Georgia Press.

Foster, E., & Kerr, P. (2024). Queer/Green collaboration as a radical response to climate crises: Foregrounding the green stripe. *Global Political Economy, 3*(1), 73–91. https://doi.org/10.1332/26352257Y2024D000000013.

Garrard, G. (2010). How queer is green? *Configurations, 18*(1), 73–96. https://muse.jhu.edu/pub/1/article/429843.

Grant, A. (2017). *Originals: How non-conformists move the world.* Penguin Books.

Kahn, P. H. (2001). *The human relationship with nature: Development and culture.* MIT Press.

Kalms, N. (2019). To design safer parks for women, city planners must listen to their stories. *The Conversation.* Available at: https://theconversation.com/to-design-safer-parks-for-women-city-planners-must-listen-to-their-stories-98317.

Kohut, H. (2009). *The analysis of the self: A systematic approach to the psychoanalytic treatment of narcissistic personality disorders.* University of Chicago Press.

Merchant, C. (1989). *The death of nature: Women, ecology, and the scientific revolution.* Harper & Row.

Mortimer-Sandilands, C., & Erickson, B. (2010). *Queer ecologies: Sex, nature, politics, desire.* Indiana University Press.

Perera, N., & Olanipekun, O. (2022). *Flock together: Outsiders: Reclaim your place in nature.* Octopus.

Richardson, E. A., & Mitchell, R. (2010). Gender differences in relationships between urban green space and health in the United Kingdom. *Social Science & Medicine, 71*(3), 568–575. https://doi.org/10.1016/j.socscimed.2010.04.015.

Rigolon, A. (2016). A complex landscape of inequity in access to urban parks: A literature review. *Landscape and Urban Planning, 153,* 160–169. https://doi.org/10.1016/j.landurbplan.2016.05.017.

Rigolon, A., Browning, M., & Jennings, V. (2018). Inequities in the quality of urban park systems: An environmental justice investigation of cities in the

United States. *Landscape and Urban Planning, 178*, 156–169. https://doi.
org/10.1016/j.landurbplan.2018.05.026.

Runte, A. (1990). *Yosemite: The embattled wilderness*. University of
Nebraska Press.

Thomas, L. (2022). *The Intersectional Environmentalist: How to Dismantle
Systems of Oppression to Protect People + Planet*. Hachette UK.

Wu, J., Xu, Z., Jin, Y., Chai, Y., Newell, J., & Ta, N. (2022). Gender disparities in
exposure to green space: An empirical study of suburban Beijing. *Landscape
and Urban Planning, 222*, 104381. https://doi.org/10.1016/j.landurbp
lan.2022.104381.

About the Author

Eugene Hughes is a psychologist and clinical psychotherapist working in private practice in the UK and a guest lecturer in academia worldwide.